Dark
Thoreau

Dark
Thoreau

Richard Bridgman

UNIVERSITY OF NEBRASKA PRESS
Lincoln and London

Publishers on the Plains

UNP

Publication of this book was aided by a grant from The Andrew W. Mellon Foundation.

Manufactured in the United States of America

Frontispiece: Henry Thoreau, daguerreotype by B. W. Maxham, 1856. Courtesy of The Thoreau Society, Inc.

The paper in this book meets the guidelines for permanence and durability of the Committee on Production guidelines for Book Longevity of the Council on Library Resources.

Library of Congress Cataloging in Publication Data

Bridgman, Richard.
  Dark Thoreau.

   Includes bibliographical references and index.
   1. Thoreau, Henry David, 1817–1862—
Criticism and interpretation. I. Title.
PS3054.B7   818'.309   81–4788
ISBN 0–8032–1167–8   AACR2

For Quee
  Joel
    and Roy—
Seamless.

Contents

The artist and his work are not to be separated. . . . the deed and the doer together make ever one sober fact.

A Week on the Concord and Merrimack Rivers, pp. 312−313

Preface

Since we already possess what would seem to be a sufficiency of Thoreau studies, the prospect of yet another may be discouraging. I am impelled to offer one because Thoreau's writings raise certain questions that have not often been addressed, even though they bear centrally on the terms of his received reputation. In consequence, our present understanding of Thoreau strikes me as somewhat distorted. For example, it is generally accepted that Thoreau is the rhetorically powerful advocate both of the supreme value of the individual and of the benign glory of nature—declarations of faith that have increased in attractiveness with the growth of oppressive social institutions and urban wildernesses—but to verify these ideas in Thoreau one must read him very selectively. Many of Thoreau's statements and images qualify, undermine, and even directly challenge these ideas, but those that do so have regularly been ignored on behalf of his affirmations or, when mentioned, have been interpreted positively or regarded as at worst no more than temporary aberrations. As something of a counterbalance, then, I mean to consider these neglected portions of Thoreau's work. His darker sentences, journal entries, and poems will constitute the central weight of this study. To that extent, it is as partial as its predecessors.

I shall be making several points about Thoreau in the following pages: among them, that he was a deeply pessimistic man who could rarely bring himself to admit it; that he had a hostile, punishing streak in him, manifested most vividly in his imagery; that severe tensions necessarily existed between his temperament and his acquired idealism; and that, in consequence, his writings contain a good number of opaque and sometimes bizarre moments that can be attributed to these conditions of psychological strain. The cost of ignoring these symptoms of Thoreau's humanity is a skewed understanding of his accomplishments as a writer.

For a representative instance, let us begin with a sentence that appears toward the end of *Walden*'s troubling chapter on spring. Initiated by the presence of the body of a horse that lay rotting and malodorous near Thoreau's path, the sentence occurs as Thoreau is in the process of enlarging the general point that it inspires us to encounter the vigorous and creative destructiveness of nature, such as its flood-producing rainstorms and its rotting carrion. He had begun the argument with a memorable abstraction—"the tonic of wildness"—one that is often appreciatively cited. But then, as the passage continues, his commentators drop discreetly away, and not surprisingly, for the prose coarsens and in its aggressive celebration of pain offers anything but a salutary tonic. Earlier in the passage, Thoreau had said that he was "refreshed" and "cheered" by evidences of nature's power. Now, his response became actively, enthusiastically, "I love . . ."

I love to see that Nature is so rife with life that myriads can be afforded to be sacrificed and suffered to prey on one another; that tender organizations can be so serenely squashed out of existence like pulp—tadpoles which herons gobble up, and tortoises and toads run over in the road; and that sometimes it has rained flesh and blood! (318)

The clumsy echo in the phrase "rife with life" is the first signal that Thoreau was becoming mesmerized by his own developing imagery and the zest of the verbs that follow confirms it: "squashed," "gobble up," "run over," and "rained." In their colloquial excitement they are out of keeping with the philosophic point Thoreau meant to illustrate. However, as we shall see, they are altogether consonant with his behavior when his feelings overran his defenses.[1]

Flesh and blood did rain, following the explosion of the powder mills near Assabet on January 7, 1853, to which disaster Thoreau hastened, to discover, as he coolly put it, that "some of the clothes of the men were in the tops of the trees, where undoubtedly their bodies had been and left them." He could, however, still discern "some limbs and bowels here and there, and a head at a distance from its trunk." After carefully recording other such macabre details in his journal, Thoreau concluded on a practical note: "Put the different buildings thirty rods apart, and then but one will blow up at a time" (*J*, IV, 455).

Throughout his life, the mutilated bodies of men, animals, birds, and reptiles, the battered remnants of destroyed life, repeatedly absorbed Thoreau's attention and evoked a response that might be curious or excited but never compassionate, for, as he remarks near the end of the "Spring" passage: "Compassion is a very untenable ground" (318). Six months after the powder mill explosion, Thoreau reflected that some of its timbers must have floated into the Gulf Stream by then, or might even have been cast up on the Norway coast. Then, without transition, those timbers metamorphosed into a drowned man, "lying all bare, lank, and tender on the rocks, like a skinned frog or lizard! We did not suspect that he was made of such cold, tender, clammy substance before" (*J*, V, 212). Something in Thoreau demanded that he invent that cruelly objective imagery.

To return to *Walden*: after his fantasies of flesh squashed into a pulp, Thoreau observes that "the impression made on a wise man is that of universal innocence. Poison is not poisonous after all, nor are any wounds fatal." This is a version of Emerson's often-mocked conclusion to *Nature*, in which he asserted that an influx of spirit was sufficient to cause "all disagreeable appearances, swine, spiders, snakes" and the like to vanish, for "they are temporary and shall be no more seen."[2] But whereas Emerson's is an instance of emphasized idealism, Thoreau's version does not prophesy the disappearance of suffering, but rather takes its presence as instructive. In this respect, Thoreau may seem the more faithful to the predatory actualities of life, and yet his apparent exultation in the absolute indifference of the natural system, in its operating by means of flesh torturing flesh, must give us pause. Natural survival may have led Indians to drive herds of bison over cliffs and modern war may have exploded thousands of people into burning rains of flesh and blood, but such occasions have never been celebrated as the tonic of wildness, nor as reassurances of universal innocence.

If Thoreau's vivid imaginative cruelty is a central feature of his writing, no less striking is his frequent verbal opacity. For example: "The stars so low there seem loth to depart, but by a circuitous path to be remembering me, and returning on their steps" (*Week*, 331). One of the first things one notices about Thoreau's writing is that in aggregate (as opposed to the single strong sentence) it is often quite difficult to read: "And yet we have not seen pure Nature, unless we have seen her thus vast, and drear, and inhuman, though in the midst of cities" (*MW*, 70). Close examination often reveals that ambiguous syntax, vague pronoun references, and a shifting subject and tone are responsible for the difficulty, not the complexity of thought. To speak only of his contemporaries, in reading De Quincey, Carlyle, Emerson, Ruskin, or Melville one may be puzzled by their topical references, or disagree with their arguments, or be perplexed by the reach of their verbal ambitions, but one will not regularly encounter mechanically awkward sentences, or ideas evaded or insufficiently thought out: "It is said that the British Empire is very large and respectable, and that the United States are a first-rate power. We do not believe that a tide rises and falls behind every man which can float the British Empire like a chip, if he should ever harbor it in his mind" (*Walden*, 332). No wonder that when a translation of *Walden* was being serialized in Moscow in 1887, Chekhov should have remarked: "This Thoreau fellow . . . sounds quite promising. . . . He's got ideas and a certain freshness and originality about him, but he's hard to read. The architectonics and construction are impossible."[3] In a more recent reaction to *Walden*'s style, Donald Ross, Jr., observed that its unity must be sought in "networks of repeated key words and metaphors," for "Thoreau's syntax is ultimately not conducive to reasoned argument or to clear description—it is too asymmetric and too irregular. When short passages are isolated for reading out of context . . . they often seem confused, involuted, pointless and muddled."[4] In general, that accords with my own impression of Thoreau's most famous literary work. It is understandable that such unkempt moments should have been ignored on behalf of a more coherent and positive picture of Thoreau; nonetheless, they are important revelatory signals, emanating from the innermost privacies of the man.

Some of Thoreau's opacity is caused by an unwillingness to admit threatening truth. Elsewhere, however, the explanation proves no more complicated than that Thoreau stated the matter poorly at the outset, then neglected to improve it. For example, in "Ktaadn" he tells us: "Here it fell to my lot, as the oldest mountain-climber, to take the lead" (*MW*, 56). Now, one may decide that by "oldest," Thoreau meant that he was the most *experienced* mountain-climber in the party, but not until forced unnecessarily to consider whether perhaps the oldest in years might be asked to go first in order to set the pace most comfortable for him. This example can stand for innumerable blurred sentences, some, such as this one, merely mechanically so, but others caused by Thoreau's inner turmoil. Early on, he enunciated a principle that bears on the problem: "We should not endeavor coolly to analyze our thoughts, but, keeping the pen even and parallel with the current, make an accurate transcript of them. Impulse is, after all, the best linguist" (*J*, I, 35). Unfortunately, impulse did not always provide the best medium for communication with others.

Among other considerations in this study, I shall also try to show how much incoherence is present in Thoreau's full-length works. As a master of the aphorism, he could generate an authentically original force in localized moments. But the whole of any of his poems, essays, chapters, or books rarely exhibited a sustained imaginative effort. For this reason, I have not organized my observations thematically, for to have done so would have been to forfeit the means of illustrating what I understand to be the sequential disorder of Thoreau's work. By following the course of his literary career, I hope to show the underlying associated relationships of ideas and images within his works that persistently conspire to create sterile contradictions. They conform to certain psychological patterns, visible from the start but rarely consciously addressed by Thoreau, for his most crippling feature was that he dared not be a deeply reflective man.

Abbreviations

Citations from Thoreau's works will be identified parenthetically in the text, using the abbreviations shown below, plus a page number—for example, (*MW*, 325)—but, if the title is clear from the context, then by the page number alone.

Princeton University Press edition of *The Writings of Henry D. Thoreau.*

EE   *Early Essays and Miscellanies,* ed. Joseph J. Moldenhauer and Edwin Moser, with Alexander Kern (Princeton, 1975).

MW   *The Maine Woods,* ed. Joseph J. Moldenhauer (Princeton, 1972).

RP   *Reform Papers,* ed. Wendell Glick (Princeton, 1973).

Walden   *Walden,* ed. J. Lyndon Shanley (Princeton, 1971).

Week   *A Week on the Concord and Merrimack Rivers,* ed. Carl V. Hovde, William L. Howarth, and Elizabeth Hall Witherell (Princeton, 1980).

Other editions

W   *The Writings of Henry David Thoreau,* Walden edition (Boston: Houghton Mifflin, 1906).

Cape Cod *Cape Cod and Miscellanies,* IV, *The Writings.*

J   *The Journal,* VII–XX, *The Writings,* but separately numbered I–XIV.

Yankee   *A Yankee in Canada, Excursions and Poems,* V, *The Writings.*

CinC   *Consciousness in Concord: The Text of Thoreau's Hitherto "Lost Journal" (1840–1841),* Together with Notes and a Commentary by Perry Miller (Boston: Houghton Mifflin, 1958).

Corr.   *The Correspondence of Henry David Thoreau,* ed. Walter Harding and Carl Bode (New York: New York University Press, 1958).

HM   Manuscripts held at the Huntington Library, San Marino, California.

Poems   *Collected Poems of Henry Thoreau,* ed. Carl Bode (Baltimore: Johns Hopkins University Press, 1970).

Rags and Meanness:
Journals, Early Essays,
Translations, and Poems

> When we speak of a peculiarity in a man or a
> nation, we think to describe only one part, a mere
> mathematical point; but it is not so. It pervades all.
>
> *Journal,* I, 16

MUCH OF WHAT Thoreau felt in his early years is concentrated in his poems and journals. They initiate the terms of his confusions and they help to explain both the violence and the evasions present in his writing. On the positive side, he idealized friendship and exulted in the diversity of nature. On the negative, he discovered little that was attractive in himself or in the social realities around him, and so dwelt obsessively on viciousness, destruction, and dissolution. Given these strained conditions, absorption in nature was a relief from quotidian irritations, not to say from himself. He once testified passionately: "I love Nature partly *because* she is not man, but a retreat from him. . . . In her midst I can be glad with an entire gladness" (*J*, IV, 445). However, Thoreau suffered from the transcendental dilemma: nature wore the colors of the spirit;

1

the world could but reflect his moods. "Packed in my mind lie all the clothes / Which outward nature wears" (*Poems*, 74). And although he enjoyed periods of authentic happiness, he also suffered moments of the utmost grimness, when he believed that "Death cannot come too soon / Where it can come at all" (*Poems*, 131).

Thoreau often asserted his indifference to political argument, saying that the brave man does not even hear the idle clashing of swords in the outer world, so "infinite" is the "din" within his spirit. "Is he not at war?" (*J*, I, 247). Thoreau was. Still, he rarely focused directly on that internal uproar, for, paradoxically, the inner self also constituted a central refuge for him. "For an impenetrable shield, stand inside yourself," he counseled, and did just that for a good part of his social life (*J*, I, 106; repeated on 154). Yet the tensions continued to harass him behind that shield. One can hear the anxiety in his question, "How shall I help myself?" The immediate answer was: "By withdrawing into the garret, and associating with spiders and mice, determining to meet myself face to face sooner or later" (*J*, I, 132–133). This curious (and unfulfilled) vow essentially repeated a declaration Thoreau had made at the opening of his journal three years earlier: "To be alone I find it necessary to escape the present,—I avoid myself. . . . I seek a garret. The spiders must not be disturbed, nor the floor swept, nor the lumber arranged" (*J*, I, 3). Thoreau was distracted by daily life and, moreover, he realized that this very distraction permitted him to evade himself. The solution conceived was a retreat. If in 1837 Thoreau's prescription for self-health was a solitary environment among other reclusive creatures, by 1840 he had realized that he was still avoiding himself and that, worse yet, he needed the shock of self-confrontation that he alone could provide. It would take him five years more, however, to find the appropriate retreat in the cabin at Walden Pond—and even then he would only go part way toward meeting himself "face to face."

Again and again in his life, Thoreau returned to this

prescription of confronting or revealing himself, but always in secret. If the house is "the very haunt and lair of our vice," he also acknowledged it to be "a great relief when . . . we can retire to our chamber and be completely true to ourselves. . . . In that moment I will be nakedly as vicious as I am" (*J*, I, 240, 241). Sometimes he felt that he did not understand himself, but that retirement would enable him to unveil the mystery. At other times, he felt that he knew all too well who he was, and sought the relief of confessing it in private. At yet others, he found solace in the idea that such candor would be the first step upward: "If we only see clearly enough how mean our lives are, they will be splendid enough." But to this he at once added a warning against excessive idealizing: "Let us remember not to strive upwards too long, but sometimes drop plumb down the other way, and wallow in meanness" (*J*, I, 146). All this speculative bravado yielded at last to ugly resignation: "At any rate, a carcass had better lie on the bottom than float an offense to all nostrils" (*J*, I, 146).

The affirmation that the rotting carcass is "an offense to all nostrils" clashes of course with the representation of the dead horse near his path as a "tonic of wildness." But Thoreau's imagination was ranging back and forth, trying to come to terms with the inadmissible. The root problem seemed to him his body proper, that unfortunate corporeal reality on which he had to depend. "I must confess there is nothing so strange to me as my own body. I love any other piece of nature, almost, better" (*J*, I, 321). And yet Thoreau realized that the full dimensions of his being were not to be found even in private. "The nearest approach to discovering what we are is in dreams" (*J*, I, 253). But if true, dreams were too unreliable, too sporadic and uncontrolled a source of knowledge for him. When he did manage to look within, what he saw forced him to ask himself: "Did you ever remember the moment when you were not mean?" The occasion for this particular question came during an especially dark mood. Two more somber questions followed: "Is it not a satire to say that life is organic?"

And: "Where is my heart gone? They say men cannot part with it and live" (*J*, I, 349, 350).

As for meanness, it was a condition Thoreau sometimes chose to praise as at least smacking of reality and, at other times, to curse in others and lament in himself. For Thoreau, the significance of certain key terms could shift radically, and not just over an extended period of time. Mutually exclusive ideas came to rest in words of special power for Thoreau. "Meanness" was one of them. One Thoreau, for example, regarding himself as low and degraded, found the concept applicable to himself. "I am sure that my acquaintances mistake me," he told his journal in 1850. "I am not the man they take me for. On a little nearer view they would find me out. . . . If I should turn myself inside out, my rags and meanness would appear" (*J*, II, 46). In *Walden*, though, meanness was memorably offered as the possible essence of life. If so, then Thoreau intended to "get the whole and genuine meanness of it, and publish its meanness to the world" (91). Such a salutary acknowledgment of the hardpan reality of existence was not possible for Thoreau for a long time, however, because he found himself incapable of giving full assent to those of his perceptions that failed to harmonize with the idealism he had learned, even when he felt their accuracy.

Thoreau's early journals furnish plentiful evidence of his dissatisfaction with himself. He lamented his physical being, his creative inadequacies, and the stunted condition of his heart. At age twenty-two, he was already sounding a mournful note of sterility in a poem: "The birds have sung their summer out, / But still my spring does not begin" (*J*, I, 127). That melancholy expression of thwarted growth was reflected in his vocational frustration. By 1840, aside from his journal, Thoreau had written only a few essays and poems, and, although just on the edge of being published in *The Dial*, he had absolutely no reputation as a writer. But the best he could do about his dissatisfaction was to persist in constructing in his journal an ideal of behavior, accompanied by an undercurrent of doubt that indicated his awareness of the warring elements in his nature.

Lacking human closeness outside his family, Thoreau felt frozen, whereas the affectionate life of others seemed to flourish. "The days of tilts and tournaments has gone by, but no herald summons us to the tournament of love" (*J*, I, 102). He turned his seasonal metaphor specifically to love. "Any exhibition of affection—as an inadvertent word, or act, or look—seems premature, as if the time were not ripe for it" (*J*, I, 191–192). Yet Thoreau felt he needed human intimacy. "How insufficient is all wisdom without love! . . . Our life without love is like coke and ashes,—like the cocoanut in which the milk is dried up" (*J*, I, 348). But the question of where he might derive that needed love was distinctly a problem for him. At a pitch of feeling, he remarked: "Love is so delicate and fastidious that I see not how [it] can ever begin." Then, as an indication of one way in which intercourse was blocked: "Did I ask thee to love me who hate myself?" Thoreau's advice to his potential lover was to share his enthusiasms: "No! Love that I love, and I will love thee that lovest it" (*J*, I, 329). This was love by indirection. Thoreau could not express his yearnings in terms of a heterosexual union. The feminine was virtually a non-existent gender for him, except when he was complaining about its trivialities. When his hunger for companionship surged through him, the best expression he could manage was a neutralized desire: "I would live henceforth with some gentle soul such a life as may be conceived, double for variety, single for harmony" (*J*, I, 113). The desired state was ambiguous, as indeterminate as the gender.

In this connection, Thoreau's translation of the most famous of Anacreon's poems becomes significant. Anacreon had directed his sardonic lyric toward a proud young woman who persisted in ignoring him. His conceit was to address her as a young mare whom, if he wished, he could master and ride. In a standard modern prose version:

> Pray, why do you look askance at me, my Thracian filly, and shun me so resolutely as though I knew nothing of my art? I would have you to know I could bridle you right well and take rein and ride you about the turning-post of the course. But instead you graze in the meadows and frisk and frolic to your heart's content; for you have not a clever breaker to ride you.[1]

The poem has been translated many times. For our purposes the opening is the crucial part. In the eighteenth century:

> Why with Scorn-reverting Eye,
> Pretty *Thracian Filley*, Why
> Me as skill-less and unwise
> Fly you . . .

At the beginning of the nineteenth:

> Like some wanton filly sporting,
> Maid of Thrace! thou fly'st my courting,
> Wanton filly! tell me why . . .

Now, the very fact that Thoreau should have selected a poem in which the voice asserts its superiority to a disdainful woman is certainly meaningful in itself. Moreover, the existence of a classical model freed him to be much bolder and more direct in his translation than he could ever bring himself to be in his own right. But consider *his* version of the opening lines:

> Thracian colt, why at me
> Looking aslant with thy eyes,
> Dost thou cruelly flee . . ."
> (*Week*, 230)

Thoreau has neutralized the gender of the filly. He knew Greek sufficiently well not to have made such a fundamental error in his translation. It is true that "colt" has been used elsewhere to designate a young mare, as in the *Oxford English Dictionary*'s citation of Tennyson writing in 1858: "She's yet a colt—Take, break her." But the *OED* also shows that since as early as 1400 "filly" had been the standard term used to distinguish the young female horse. Edith Seybold, in her study of Thoreau's engagement with the classics, has commented on his occasional willfulness in translation, contending that he sometimes "deliberately mistranslated, knowing quite well that the lines meant one thing as Horace and Persius wrote them but finding a second meaning more acceptable to himself."[2] In this instance, Thoreau's transformation of the "filly" into a "colt" effectively muted the force of Anacreon's bridling and riding a woman.

The precise significance of this change for Thoreau's mind is of course impossible to determine. But the Anacreon translation seems to me related to a more general confusion of genders in Thoreau's writing, particularly that involving his well-known elegy, "Lately, alas, I knew a gentle boy" (*Poems*, 64–66). This poem laments Thoreau's estrangement from a boy "whose features all were cast in Virtue's mould." So smitten had he been with this boy that he "quite forgot my homage to confess." Because of this oversight, he was now "forced to know, though hard it is, / I might have loved him had I loved him less" (64).

Thoreau's "gentle boy" probably was the eleven-year-old Edmund Sewall, although we have no particular indication why Edmund should have inspired such a poem. In fact, the little evidence surviving runs in the contrary direction. The Sewall family remembered Edmund's being irritated at being referred to as "the gentle boy."[3] Further, it is not clear why there was no Thoreauvian rhapsody when later, in March 1840, Edmund was not only enrolled in Thoreau's school but also came to live for the term in the Thoreau household.[4] Perhaps the feelings had changed. In spite of these questions, Edmund remains the most likely candidate as the subject of the poem. He is certainly a more plausible identification than the assertions of Thoreau's contemporaries and early biographers that the poem referred to *Ellen* Sewall, apparently because they were unwilling to accept the idea that Thoreau's intensity could have been directed toward her barely adolescent brother.[5]

Although H. S. Canby argued that inasmuch as Ellen did not arrive in Concord until a month after the poem was written, Edmund must have been its subject, he then assigned the poem "Nature doth have her dawn each day" to Ellen Sewall, even though in *it* the masculine pronoun is used in connection with "my mate."[6] And, to construct the case that the poem "I'm guided in the darkest night" is also addressed to Ellen, the chronology of her visits to Concord, as well as the November 18 letter to Prudence Ward in which Ellen describes turning down "H. T.," have been used. Once this hypothesis of Thoreau's having wooed Ellen is established, it is then further used to interpret several of Thoreau's journal entries as also referring to her. What must again give us pause is that these interpretations, like that of the "gentle boy" poem, oblige one to change the gender of the pronouns in the journal entries. For example, Thoreau writes on October 17, 1840: "In the presence of my friend I am ashamed of my fingers and toes. I have no feature so fair as my love for him" (*CinC*, 176). But why should Thoreau disguise the pronoun in this entry? In what respect would he be more vulnerable if he referred to "my love for *her?*" In any case, were Thoreau infatuated with Ellen, those of his family or friends who might read his journal would presumably recognize its subject, despite the change in the pronoun's gender.

Next, an entry for October 19, 1840: "My friend dwells in the distant horizon as rich as an eastern city there" (*CinC*, 177). Even though the pronouns that follow are masculine, it has been argued that, because Ellen lived in Scituate, southeast of Concord, this entry also refers to her. It continues: "There he sails all lonely under the edge of the sky," but although eventually "he rides in my roadsted . . . never does he fairly come to anchor in my harbor. Perhaps I afford no good anchorage" (*CinC*, 177). Finally, Thoreau shifts to a sun image: "He seems to move in a burnished atmosphere, while I peer in upon him from surrounding spaces of Cimmerian darkness" (*CinC*, 177).

No matter how one judges the merits of these arguments based on biographical detail, what is significant is what generated them. The pattern in Thoreau's writing is that when he was driven to express passionate feelings, either a general ambiguity of reference obtained or males were the object of those feelings. This inevitably raises the issue of homosexuality, but not very usefully, I think. On the basis of several quotations illustrating the "theme of same-sex intimacy," Jonathan Katz has appropriated Thoreau for his anthology *Gay American History*, and one can see why, though at the same time feeling that the term limits our understanding of Thoreau.[7] There are moments enough in his writing to be woven into such an interpretation. For example, on the water, Thoreau once noted that "There sits one by the shore who wishes to go with me, but I cannot think of it. I must be fancy-free. . . . I could better afford to take him into bed with me, for then I might, perhaps, abandon him in my dreams" (*J*, IX, 46). The imagery is odd and not necessary to make the point that Thoreau seems to be making—that he wishes to remain independent, whereas even offering a boat-ride entails responsibilities. But even as with the journal entries discussed earlier, the possibility of sensual involvement pulsates in the background.

There is no evidence, however, that Thoreau was ever sexually intimate with a man. He did have youthful attractions to women, primarily older, maternal ones. But, on the whole, Thoreau was clearly unsettled by women, as he was in general by any close physical proximity. Other people's bodies troubled him as much as did his own. Further, it was clear to him that marriage would bring fleshly obligations such as he could not easily entertain, not to speak of dubious entanglements of material responsibility. But Thoreau's erotic feelings flared up from time to time in the presence of boys, men, and nature.

Throughout his life, Thoreau's remarks show that he almost invariably regarded sensual love with suspicion if not outright disgust. "Can love be in aught allied to dissipation," he asked. "Let us love by refusing not accepting one another." The reason? "There is a danger that we may stain and pollute one another" ("Chastity & Sensuality," *EE*, 275, 276). Accordingly, Thoreau's formula for marriage was a severe one. "If it is the result of a pure love, there can be nothing sensual in marriage. Chastity is something positive, not negative. It is the virtue of the married especially. All lusts or base pleasures must give place to loftier delights. They who meet as superior beings cannot perform the deeds of inferior ones" (*EE*, 274–275).

Once Thoreau had more or less permanently established chastity for himself, he elevated it and imposed it imaginatively on his friends. To be sure, such repression was hardly unusual in Thoreau's century. Its concealments of sex were sufficient for him to have remarked that "one of the most interesting of all human facts is veiled more completely than any mystery" (*EE*, 274). He himself had experienced an idealized but elusive version of it. "The intercourse of the sexes, I have dreamed, is incredibly beautiful, too fair to be remembered. I have had thoughts about it, but they are the most fleeting and irrecoverable in my experience" (*EE*, 277). Still, Thoreau could fantasize that communion with one's beloved might involve bewitching threats to one's self-control: "What if the lover should learn that his beloved dealt in incantations and philters! What if he should hear that she consulted a clairvoyant!" ("Love," *EE*, 271). And he could not countenance another's curiosity. Any questioning, even of the most innocent sort, seemed to violate his privacy. "I require that thou knowest everything without being told anything. I parted from my beloved because there was one thing which I

had to tell her. She *questioned* me. She should have known all
by sympathy" ("Love," *EE*, 271). A decade later, in curious
image, Thoreau reiterated that position, this time in respect to
friends. "My friend is he who can make a good guess at me, hit
me on the wing" (*J*, IV, 359).

Given the power of his inhibitions, Thoreau had to suppose that his feelings could be intuited. As he put it in an
unfortunate piece of doggerel:

> . . . if the truth were known, Love cannot speak,
> But only thinks and does;
> Though surely out 'twill leak
> Without the help of Greek,
> Or any tongue.
> (*J*, I, 41; *Poems*, 89)

Thoreau eventually reconciled himself to his bachelor-
hood. In 1851 he told his journal: "I am sure that the design of
my maker when he has brought me nearest to woman was not
the propagation, but rather the maturation, of the species.
Man is capable of a love of woman quite transcending marriage" (*J*, II, 185). He became habituated to conceiving of
love and friendship as if they were synonymous. Thoreau did
have a number of intimate friendships of considerable depth
and intensity, beginning in his family, but he commonly displayed such reticence that when he refers to "my friend" we do
not necessarily know whether he means male or female, relative or close companion. In some few cases, this uncertainty
may be the result of editorial discretion, observed, as an editor
of the journals explained, "out of regard for the feelings of
possible relatives or descendants of the persons mentioned"
(*J*, "Preface," 5). However, Thoreau normally observed a
prudent distance in his references. Typically, we do not even
know whether the famous opening question of the whole huge
journal can be positively attributed to Emerson or not: " 'What
are you doing now?' he asked. 'Do you keep a journal?' " (*J*, I,
3). And when Thoreau's brother John died of lockjaw, fol-

lowed shortly by the death of the Emersons' son, Waldo, only an ellipsis of forty-one days appeared in Thoreau's journal, from January 9, 1842, to February 18. We know from other sources that Thoreau himself was ill with a psychosomatic case of sympathetic lockjaw during a portion of this period, so severe was his bereavement (and possibly guilt because of his having courted the same young woman his brother loved).[8] The most Thoreau said was in a letter: "I have been confined to my chamber for a month with a prolonged shock of the same disorder" (*Corr.*, 66). When he recommenced his journal, he made but a few perfunctory remarks to the effect that the death of "friends" should inspire us, since good can never disappear (*J*, I, 321). He does admit that his "soul and body have tottered along together of late," but his only deep acknowledgment of the profundity of the trauma is the wonderful sentence: "I am like a feather floating in the atmosphere; on every side is depth unfathomable" (*J*, I, 322, 321).

In the powerfully yearning days of his youth, Thoreau preferred to believe that friendships were fated and irresistible, "like air bubbles on water, hastening to flow together" (*J*, I, 113). And he asked why such classic friendships as those of Orestes and Pylades, or Damon and Pythias, should not be put to shame by a present-day community (*J*, I, 113). But his imagery betrayed the insubstantiality of his conceptions, for air bubbles are doomed to burst, and he could not assert that modern friendships would be superior to classical ones, but could only question why they should not be.

In those days, Thoreau also chose to believe that the attitudes of one's friends were of no moment. One's idealizations and subjective extensions were the only reality. Temporal disagreements were of no consequence. "What matter a few words more or less with my friend,—with all mankind;—they will still be my friends in spite of themselves. Let them stand aloof if they can!" (*J*, I, 108). Ultimately these brave words proved of no practical value for Thoreau in subduing the anxiety of loneliness. Friendship remained a problem for him, even though, by 1842, he was dealing more complexly with its actualities. At the same time, he continued to rationalize away difficulties. "My friend is cold and reserved," he remarked, "because his love for me is waxing and not waning," a sanguine conclusion that would not normally be drawn from such chilly evidence. Thoreau then pursued a Stendhalian crystallization analogy: "These are the early processes; the particles are just beginning to shoot in crystals." Then, restlessly dropping this unpromising image, Thoreau turned to a declaration of the satisfaction that he took from withheld friendship: "If the mountains came to me, I should no longer go to the mountains. So soon as that consummation takes place which I wish, it will be past." Finally, Thoreau reverted briefly to his preference for postponed fulfillment: "Shall I not have a friend in reserve? Heaven is to come. I hope this is not it" (*J*, I, 339).

This sequence strikes me as an altogether representative instance of Thoreau's thinking, in that it presents a series of disconnected and not especially apt images in the service of explaining away disappointment. To look ahead a bit, by 1851 Thoreau had incorporated this generalized observation into a particular and positive truth about himself: "I find that I postpone all actual intercourse with my friends to a certain real intercourse which takes place commonly when we are actually at a distance from one another" (*J*, II, 266). In this formulation, fulfillment was not postponed and happily anticipated. Rather, the *imaginary* intercourse with the friend was now described as "real" compared to the crude actuality of their physical encounters.

Thoreau composed several poems on various aspects of friendship, some of them among his most intriguing. None is without interest, nor is any without its problems. When these poems have been noticed, it has primarily been to tease biographical revelations out of them, but they also confirm that

Thoreau's vision of friendship almost invariably entailed separation. Early in his manhood, he was able to identify friendship as that condition in which one shared "a kindred nature" with another, so that "each may other help, and service do" (*Poems*, 90). But even in this 1838 poem, "Friendship," this familiar conception underwent revision. "Two sturdy oaks, I mean," Thoreau writes in clarification, which "barely touch." Only deep in the ground are "their roots . . . intertwined / Insep'rably" (*Poems*, 90, 91). If this assertion of covert intimacy were not austere enough, even that much Thoreau could not long believe or accept. It was much more characteristic of him to envision friendship as "a double star" fixed in the heavens and revolving "about one centre" (*Poems*, 109). It is true that here, in 1839, he could still assert that the revolving was accompanied by "spheral song," but soon enough that harmony yielded to sterner realities about intimacy. Should he roll near the path of another, "with a pleased anxiety," he would feel the other's "purer influence on my opaque mass," yet he was always doomed to learn that ultimately he had "scarce changed its sidireal [sic] time" (*Poems*, 140). These feelings of inferiority and ineffectuality accurately reflected Thoreau's troubled condition.

The 1838 poem, "Friendship," said that possession of the same "loves and hates" would prove that the two persons were "mates" (*Poems*, 90). If the needs of rhyme seem to have triumphed over psychological insight here, eventually Thoreau was obliged to assert that hate was the positive element in a relationship, so that he might justify his feelings, as well as those of his Concord neighbors. The central poem on this topic is "Let such pure hate still underprop" (*Poems*, 71). Its central and startling conceit appears in the opening stanza:

Let such pure hate still underprop
Our love, that we may be
Each other's conscience,
And have our sympathy
Mainly from thence.
(*Poems*, 71)

The balance of the poem expresses familiar Thoreauvian themes: that human beings, even when attracted by deep bonds of sympathy, remain solitary stars; that love does not communicate by words, for none is sufficient to bridge the "gulf of feeling," except by "decrees of fate"; that love shines serenely on above the clouds and is irresistible (*Poems*, 72). Thoreau was ever trying to establish the imperial indifference of love toward temporary confusions and setbacks. Being all too well aware of the flaws and obstacles that threatened such friendships as he had experienced, he insisted all the more on friendship's austere and fated triumph.

Hanging over the whole argument was that harshly moralistic opening, "Let such pure hate still underprop / Our love. . ." Having detected hate in his human relationships, or, if not hate, then some reduced versions of it—disapproval, envy, rancor—and finding himself incapable of purging himself (or the other) of that negative emotion, he sought to incorporate it into his model by idealizing it into a "pure" hate. That Thoreau possessed a plenitude of violent feelings cannot be doubted. One of the most famous incidents associated with him is normally recounted as an instance of his independence; it seems to me to tell quite another tale. It occurred after Thoreau was newly graduated from Harvard College and was teaching in the Concord Town School. Admonished by an observing committeeman and deacon to thrash his pupils, Thoreau at first refused, then took six of them ostensibly at random (including, disconcertingly enough, "the maid-servant in his own house"), used the ferule on them, and resigned his position.[9] A moment's thought will suggest that *six* of the innocent was a somewhat excessive number to punish so that Thoreau might prove his contempt for his judges. Evident in this episode is the explosive fury normally suppressed by Thoreau but sporadically appearing with alarming metaphoric force in his writing. He managed to control his furious resentments for the most part (or, by retiring from company, to reduce the potentiality for their exacerbation), but the strain on him was evident. His former, admiring pupil, Horace

Hosmer, reported that "Henry was not loved. He was a conscientious teacher, but rigid."[10] Another student, one of the six arbitrarily punished, was still alive in 1917 and, according to Edward Emerson, "all through life has cherished his grievance, not understanding the cause."[11] Still, the younger Emerson, who knew Thoreau intimately, was anxious to make the point that "Thoreau, although brusque on occasions, was refined, courteous, kind and humane."[12] This seems to have been the case, at least with people who made no serious demands on him, such as children and the old.

Others, though, even friends who were not readily inclined to judge him, proved more taxing. Over and over he insisted on the necessity of hate as a component of love. "I need thy hate as much as thy love. Thou wilt not repel me entirely when thou repellest what is evil in me" ("Love," *EE*, 272). The responsibility was exigent: "Love is a severe critic. . . . They who aspire to love worthily, subject themselves to an ordeal more rigid than any other" (*EE*, 270). And in a journal entry for December 31, 1840, after considering the alternative to this harsh, if elevated, conception of love, Thoreau dismissed it contemptuously: "This sickly preaching of love, and a sympathy that will be tender of our faults, is the dyspepsia of the soul" (*CinC*, 202).

The paradox is evident. Thoreau resented criticism but at the same time, privately charged with self-disgust, felt the need for it. But his championing of hate as an essential component of friendship reached such obsessive proportions at times as to become grotesque:

> Surely, surely, thou wilt trust me
> When I say thou dost disgust me.
> O, I hate thee with a hate
> That would fain annihilate . . .
> (*Poems*, 181)

These lines, intended altogether seriously, display the power of Thoreau's feeling, not against a bureaucratic state, nor a slaveholder, nor a businessman—all objects of Thoreau's wrath at one time or another—but against someone he designates in the poem as "my dear friend." "Yet sometimes against my will / My dear friend, I love thee still." But immediately following this confession of lingering susceptibility, Thoreau returns to underscore the obligatory nature of his disgust:

It were treason to our love,
And a sin to God above,
One iota to abate
Of a pure impartial hate.
(*Poems*, 181)

Hate also appears in a friendly letter Thoreau wrote to the Emersons during his absence on Staten Island in 1843. This was shortly after he had left their household after a stay of two years, at which time he had thanked them "for your long kindness to me" (*Corr.*, 78). In the letter in question, Thoreau warmly recalled "sacred" walks in the woods with his sponsors, then continued:

But know, my friends, that I a good deal hate you all in my most private thoughts—as the substratum of the little love I bear you. Though you are a rare band and do not make half use enough of one another." (*Corr.*, 124)

From that quite unexpected remark, Thoreau then passed on without further comment to an analysis of the newest number of *The Dial*.

What are we to make of this passage, other than that in its abrupt candor it is altogether typical of Thoreau? The Emersons must have felt they knew how to take their protégé's words, since these remarks seem to have occasioned no concern. Emerson's next letter said that they "were all very glad to have such cordial greetings from you" (*Corr.*, 126). It is true that the letter in question immediately followed the one containing Thoreau's soulful testimony to Lidian Emerson that "the thought of you will constantly elevate my life" (*Corr.*, 119). It is also true that Thoreau's next letters were notably dampered, and it may be that he brought forth his testimony of hate as a means of laying to rest the indiscretion of his sentimental overreaction. The quantity of hate, we see, is "a good deal"; of love, "a little."

Since for Thoreau hate could be the expression of conscience and therefore operate in the service of the good, one might assume that the "higher" function of hate was operating in the paragraph from the letter to the Emersons. However, Thoreau also had reasons for being resentful toward them, especially toward Emerson himself. When he was absent, then Thoreau could play the attractive role of father to the Emerson family. He genuinely enjoyed their children and had inclinations toward imaginative appropriation. For example, in 1843 he wrote Emerson that his daughter Edith "says 'papa' less and less abstractedly every day, looking in *my* face" (*Corr.*, 76). Some four years later, he again wrote to the absent breadwinner that his son Eddy "very seriously asked me, the other day, 'Mr. Thoreau, will you be my father?'. . . So you must come back soon, or you will be superseded" (*Corr.*, 189). There is no little complacency in those reports.

But now Emerson had been the agent, however well-meaning, of exiling Thoreau in the inhospitable environment of Staten Island. And Lidian had evidently retreated from that original "trustful" mood expressed in the letter from her that had so stirred Thoreau's feelings (*Corr.*, 119). In his June 20, 1843, reply Thoreau admitted to Lidian that "I, perhaps, am more willing to deceive by appearances than you say you are; it would not be worth the while to tell how willing—but I have the power perhaps too much to forget my meanness as soon as seen, and not be incited by permanent sorrow. My actual life is unspeakably mean" (*Corr.*, 120). I suspect that a component of the meanness Thoreau observed in himself was that rankling resentment he tried to elevate into a virtue. So, when Thoreau told the Emersons that he hated them a good deal "in my most private thoughts," he probably meant it, even though his designation of hate as the agent of conscience underpropping love would protect him should offense be taken.[13]

For all his attempts at rationalization, Thoreau felt himself in most respects seriously out of phase with his world. His writings tell us that he often perceived no goal, no hope, and no inspiration in that world and, moreover, that the problem extended to the subjective level of existence. When he consulted his inner condition, he heard an "infinite din within," but he tried to convince himself that, even if he reproached himself for not actively engaging in the struggles with the outer world, for not allowing "the indignation which has so long rankled in his breast" to "take to horse and to the field," still, the true vocation of the brave man was in fact internal battle. "Is he not at war?" (*J*, I, 246–247). And in another journal entry he confirmed this sense of psychic strife by observing sternly: "I have a deep sympathy with war, it so apes the gait and bearing of the soul" (*J*, I, 156). Thus a change of scene or of occupation could not eliminate Thoreau's malaise. Residence at Walden Pond could perhaps clarify his ideas somewhat, but it could not still the internal uproar. Much of the distress of the young poet remains visible in *Walden*, even if that book's surface optimism has shone so brightly as to blind us to its caves of darkness.

Often impatient with his contemporaries, Thoreau gravitated to the classics for inspiration and guidance. One of his early projects was a translation of Aeschylus' *The Prometheus Bound*. Although Emerson had requested it, both the author and the subject attracted Thoreau. In a little sermon composed for his 1839 journal, he had reflected that Aeschylus was a man who had "lived his own healthy Attic life," who had disregarded rhetorical display to speak genuinely, and who "like every genius ... was a solitary liver and worker" (*J*, I, 93). Feeling a sympathetic relationship, then, Thoreau returned a few weeks later to expand on Aeschylus' greatness. He "had a clear eye for the commonnest things." Further, it seemed to Thoreau that "the social condition of genius is the same in all ages. Aeschylus was undoubtedly alone and without sympathy in his simple reverence for the mystery of the universe" (*J*, I, 116, 117). So, already respectful of the poet, Thoreau turned willingly to his dramatization of a demi-god sacrificed for helping man. The role of the stoic under sentence of perpetual torture for his good deeds supplied a certain appealing parallel to his own situation. "O revered Mother, O Ether / Revolving common light to all," reads Thoreau's version of the play's concluding lines, "You see me, how unjust things I endure!" (*W*, V, 375).

Thoreau readily identified with such figures as Prometheus who were noble and inspired but obliged to endure some torment or bondage. "The god Apollo (Wisdom, Wit, Poetry) condemned to serve, keep the sheep of *King* Admetus" constituted a favorite analogy in his mind (*J*, I, 391). "Who is King Admetus? It is Business, with his four prime ministers Trade and Commerce and Manufactures and Agriculture. And this is what makes mythology true and interesting to us" (*J*, II, 378). Thoreau saw the social applicability, but he also identified directly with the subjugated Apollo. "I am thinking what an elysian day it is, and how I seem always to be keeping the flocks of Admetus such days—that is my luck" (*J*, VI, 185; see also II, 375, III, 5, and IV, 114, for other references to Admetus).

Thoreau was trying to *make* himself, to construct a mode of life that would be both satisfying and defensible, while at the same time he suffered from guilt, loneliness, and despair. For example, although his essay "The Service" offers a rather complacent series of declarations concerning what the brave man is in comparison to the coward, embedded within it is a quatrain expressing chagrin and regret:

> Each more melodious note I hear
> Brings this reproach to me,
> That I alone afford the ear,
> Who would the music be.
> (*RP*, 9; *Poems*, 119)

The moon afforded Thoreau an example of cosmic ease and beauty that he longed to emulate. "The moon moves up her smooth and sheeny path / Without impediment." But that was not the case with him: "My cares never rest . . . my current never rounds into a lake" (*Poems*, 226). The moon has a serene indifference to all terrestrial suffering such as his own:

> She does not wane, but my fortune,
> Which her rays do not bless,
> My wayward path declineth soon,
> But she shines not the less.
> (*Poems*, 11)

Even when the moon pales, she remains "alway in her proper sphere / She's mistress of the night" (*Poems*, 11). By contrast, Thoreau felt uncertain, out of place, unfulfilled. He sometimes tried to convince himself that the wisest course was passivity in the face of the inevitable. "What first suggested that necessity was grim, and made fate so fatal," he asked himself in his journal. "The strongest is always the least violent." Then, memorably: "Necessity is a sort of Eastern cushion on which I recline" (*J*, I, 168).

But, too regularly agitated to be able to accept the condition of Oriental ease, Thoreau plunged again and again into the fields and woods for relief. These daily walks helped, for however random the experience they furnished might be, they organized existence without greatly organizing it. The bits and pieces of experience they offered did not require difficult assimilation to be appreciated. And, if one considers the literary forms on which Thoreau relied, one can see that they either furnished the structure that was missing or, as with the journal, sanctioned randomness and improvisation. Translation most obviously frees the writer from the burden of original organization. Reviews such as "Paradise (To Be) Regained" and assessments of careers like "Sir Walter Raleigh" and "Thomas Carlyle" also provided stable, fixed entities on which Thoreau could elaborate. His descriptions of walks as well as the narrative skeleton of the *Week* were provided coherence by the movement across a landscape and by the passage of time, and *Walden*, of course, depended on a seasonal calendar for its ordering form.

But, as Thoreau learned, his confusions were only contained, not resolved, by these contingent forms. "I am a parcel of vain strivings tied / By a chance bond together." These, the opening lines of "Sic Vita," one of his most imagistically effective poems, sum up Thoreau's condition as a young man. Of no moment; expending effort without success; and existing, not in conformance to some grand conception, but randomly. The poem itself was supposedly thrown in the window of Mrs. Lucy Jackson Brown, but it is hardly a love lyric. Bronson Alcott, in fact, read it at Thoreau's funeral (Canby, *Thoreau*, 439). Nor is it, as Canby suggests, a poem in which Thoreau indicates that he will mature—that "give him another year, and freedom, and then his vain strivings will have strengthened his character, and have made more virile the stock of talent in his mind" (*Thoreau*, 73–74). Quite the contrary. In the poem there is no specified recipient of the bouquet, nor any gratified response to its presentation. Rather, the speaking nosegay is placed in a bare cup where its tender buds mimic life, for they will not, they cannot, develop.

There *is* a resolution—the very oddest sort of rationalization. The speaker, it turns out, is to be regarded as a sacrifice, one that is necessary for the improvement of the plant. "Thus thinned," the parent stock will bear "more fruits and fairer flowers," "while I droop here" (*Poems*, 82). Now although the poem's opening lines surely capture Thoreau's own sense of hopelessness and lack of purpose, this resolution is both specious and internally contradictory. Thoreau has specified the nosegay as composed of a mixture of violets and sorrel, seized "in haste" from the fields. So not only are the prophesied *fruits* inappropriate to the specific plants mentioned, but the spontaneous and hasty act of picking them can hardly be described as the deliberate thinning a gardener might perform. But Thoreau needed some positive explanation, some understanding of why, in an ostensibly harmonious world, he should feel himself no more than a motley collection of frustrated impulses, and so he generated this fable of productive sacrifice that supplied the poem with a formal but distinctly unsatisfactory conclusion.

Given the state of his frustration, Thoreau could not always uphold the strenuous position that insisted that the striving was all. Instead, like a village Hamlet, he sometimes longed for his sullied flesh to thaw and resolve itself into a dew. In 1839:

> Fain would I stretch me by the highway side,
> To thaw and trickle with the melting snow,
> That mingled soul and body with the tide,
> I too may through the pores of nature flow.
> *(Poems, 107)*

The relief of such a dissolution was, however, denied Thoreau. "But I alas nor trickle can nor fume" (*Poems*, 107). Therefore, once more as in "Sic Vita," he attempted a positive resolution. His role, he decided, was "to hearken while these ply the loom, / So shall my silence with their music chime" (107). One cannot help but note how often Thoreau will attempt to make his negative qualities—his silence, his passivity, his distance, his frozenness—into virtues. Typically: "The most positive life that history notices has been a constant retiring out of life, a wiping one's hands of it, seeing how mean it is, and having nothing to do with it" (*J*, I, 133).

On the other hand, the desire to be literally absorbed into the all remained with him. One eccentric version of it was his evocation of the imagined pleasure of standing all day up to the chin in a swamp (*J*, I, 141). A more common experience took place in 1839, when "drifting in a sultry day on the sluggish waters of the pond, I almost cease to live and begin to be. . . . I am never so prone to lose my identity. I am dissolved in the haze" (*J*, I, 75). That condition was clearly at once a union and an escape.

At the other extreme was Thoreau's celebration of crisp winter when each object had its firm definition. Such marble selfhood brought him reassurance. Melting was a rare phenomenon for him and generally one neither sought nor desired. In his hardened Roman state, Thoreau not only was armored against a wounding world but also evinced an indifference to suffering. He could look with fatalistic objectivity on a scene of disaster, transcending the pain of others and, by utilizing the same formula of paradox he employed with himself, could actually assert the attractiveness of such a scene. "When a freshet destroys the works of man, or a fire consumes them, or a Lisbon earthquake shakes them down, our sympathy with persons is swallowed up in a wider sympathy with the universe. A crash is apt to grate agreeably on our ears" (*J*, I, 135).

Nonetheless, at times such defenses failed, whereupon Thoreau was compelled to ask the question direct: "My friends, why should we live?" His gloomy perception was that "Life is an idle war a toilsome peace." If his metaphor for existence was military, his tone was pessimistic, not because he felt defeated but because he felt useless. "Shall we out-wear the year / In our pavilions on its dusty plain . . .?" As the signal never comes "To strike our tents and take the road again," we are denied even the pleasure of purposeful movement. The poem's concluding stanza is utterly without hope, proposing as it does a wearisome and useless lifetime of illusory activity:

> Or else drag up the slope
> The heavy ordnance of nature's train?

Useless but in the hope,
Some far remote and heavenward hill to gain.
                              (*Poems*, 137)

Although these sentiments are far from the whole of Thoreau, they do constitute a major component of his general mood—that there was neither purpose nor hope in a life that was marked by labor dedicated to a markedly dubious end. "Vain" then became an important operative term for him. "In vain I see the morning rise, / In vain observe the western blaze" (*Poems*, 78). These lines come from "The Poet's Delay," Thoreau's lament for his unresponsiveness to the presumably inspirational natural world. Nature may be boundlessly wealthy, but "I only still am poor within." Nature may celebrate fecundity, growth, and promise, "But still my spring does not begin" (*Poems*, 78).

Such laconic desolation was a recurrent feature of Thoreau's imagination. But, although he could describe his personal distress or embody his world in a bleak image, he rarely drew any explicit conclusions. Here is a complete poem:

Between the traveller and the setting sun,
Upon some drifting sand heap of the shore,
A hound stands o'er the carcass of a man.
                              (*Poems*, 206)

So, if not the bay horse and turtle-dove, Thoreau did at last find his hound. But he refused to interpret its significance. There was merely silence and stilled motion: sand, a hound, a human carcass, and beyond these the setting sun.

Here, then, is a background against which to read Thoreau's major writings. Highly personal, uncertainly ordered, and often perplexing compositions, they emerge out of such distress and confusion as these early pieces reveal. This study describes no sequential success story, but rather follows an intermittent struggle that is sometimes impressive, sometimes irritating, and often quite poignant in its urgency. Thoreau did manage some modest victories in time, as well as a quiet truce with himself and with the failings of those others who so regularly exasperated him. But self-conquest was a fantasy, and even that self-knowledge that Thoreau resisted so strenuously was a solvent of distinctly limited powers. Until his death Thoreau harbored demons of anxiety and resentment that he tirelessly tried to rationalize but that would not be stilled. Sometimes he rarefied his arguments to a point difficult to reconcile with his supposed commitment to the actualities of existence; at other moments, his prose grew opaque, evasive, and strangely insufficient. Pessimism, aggressive anger, and incoherence are all prominent features of Thoreau's writing, but because they fail to accommodate themselves to those positive versions of the man ranging from the gentle naturalist to the fiery independent, they have been largely overlooked. Still, they are symptoms of inner conflicts of a magnitude and endurance hardly acknowledged, and they mark his writing everywhere.

Uneasy Drifting:
The *Week*

A bustling camp and an embattled host
Extending far on either hand I saw,
For I alone had slumbered at my post,
Dreaming of peace when all around was war.

Poems, p. 387

AFTER YEARS of writing incidental pieces, in 1845 Thoreau tried for the first time to create a full-length narrative. *A Week on the Concord and Merrimack Rivers* was initially written during that period of extraordinary productivity Thoreau enjoyed at Walden Pond, or rather it was largely constructed there of materials already extant in his journals that he then revised and expanded. Because he was drawing so heavily on ideas already verbally formulated as far back as seven years, one may say that composition of the *Week* partially hampered Thoreau's development, since, by the power of their prior existence, his own words tended to coerce him into positions he was already prepared to go beyond.

At the same time, Thoreau's general mood was regressive. He was engaged in a double withdrawal—not only to

27

Walden Pond, but also into the past, sailing in memory down the Merrimack, away from the failures and loneliness of his life and away from the disapproval of a Concord society that he could not bring himself to leave permanently. The result is an indifferent success, a potpourri of ideas that are often quite flat and inconsequential and, at their deepest level, in unacknowledged contest with one another. Ostensibly the *Week* memorializes an idyllic journey taken in 1839 with Thoreau's cheerful, outgoing, but now deceased brother John, but, so anonymous is the presence of Thoreau's companion on the trip as recounted, we can begin by declaring that it is no tribute to John.[1] But neither is it finally a lyrical outing, for, despite Thoreau's attempt to escape into the optimism of retrospect, his fundamental pessimism kept rising up to flood the landscape.

The rueful tone commences with the epigraphs, one of which is Thoreau's equivocal quatrain:

I am bound, I am bound, for a distant shore,
By a lonely isle, by a far Azore,
There it is, there it is, the treasure I seek,
On the barren sands of a desolate creek.
(*Week*, 3)

The setting in which Thoreau imagines the discovery of a brilliant recompense is singularly dreary. It is "distant," "lonely," "far," "barren," and "desolate." The negative force of these descriptive terms far outweighs the treasure perceived but not yet reached, giving one a glimpse at the outset of the desolate inner landscape through which Thoreau moved, year after year, in search of something he could count precious. The natural world might temporarily divert him from his sense of pervasive desolation, but it could not permanently correct it.

Even in the meandering prologue to the *Week*, "Concord River," Thoreau's imagination is drawn to instances of suffering. Although he was suggesting the value of following the

Concord River in order to see the sights, those sights included ducks "all uneasy in the surf, in the raw wind," and muskrats "swimming for dear life, wet and cold." And he imagines that one may run aground and "get as good a freezing there as any where on the North-west Coast" (7). To be sure, Thoreau included other images possessing less emotional content—great hills, a hundred brooks, haystacks, wheeling gulls—and called the totality "such healthy natural tumult as proves the last day is not yet at hand" (7). Thoreau did generally react positively to the testing of life, but without pondering why apprehension and pain were obligatory nor what the implications of their presence might be.

He himself clearly initiated some of the suffering. For example, embarking on a catalogue of local fish, he observed that he had seen small fish "when frightened by something thrown into the water, leap out by dozens, together with the dace, and wreck themselves upon a floating plank" (30). So, too, we learn that the horned pout "are extremely tenacious of life, opening and shutting their mouths for half an hour after their heads have been cut off," and that the eel, "a slimy, squirming creature," will continue, as it is cooked, "squirming in the pan" (31, 32). As for the common sucker, Thoreau tells us that they may be caught by jerking them out of the water with "a hook fastened firmly to the end of a stick, and placed under their jaws" (32). No doubt these details require no justification beyond their realism for being included. Still, Thoreau had a marked zest for the hard and the macabre. Speaking of pickerel, he observed, "I have caught one which had swallowed a brother pickerel half as large as itself, with the tail still visible in its mouth, while the head was already digested in its stomach" (31). Although Thoreau would regularly offer his readers such details drawn from his patient observation of nature, he rarely attempted to utilize such grotesque instances of nature's savagery as emblems of a higher meaning, nor did he ponder why they should be exempt from such exercises in interpretation.

As the Concord River bore Thoreau away from the "ignoble town," he expressed his regret at the disappearance of a
generation of revolutionary patriots. "The men who stood on
yonder height / That day, are long since gone" (17, 18). He
also sentimentalized the now "extinct" race of professional
fishermen who had formerly piled the river's banks with
"heaps uncountable" of shad and alewives. They were distinctly superior in his mind to the casual present-day fisherman, "skulking through the meadows to a rainy afternoon
sport" (34). In short, the contemporary generation deserved
dismissal for being conventional and prudent. The *Week*
served as an imaginative escape from his ignoble neighbors,
who built factories in Lowell and a dam at Billerica that
Thoreau thought should be leveled because it flooded the
meadows and destroyed the fisheries (33, 38). He suggested
that a crowbar might properly be turned against the dam, but
even if such force should fail, he remained assured that nature
would have destroyed it "after a few thousand years" (37).

Despite these aggressive thoughts, the inception of the
voyage itself is markedly passive. Thoreau had long contemplated the Concord's slow-moving current, until at last he
"resolved to launch myself on its bosom, and float whither it
would bear me" (13). And it is into a dream world that the
brothers drift. The first night they pitched their tent where,
"for the most part, there was no recognition of human life in
the night; no human breathing was heard" (40). It is an ideal
situation, because away from men. Thoreau emphasizes that
he and his brother represent "the first encroachment of commerce on this land" (40). Yet he also realized that the re-
created trip was a forced act of the imagination. In one of those
queer little quatrains he inserted here and there in the book,
he wrote:

> But since we sailed
> Some things have failed,
> And many a dream
> Gone down the stream. (18)

John was one of those lost ideals, and his own hopes were another. And there was nothing to be done about it, save float where the river would bear him, displaying a wise passivity before the inevitable.

In considering the structure of the *Week*, no one has ever given it high marks for coherence. An assemblage of materials barely stitched together and minimally connected with the journey on the two rivers, the book discusses subjects we must assume were of central importance for Thoreau, since he had an abundance of time available for composing and polishing it. Unlike Poe or Melville, he was not driven by financial exigencies to churn out indifferent prose for a livelihood. Nor was there a public avid for the latest Thoreau. He had to force his way into publication. After unsuccessful negotiations over the *Week* with Wiley & Putnam, Harpers, Crosby & Nichols, Ticknor & Co., and still others, he finally accepted an arrangement with James Munroe & Co., in which he agreed to defray the full costs of the printing, which he hoped to recover through royalties, although, as it finally turned out, it was the sale of pencils that made up the deficit (Harding, *Days*, 243–246, 254).

Sunday had a particular resonance for Thoreau. It was the day when his materialistic fellow-citizens were abroad, pretending to virtue. The sun liberated the day itself from "a dense fog," making the atmosphere "more of the auroral rosy and white." It seemed "as if it dated from earlier than the fall of man, and still preserved a heathenish integrity" (43). That statement commences the symbolic spine of the chapter "Sunday": an espousal of a world superior to Christianity's, and to home. Like the village that shared its name, the Concord River was "a sluggish artery" to Thoreau, "a deep, dark, and dead stream" (11, 43). Despite some superficially positive gestures toward his native river, Thoreau's conveyed sense of it was persistently unpleasant. Only when he had descended through the locks into "the freedom of the Merrimack" did his imagery brighten (79). Then, gliding over its "broad bosom," he refers to the Merrimack's village harbors as "smooth and fairy-like," and the houses on its banks seem "the dwellings of noble, home-staying men" (80).

While the matutinal mood was on him, Thoreau felt "as if it were a natural Sabbath" (46). In his lyrical exaltation, he asked why our lives should not be both "fair and distinct," whereupon his imagination characteristically veered to a modification of the ideal, to such qualification as experience forced on him. Our lives "should at least, like the life of the anchorite, be as impressive to behold as objects in the desert, a broken shaft or crumbling mound against a limitless horizon" (46). As we shall repeatedly have occasion to see, those images come closer to Thoreau's deepest sense of things. He was quite capable of a rhapsodic appreciation of his surroundings, as when, just before evoking the broken shaft against the infinite desert horizon, he says that there are times when the course of our lives seems "to wind on before us like a green lane into a country maze, at the season when fruit trees are in blossom" (46). One cannot doubt that Thoreau experienced such moments of organic plenitude. But because they did not match his general sense of his own life, his imaginative integrity generated those images of the broken shaft and the crumbling mound.

Christianity came to spoil Sunday in a pair of intrusive moments of the sort that were always certain to annoy Thoreau. First, as his boat passed under a bridge, some impudent young men leaned over "to pry into our concerns" (63). Thoreau stared them down. Not long after, though, people coming out of church also paused on another bridge "to look at us from above" (63). So sensitive was Thoreau to the judgments of the godly that he assumed these spectators were criticizing them—"and apparently, so strong is custom, indulged in heathenish comparisons" (63). As such unspoken condemnations could not be fended off with a fiery glance, they propelled Thoreau into a very long series of rather disconnected observations on Christianity. He proclaimed Pan as the monarch of his Pantheon and established "my Buddha" as equal to "their Christ" (65, 67). He insisted that he found not "the least vestige of authority" for settled dogmas such as the Trinity (70). He referred admiringly to the New Testament—"I love this book rarely"—but noted pointedly that despite the superficial favor it enjoyed, it was generally unpopular (71). His conclusion was that there was no greater infidelity these days than "that which prays, and keeps the Sabbath, and rebuilds the churches" (76). Even as it pushed off into a world of escape, the *Week* was being used to score off conventional life wherever possible. Predictably, most of the negative criticism of the book, even from those receptive to it as a river journey, concerned its facile paradoxes, such as: "It is necessary not to be a Christian, to appreciate the beauty and significance of the life of Christ" (67).

The meaning of that life was by no means clear in Thoreau's mind, for the main function of its specification was to stand in opposition to those who took Christ's name. "If it is not a tragical life we live, then I know not what to call it," Thoreau remarks, beginning a new paragraph. "Such a story as that of Jesus Christ and the history of Jerusalem, say, being a part of the Universal History." It is not certain whether Thoreau meant the reader to understand that the fate of Jesus was a universal one. His extension of the imagery does not appreciably diminish the uncertainty: "The naked, the embalmed, unburied death of Jerusalem amid its desolate hills,—think of it." Although the paragraph continues—"In Tasso's poem I trust some things are sweetly buried. Consider the snappish tenacity with which they preach Christianity still"—the initial conception is completed, but without ever illustrating that this was a tragical life (67). In fact, his initial statement had emerged conditionally—if it isn't tragic, I don't know what to call it. Nor did he. Nor would he think it through. That was at the heart of his rhetorical problem.

There was no mistaking his bitterness, however. "Think what a mean and wretched place this world is; that half the time we have to light a lamp that we may see to live in it. This is half our life. Who would undertake the enterprise if it were all?" So opens Thoreau's penultimate paragraph of this section. But surely daytime is superior? No, it only offers, he says, "a lamp that burns more clear . . . so we may pursue our idleness with less obstruction." That characterization does not markedly improve the state of man's existence. Still, says Thoreau with an astonishing irony, since he is mocking precisely that area he has marked out for worship: "Bribed with a little sunlight and a few prismatic tints, we bless our Maker, and stave off his wrath with hymns" (68–69).

He then provides a poem, "I make ye an offer, / Ye gods, hear the scoffer," the burden of which is that although the gods admittedly created him, he remains a proud and independent creature. He will neither "toil blindly" nor will he be slave to any god. What he *will* agree to do, he announces in this poetic manifesto, is to strive, but only on the condition that the gods "will discover, / Great plans to your lover, / And give him a sphere / Somewhat larger than here" (69). The terms emanate from discontent. Thoreau finds the world as given to be inadequate, and should there be acceptable plans for its improvement he has yet to discover them. Therefore, Thoreau concludes this section of "Sunday" with a quotation from Sadi's *Gulistan*: "Verily, my angels! I was abashed on account of my servant, who had no Providence but me; therefore did I pardon him" (69). Pardon is forthcoming because the master realizes his own deficiencies. There is no question of a superior order.

These sentiments contradict by implication the main line of Thoreau's argument: that a lovelier, higher world is available to him who will give up the values of the village and its theology. But, as Thoreau himself acknowledged: "A man's real faith is never contained in his creed" (78). If his skepticism cannot be reconciled with his idealism, one can see that they both issue from a single man and move through much of his writing. He attacks and dismisses popular standards; he asserts the superior reality of both his practical and his transcendental values; and occasionally he emits an expression of despair concerning the intractable mystery with which he struggles.

When the day is over and the brothers have beached their boat, put up the tent, started a fire, and supped, there comes a remarkable last paragraph that affords a typical conjunction of Thoreau's first giving vent to alarming doubts, then explaining them away. "One sailor," he begins, referring to himself, "was visited in his dreams this night by the Evil Destinies, and all those powers that are hostile to human life, which constrain and oppress the minds of men, and make their path seem difficult and narrow, and beset with dangers, so that the most innocent and worthy enterprises appear insolent and a tempting of fate, and the gods go not with us" (116). This is a strong description of the anxious atmosphere of a dream, but Thoreau can locate its source only in the capitalized "Evil Destinies." Although he did not know the source of his misery, he had to air it, then carefully negate it, which he does here by describing his brother as passing a serene night of "happy natural sleep" then saying that he was "soothed and reassured" by his brother's "cheerful spirit . . . for whenever they meet, the Good Genius is sure to prevail" (116).

Would that it were true. This was mere sentimental evasion of those hard questions about the self and the world that persisted in troubling him, but it was also typical. The "Monday" chapter of the *Week* also ends with a variant conceding the existence of destructive forces abroad in the world—in this case a high wind in the night that Thoreau later learned did "much injury to the corn-fields." But he added that he and his brother were spared its onslaught, "as if it had no license to shake the foundations of our tent" (178). Thoreau preferred to believe in providence, but his uneasiness betrayed itself in the fear that this world, which he purported to read as a harmonious symbol of a greater good, might ultimately prove to be destructive or, even worse, meaningless.

When the new day commenced, it was again with epigraphs that encapsulated Thoreau's mixed attitudes. Gower contributed a verse that spoke Thoreau's aspiration: to perceive insofar as possible the perennial freshness of the world.

> I thynke for to touche also
> The worlde whiche neweth everie daie,
> So as I can, so as I maie. (117)

The last line admits the possibility of constraints, to which, with a somewhat oblique mysteriousness, the next two quotations turn in the ballads of Robin Hood:

> The hye sheryfe of Notynghame,
> Hym holde in your mynde.

These two lines—all that are quoted—suggest that one must take into consideration the power of the laws of the state, which here, in the context of Robin Hood, would be seen as negative, although potentially of real consequence. Still, the next quotation reads:

> His shoote it was but loosely shott
>   Yet flewe not the arrowe in vaine,
> For it mett one of the sheriffe's men,
>   And William a Trent was slaine.

So Thoreau suggests that the repressive forces can be diminished, almost as if by divine guidance, yet the force of this quotation is not dominant. William a Trent's death is a very minor triumph. I think this accounts for the last epigraph (from William Browne's *The Shepheard's Pipe*)[2]:

Gazed on the Heavens for what he missed on Earth. (117)

This action of gazing on the heavens is not a matter of selecting and interpreting the data given in this world so as to arrive at a positive transcendental reading. Rather, it involves a looking *beyond* the immediate in order to find satisfactory recompense.

In the actual opening of the "Monday" chapter, one can feel the continuing pressure of troubling perceptions. At dawn, "all men, having reinforced their bodies and souls with sleep, and cast aside doubt and fear, were invited to unattempted adventures" (117). But the casting aside of doubt and fear did not diminish their reality, the ambiguities persisted, and the day commenced with "rowing through the fog as before" (118).

Although "Monday" begins with angry and contentious men—first, an "impatient traveller pacing the wet shore with whip in hand, and shouting through the fog," followed by the Indian fighter, Captain Lovewell—the book was in fact already beginning to slow down and to enter a condition of stasis (118). First, though, Thoreau had to make his way through a portion of the region's history. The passage is deceptive in tone, apparently straightforward but probably ironic. Thoreau fixes on a young chaplain in an old ballad: "he many Indians slew, / And some of them he scalped, while bullets round him flew" (120). Thoreau's comment is, "Our brave forefathers have exterminated all the Indians, and their degenerate children no longer dwell in garrisoned houses, nor hear any warwhoop in their path. It would be well, perchance, if many an 'English Chaplain' in these days could exhibit as unquestionable trophies of his valor as did 'good young Frye' " (120). Were this not Thoreau, we might suppose him to be serious. He *is* serious in part, for we may be sure that Thoreau did wish contemporary preachers possessed more valor. But we are equally certain that Thoreau does not approve of the extermination of Indians and that he well understands the inappropriateness of a Christian scalping an Indian. In sum, then,

Thoreau perceives his modern fellows as degenerate versions of their brutal ancestors.

He continues his indirect criticism with a quotation from a local historian who said that "new lights" and free-thinkers inhabited the region. Moreover, although most espoused Christianity, the historian also noted the presence of "a sort of *wise men*, who pretend to reject it; but they have not yet been able to substitute a better in its place" (123). Thoreau does not comment directly on this criticism of men like himself; instead, he follows it with a new paragraph that reads in its entirety: "The other voyageur, perhaps, would in the meanwhile have seen a brown hawk, or a woodchuck, or a musquash creeping under the alders." (124).

Here is another model of the operation of Thoreau's mind. Although there are times when he will strike out angrily at something he loathes, his preferred method is to correct through irony (as with the account of the scalping chaplain) or through silent comparison (as here). Thoreau was not prepared to assert that the world of the hawk, woodchuck, and muskrat was superior to Christianity, although the implication was there.

In any case, at this point in his life Thoreau was not as belligerent as he became in "Life Without Principle" and "Slavery in Massachusetts." Rather, he extolled freedom from "all anxiety and stated toil," recapturing the lazy ease of eating melon slices with the boat tied up in the noonday heat. So blissful, so important, was this mood of repose, Thoreau asserted, that he "could find some apology even for the instinct of opium, betel, and tobacco chewers" (125, 126). He lauded escape from the reformers, preferring the calm, waiting peace of the trustful, those who were confident that all would turn right without the necessity of one's anxious involvement. There was the central mode of the *Week*: passive drift.

In more vigorous moments, Thoreau praised not opium-like trances but the virtue of being awake, "though it be stormy" (134). Feeling oppressed by the past, he expressed his feeling in that morbid fashion his imagination had ready to hand: "we bear about with us the mouldering relics of our ancestors on our shoulders" (131). During "Monday," Thoreau was searching for proper action. The search forced a dialectic: on the one hand, he acknowledged the contemplative East, uttering "the mystic 'Om,' " but it seemed to him "infinitely wise, yet infinitely stagnant." On the other, there was the practical reform espoused by Christianity, the conscience of humanity (136, 137). But Thoreau could not long praise Christians. They had voice enough in his world. He elected contemplation, not action: "The things immediate to be done are very trivial. . . .The most glorious fact in my experience is not anything I have done or may hope to do, but a transient thought, or vision, or dream, which I have had" (140).

Thoreau could never, however, continue long in the affirmative. Passing some time with sailors on a scow heading for the sea became the occasion for a poem with a strikingly pessimistic point. It proposed that one should not leave one's native land, because one's fortune will inevitably follow one. His extended image concludes that one's vessel, no matter how propitious the weather or what kind of cargo it carries, will sooner or later sink. "Beneath her copper [she] bears a worm" that will ultimately bore through the hull "and sink her in the Indian seas, / Twine, wine, and hides, and China teas" (145, 146). Whether the worm be regarded as original sin, or a fatal flaw, or human mortality, the position is close to the severe indigenous Calvinism Thoreau was trying to escape.

One source of relief was the Eastern commitment to the now. "Noontide" was that mysterious transition point on the tyrannical clock when all was suspended, so that one might ask of the present, "How broad a line is that?" (153). Thoreau imagined that all history was simultaneous, so that "if I listen, I hear the peep of frogs which is older than the slime of Egypt" (153). But antiquarian efforts to resuscitate the past were fruitless. We should "not try to make these skeletons stand on their legs again" (155). The past exists in the living present, so that creation means that "the hawk . . . over the top of the wood, was at first perchance only a leaf which fluttered in its aisles" (160). But, Thoreau says laconically, "we do not know much about it" (158).

Given the depth of the mystery, only resolution could endure the daily buffets. In the neighborhood, the noblest representative of stoic grandeur being Wachusett Mountain, Thoreau introduced a long poem, "With frontier strength ye stand your ground." In it, he praised the mountain for western virtues akin to the eastern ones. The mountain is firm and cool, "as Time had nought for ye to do" (163). "I fancy even," Thoreau says, that "through your defiles windeth the way to heaven." But as his wording—"I fancy even"—reveals, the conception is an exaggerated one. Thoreau needed to eliminate from his mind the supposition that there was some final Valhalla to which he could aspire, and it was his love of the local forest and meadows that would eventually assist him to attain a state of approximate existential sufficiency. Here, though, all he could do was commend Wachusett because "like me" [thou] "standest alone without society" and "know'st not shame nor fear" (164, 165).

Bad dreams, doubt, shame, fears: the psychological pressures on Thoreau were severe. Nonetheless, he tried in the conclusion of the chapter to rise to a pitch of affirmation: "Heal yourselves, doctors; by God I live" (173). But his consciousness still remained troubled. Even the smallest images betrayed the distraction. What wakened him in the night? A cricket "shrilly singing on his shoulder . . . a hunting spider in his eye" (172). Thoreau's life was filled precisely with such annoyances, not to say ugliness and threat, which he could not translate into affirmation but which he ignored or excluded at his psychic peril. The tension was everywhere evident. Having endured "some tyro beating a drum incessantly," he tried to unfold a cosmic spectacle. The impression the sound made on him, he said, was of an opening into infinity, "as if the plow had suddenly run deeper in its furrow through the crust of the world," or as if it had opened "a bottomless skylight in the bog of my life" (173). Bog? Save for those meditative interludes when he could escape into an ecstatic realm, Thoreau felt himself mired in existence. And even when he experienced exultation, the feeling was "a sad cheer . . . perchance because we that hear are not one with that which is heard" (175).

"Perchance." The qualification was habitual for Thoreau. It and similar locutions prudently held him back from full verbal commitment. Sometimes the forceful affirmation was qualified implicitly by the action that succeeded it. The "Monday" chapter ends, for example, with a somewhat ambiguous poem of chivalric antecedents that concludes, directly enough, with Thoreau proclaiming that should Heaven "lose her champion true," it should not despair, "for I will be her champion new, / Her fame I will repair" (178). That stance was imaginatively comfortable for Thoreau. It promised that he would fulfill his goal of being an active idealist. But the bold vow of the poem is immediately followed by the chapter's last paragraph, that account of a high wind "which we afterwards learned had been still more violent elsewhere." In the face of it, a characteristic Thoreauvian prudence obtained. "We only laid our ears closer to the ground, while the blast swept on to alarm other men" (178).

"Tuesday" begins in domestic uproar, quite clearly intended to assert dominion over nature. Ranging abroad, "hatchet in hand," the brothers "made the yet slumbering and dreaming wood resound with our blows." With the fuel obtained, they "burned up a portion of the loitering night" (it was still before 3 a.m.). Next, they "tramped about the shore" to no particular purpose, save that they "waked all the muskrats, and scared up the bittern and birds that were asleep upon their roosts." They then finished their preparations for departure, all the while "talking aloud as if it were broad day" (179).

It was not, however, and this energetic busyness would never recur during the rest of the day. In fact, the bustle of the opening may have been psychologically required to offset the somber tenor of what was to come. Although the symbolic suggestion of the chapter's epigraph was that we would follow the road that runs "to many-towered Camelot," in fact Thoreau would describe two side-trips he had made in the Berkshires five years before the river journey with his brother, and they lead anywhere but to Camelot (179).

This early sentence presented Thoreau's problem: "Though we were enveloped in mist as usual, we trusted that there was a bright day behind it" (179). Or, as he put it in an accompanying lyric: "In each dewdrop of the morning / Lies the promise of a day" (179). A part of Thoreau very much wanted to believe that a heaven lay behind the obscure atmosphere of daily life, or that it could be found at the end of the arduous journey. Were these conditions true, Thoreau could then explain away the miseries of his life as being present either because one's vision was not yet able to penetrate to reality or because they were a test to make sure that only the worthy achieved Camelot. Given these two possibilities, Thoreau was temperamentally inclined to elect the one that would involve his clearing his mind of distorting vapors until he could see the truth he hoped was there. At times, he could perceive the day incipient in the dewdrop, but not always, nor even often, to judge by his writings, so that, however often it was enunciated, the optimistic assumption was repeatedly subjected to the corrosiveness of his experience.

For example, sterile wastes preoccupied Thoreau's mind during "Monday" and "Tuesday." The brothers pass "a small desert" where they learn that corn once grew, until fishermen uprooted the bushes growing on the banks to ease the hauling up of their seines, thus encouraging the winds to blow the sand up from the shore (146). Similarly, they find "another extensive desert" that had been caused rather improbably by sheep so worried by fleas that they had pawed the ground until the sod was broken "and so the sand began to blow" (198). Although Thoreau will normally note such degenerative transformations of nature without comment, here he remarks with a jocular air: "It is astonishing what a great sore a little scratch breedeth," then inquires: "Will no god be kind enough to spread a salve of birches over its sores?" (198). But he would not consider directly the implications of this "poor globe" itching "in many places" (198).

"As we cannot distinguish objects through this dense fog," Thoreau elects to interrupt the narrative of "Tuesday" almost immediately with a digression. It concerns a time when, hiking alone in the northwest corner of Massachusetts, Thoreau determined to climb Saddleback Mountain. Thunder rumbling at his heels "all the way," he ascended a valley that "seemed a road for the pilgrim to enter upon who would climb to the gates of heaven" (182, 181). Thoreau supposed that the person living highest in the valley "must be the most singular and heavenly-minded man," a mechanical supposition shortly contradicted by experience. At the next-to-last house, Thoreau encountered what may be the only sensual woman ever to appear in his work, "a frank and hospitable young woman . . . in a dishabille . . . combing her long black hair" (182). He contemplated, he wrote, returning to her place the next day, "if I could have entertainment" (182). As for the inhabitant of the last and theoretically most noble house, he took Thoreau for a peddler and called out "to know what I had to sell" (183).

Pushing up past the head of the valley, Thoreau entered a wood, then climbed easily until he reached the summit at sunset. Although there was a "rude observatory" at the top, Thoreau was not in the mood for stars (184). He was thirsty. Quite improbably, he slaked his thirst from water standing in horse tracks, insisting that it was "pure, cold, spring-like water" (184). Following this, he cooked his supper and then, surprisingly, spent the evening "reading by the light of the fire the scraps of newspapers in which some party had wrapped their luncheon" (185).

Thoreau's next action was the most extraordinary described in the *Week*. Even though this was a planned trip, and even though he had already spent one night out on Mt. Monadnock, he tells us that he had no blanket (Harding, *Days*, 171). So he gathered some wood and lay down on a board against the observatory. Then, as the night grew progressively colder, he tells us that "I at length encased myself completely in boards, managing even to put a board on top of me, with a large stone on it, to keep it down, and so slept comfortably" (186).

It is not difficult to perceive that this is a version of self-encoffinment, followed by the oblivion of death. In fact, so naturalistically improbable are the conditions Thoreau has described that it is hard to see it in any other way. The pilgrim's ascent culminated in a trance. Thoreau had arranged that he rest like an entombed hero atop a mountain. Why?

When he climbed Saddleback in that summer of 1844, Thoreau had arrived at a crucial point in his life, when the attractions of a ceremonial departure from this world were manifest. He had established only a precarious local reputation, through the assistance of his friends in publishing his work in *The Dial*, and it was now moribund. He had failed to conquer the journalistic world of New York City. More recently (earlier that same summer, in fact), he had been profoundly humiliated by setting fire to the Concord woods, thus confirming to many that he was quite as irresponsible as his refusal to take regular work indicated, and that his carelessness extended to the very woods he pretended to revere. That incident also had its connections with the Concord River, for it occurred when Thoreau and Edward Hoar set out in a boat to explore the sources of the river (*J*, II, 21). Having kindled a fire near the eastern shore of Fair Haven pond, Thoreau saw it spread rapidly through the dry grass. He ran to get help. The first man he encountered drove on, remarking, "Well, it is none of my stuff" (*J*, II, 23). The second owned the burning woods. He initially hurried to the fire, then went back toward town for assistance. Thoreau, emphasizing that he had already run over two miles himself and was "spent," and further that he could do nothing alone, climbed up Fair Haven Cliff and sat there to observe the spectacle from on high—from "the highest rock," in fact (*J*, II, 23). At first, he felt himself "a guilty person,—nothing but shame and regret." But, reflecting on it, he then rationalized strenuously, asking how these men could suppose that *they* owned the forest. "I have set fire to the forest, but I have done no wrong therein. . . . These flames are but consuming their natural food" (*J*, II, 23). So he settled down to enjoy the "glorious spectacle," until the flames rose up the side of the cliff, whereupon Thoreau joined the arriving townspeople and helped them fight the blaze, which eventually burned some three hundred acres. Returning home, Thoreau recalled that some called him a "damned rascal" and that for some years after "a flibbertigibbet or two" shouted references at him about the "burnt woods" (*J*, II, 25). But he continued to insist to himself that he must not accept the blame for their destruction.[3]

The journal entries concerning the fire, written in 1850, constitute a remarkable instance of self-justification. It is all the more significant that Thoreau should still have been brooding over the occasion six years later. Certainly his rambling trip alone across the Massachusetts landscape, culminating in his sleeping in an improvised box of boards atop the region's highest mountain, gains resonance from this humiliating local disaster of only a few months earlier.

The ascent of Saddleback is imaginatively connected with another important journal entry, one that precedes and informs Thoreau's late poem, "Forever in my dream and in my morning thought, / Eastward a mount ascends" (*J*, X, 144).

Thoreau tells us that he has had experiences that he cannot easily distinguish from dreams. This particular morning (October 29, 1857), "for the twentieth time at least, I thought of that mountain in the easterly part of our town (where no high hill actually is) which once or twice I had ascended, and often allowed my thoughts alone to climb" (*J*, X, 141). The terms of his dream-ascent in the journal resemble those of Saddleback, although they are generally more bleak. He says that his way up lay "through a dark and unfrequented wood" and that he "shuddered" as he went along. "I have," he observes parenthetically, "an indistinct remembrance of having been out overnight alone" (*J*, X, 142). The "rocky, misty summit" was not domesticated by buildings and scraps of newspapers, however, but was "awful and sublime" (*J*, X, 142). And then, as he pondered this repeated phenomenon of his dream-world, he realized that this mountain "rises in my mind where lies the Burying-Hill" (*J*, X, 143).

The Saddleback episode has yet to finish, though—"the pith of this long digression" is yet to come (188). At daylight, Thoreau once more found himself "left floating on this fragment of the wreck of a world" in "an ocean of mist" (188). With dawn, though, the mist was gradually transformed into a "new world into which I had risen in the night" (188). It was "such a country as we might see in dreams, with all the delights of paradise" (188). The earth "had passed away like the phantom of a shadow" (188–189). After the entombment, resurrection and translation into a superior world. But the paradise could not last. Before noon, the clouds again rose up "and embraced my wavering virtue," not because of some natural phenomenon, "but, alas, owing as I think, to some unworthiness in myself" (190, 189). At this point in his life, Thoreau was incapable of detaching himself and his feelings from the natural occurrence. He had to suppose that a shifting in elevation was his fault, that he did not deserve to live longer in the celestial realm and so was obliged to descend again into "the region of cloud and drizzling rain" (190).

This account of paradise gained, then lost again through unworthiness, constitutes the substance of this long digression on the fourth day of his journey. With a return to the fog-enshrouded Merrimack, Thoreau's mood changed. Now the fog or slight mist seemed to the voyagers "even fragrant and invigorating" (191). Still, by reflecting on how optical illusions are sometimes caused by water vapor in the air, so that features of the landscape seem enlarged, Thoreau comes to a surprising generalization, one that he himself was still far from being able to accept. After noting that even "the most stupendous scenery ceases to be sublime when it becomes distinct" and that the actual size of mountains and waterfalls strikes us as "always ridiculously small," Thoreau concludes: "Nature is not made after such a fashion as we would have her. We piously exaggerate her wonders" (192).

That was not quite the truth Thoreau was probing for, although it was part of it. Nature was not necessarily a material symbol of a higher spiritual truth, nor were its flaws, cruelties, absurdities, and commonplaces necessarily the result of our defective vision. They existed. But Thoreau, like his attentive contemporaries, still had to learn to accept these distasteful realities, with all the implications for human insignificance that they implied. At this point, Thoreau himself derived his philosophic recovery from some small springs he observed in the river bank. Even if the river were "yellow and tepid" and its banks "steep and clayey," it was, he proclaimed, those small, pure rills that sustained life (193).

Thoreau now returned to a still earlier stage of the Saddleback journey, this time ostensibly to illustrate that a true politeness exists beneath the surface incivility of the backwoodsman. I make no claim for the coherence of his ruminations, other than assuming they were of some felt significance for him. As he recounts his earlier walking trip, he remembers that just at nightfall he found himself enclosed by hills "in a romantic and retired valley" (203). Thoreau continued to climb toward "the last and highest of the valleys that lay in my path," where he was told that the topmost resident "was a rather rude and uncivil man" (203). Meeting this Rice, Thoreau asks if he entertains travelers and receives the gruff reply, "Sometimes we do" (204).

From this point on, Thoreau's account grows increasingly perplexing. He enters Rice's house and passes through a series of empty rooms until he reaches what he takes to be "the guests' apartment." Hearing a distant step, he returns to the first room, where he encounters a boy and a large, growling watchdog. On requesting some water from the boy, Thoreau is told abruptly, "It runs in the corner" (204). Thoreau goes then, *not* to the corner, but outside, carrying a mug in search of a well, then returns, unsuccessful, whereupon the boy seizes the mug "and going to the corner of the room, where a cool spring which issued from the mountain behind trickled through a pipe into the apartment, filled it, and drank, and gave it to me empty again, and calling to the dog, rushed out of doors" (205).

The discourtesy and enigmatic behavior are very strange. It is not clear why Thoreau first failed to see or hear the spring trickling in the corner, especially when his attention was directed to it; it is not clear what the spring pipe emptied into; it is not clear what motivated the boy's gruffness and contempt, let alone his hurried departure. It is all as arbitrary as a dream.

Soon, Thoreau continues, some of the hired men entered, drank, combed their hair, and seated themselves, whereupon some fell asleep. All this took place in silence. Thoreau remarks that although he heard "bustle" elsewhere in the house, "all the while I saw no women" (205). Nor does he ever. So far as his experience goes, it is an exclusively male preserve that he has entered.

When Rice, the owner, finally arrives, he is carrying an ox-whip and breathing hard. "When I asked him if he could give me a bed, he said there was one ready, in such a tone as implied that I ought to have known it, and the less said about that the better. So far so good" (205). Thoreau then tries to converse with Rice about his situation, but receives contradictory and irritably defensive answers. Rice was, Thoreau observes, "rude as a fabled satyr." Nonetheless, Thoreau does not take offence; indeed, he finds that Rice "had a sweet, wild way with him," even though Thoreau offers no examples that might encourage such a description (206). Equally provocative, Thoreau tells us that Rice was "a coarse and sensual man," although again he offers no specific behavior to indicate what he means. Still, Thoreau avows he knows how to appreciate such rudeness and "quite innocently welcomed it" (207).

Finally, Thoreau decides to go to bed, whereupon Rice grows overtly hospitable and leads Thoreau to his room, "stepping over the limbs of his men who were asleep on the floor in an intervening chamber" (207). How many they were, when they left the room, why they slept on the floor—none of this do we ever know. Thoreau only adds that, although shown "a clean and comfortable bed," he sits at an open window on the sultry night, listening to a little river, then rises "as usual by starlight" and departs before anyone else is awake (208).

This curious episode must surely have possessed unusual meaning for Thoreau to devote so much detail to it, and yet, whatever that meaning might have been, the episode manifestly does not illustrate what it is supposed to: namely, that "a true politeness does not result from any hasty and artificial polishing . . . but grows naturally in the characters of the right grain and quality, through a long fronting of men and events, and rubbing on good and bad fortune" (201). Rather, there is a faintly sinister and at the same time sensual air to the gruff Rice and his mysterious household of vaguely arranged chambers and all-male occupancy. Not just narrative filler as we sometimes encounter in Thoreau's writing, this material is an incomplete and veiled account of an occasion (or a fantasy) of obviously central importance for Thoreau, where hostility and domination turn to hospitality, then evaporate at the edge of the bed.

The Rice episode has a coda. Thoreau meets a very old man with a milking-pail who stops to pick raspberries not far from Thoreau, who is doing the same. But when Thoreau asks directions of the old man, he merely replies without raising his head, then goes off muttering. Then, having collected his cows from a neighboring pasture, he stops and prays aloud, including a request for Thoreau's welfare in his supplication. This emboldens Thoreau to ask for some cheese, "but he answered without looking up, and in the same low and repulsive voice as before, that they did not make any, and went to milking" (209).

This coda has almost as many puzzling elements to it as the main episode. But its principal points seem to be the following: even though the rural world is rather inhospitable—surly, repulsive in voice, and certainly not helpful (we do not know if the old man answered Thoreau's inquiry about his route, only that he replied "in a low rough voice"—still it does pray for one's welfare. That relatively unattractive and dismissive old man does verify the accuracy of Thoreau's barely acknowledged uneasiness with this world whose champion he proposed to be. And the digression of the Rice episode as well as the encounter with the old man are consistent with Thoreau's general malaise, which regularly subverted his desire to offer songs of pure praise. The very strange obliqueness of the episode conveys the obscurely conflicting movements within Thoreau more surely than any direct statement could at that time. The introduction to the Rice episode had been Thoreau's observation that, despite a yellow river and steep banks of clay, one took sustenance from the few fresh springs found in those banks. Thoreau was, at this point in his life, reaching for whatever was available, reaching and claiming, against the preponderance of evidence, that the world was hospitable toward him.

No wonder that Thoreau next meditated on the pleasures of a simple country life out of doors, and specifically on the life of a boatman. He recalled the sensation canal boats made in Concord when "once in a year or two" they would come gliding "through the meadows and past the village" (211). But this reversion to childhood mystery and awe could not last. The present impinged on it, threatening the idyll. With the railroad coming, "in a few years there will be an end of boating on this river" (213). So that outlet, that solace, was unavailable.

And yet, in the summer's heat, Thoreau kept sliding imaginatively back into a state of dreams. As long as he did not actually engage with people, his imagination was free to work. So, of the few boatmen left on the Merrimack, "we imagined that the sun shining on their bare heads had stamped a liberal and public character on their most private thoughts" (214). It was an assumption not profitably tested. Similarly, Thoreau identified the dwellers along the river as "a quiet agricultural and pastoral people," but when he assessed their lives in a couplet, their voices said:

Our uninquiring corpses lie more low
Than our life's curiosity doth go. (215)

One might expect this to introduce a Thoreauvian diatribe against the complacent inertness of his neighbors, for "uninquiring corpses" are hardly the natural extension of a "pastoral people." But Thoreau's mind glanced off in another direction. The inertness of these people struck him as sound. The truths of the world were at home, available for the asking. Travel and inquiry were but unprofitable busy-ness. "These men had no need to travel to be as wise as Solomon in all his glory, so similar are the lives of men . . . One half the world *knows* how the other half lives" (215).

As Thoreau neared the end of "Tuesday," reflections on past misery multiplied. He quoted seventeenth-century accounts of Indians in fear of one another: firing guns, breaking up canoes to prevent their use by enemies, begging protection from the governor. An Indian maiden is scalped by a Mohawk warrior. "She, however, recovered" (220). Further, Thoreau was obliged to confront the fact that he himself contributed to the misery. The woods were alive with pigeons and "their gentle and tremulous cooing" (223). But killing one for supper occasioned rueful reflections on the ugliness of plucking it, extracting its entrails, and broiling its carcass on the coals. In defense of this modest butchery he became a little coy: "We heroically persevered, nevertheless, waiting for further information" (223). The information desired was: with what harmony could slaughter possibly be reconciled?

Thoreau found himself in a perplexing situation. To be natural was to be an animal. To be an animal sometimes involved being a merciless killer. What were Heaven's intentions in so ordering the world? These tragedies did not strike Thoreau as incidental or occasional. They were "incessant" and consciously permitted by Heaven. Contemplating the fate of the living, Thoreau observed ironically, "Nature herself has not provided the most graceful end for her creatures" (224). Even the sparrows inevitably faced "a tragedy at the end of each one of their lives. They must perish miserably." True enough, Thoreau observed mordantly, none falls without our Heavenly Father's knowledge—"but they do fall, nevertheless" (224).

For a practical man with extensive experience in the woods, this was a commonplace, but it ill-suited Thoreau's theoretical beliefs, for it challenged that perpetual and final esperance that he desired with all his heart to affirm. Equally troubling, killing small game violated his fastidiousness. The limits of his commitment to natural experience lay this side of skinning squirrels. He could eat a pigeon, but the carcasses of the skinned and eviscerated squirrels he found too much to bear. "Their small red bodies, little bundles of red tissue," so disgusted the brothers that "with a sudden impulse, we threw them away, and washed our hands, and boiled some rice for our dinner" (224). He tried to comprehend carnivorousness, though. To eat the squirrels "was to perpetuate the practice of a barbarous era," but "if they had been larger, our crime had been less." But then a few lines further, he wrote with emotion about the viciousness of killing for food, observing that after all "sheep and oxen are but larger squirrels" (224). The subject of hunting, killing, and consuming flesh was always a highly charged one for Thoreau, especially since it was practiced by his theoretical exemplars of man in harmony with nature, the Indians, and in turn because of what it represented about the basic constitution of the universe, quite beyond the infamies of civilized man.

The strain of confronting these volatile issues called for repose "under these island trees." This was the psychological moment to join the company of the gods. Thoreau praises the classical poets precisely because they are now "bodiless," so that one may have converse with them "without reserve or personality" (225–226). His reiterated word to describe his encounters with the classical poets is "serene." But even as they brought him a distanced calmness, these poets also addressed subjects of particular interest to Thoreau, and did so with a candor and stability that he very much admired. Therefore, Anacreon seemed "strangely modern" to him (226).

Thoreau's choice of Anacreon, the erotic, bisexual hedonist, was as unexpected as was his insistence on Anacreon's "ethereal and evanescent" qualities (226). Anacreon's odes, Thoreau argued, were "not gross, as has been presumed, but always elevated above the sensual" (227).[4] Of the poems available to him for translation, Thoreau selected eleven, one in part only, for presentation.[5] His rationale for selection was ostensibly quality. These poems were "some of the best" (227). But one may reasonably suppose that there was a further significance, both in Thoreau's selection and in their arrangement, for they begin with the lament that, although he has tried to sing of heroes, "my lyre / Sings only loves," and end with Cupid complaining of having been stung by a bee, whereupon his mother, Venus, remarks: "If the sting / Of a bee afflicts you, / How, think you, are they afflicted, / Love, whom you smite?" (227, 231). It is notable that Thoreau did not select those odes in which Anacreon was happy, fulfilled, or feeling gaiety and pleasure. Rather, the feelings expressed concern the enslavement and toils of love.

Of these love poems, only one mentions the female sex. "On Women" argues that whereas Nature gave horns to bulls and hoofs to horses, to birds delight, and to men wisdom, to woman she gave beauty, with which she conquers "even iron and fire" (230). Others sing ruefully of how love strikes and brands lovers. Bathyllus, a young Samian of whom Anacreon was ostensibly enamoured, appears in three of the odes Thoreau translated, most dramatically in "To a Swallow," in which the singer threatens to clip the bird's feathers or tear out its tongue because its song at dawn "snatch'd *Bathyllus* from my Arms."[6] That, however, is John Addison's eighteenth-century translation. Thoreau again sanitized Anacreon, even though for him his version is quite daring: "Why with thy notes in the dawn / Hast thou plundered Bathyllus / From my beautiful dreams?" (230).

Thoreau's ambivalence is notable. He wished to sing love, for he had suffered its incursions, but he could do so only through the medium of translation. In his own right, the most he could bring himself to pronounce was "sympathy" or "friendship" as euphemisms for this torment. The meaning of his selection of odes from Anacreon was plain enough, though: love's mastery, love's pains, and, most poignant of all, love's insufficiencies. In the poem "On Love," Love takes the speaker on a run with him through nature until at last a water-snake stings him. At this point, Love approaches and in the original "cry'd, How long must I reprove? / When will you, Rebel, learn to love!" John Addison glosses the remark: "By this expression *Cupid* would intimate that if he had submitted sooner, he should have suffered less."[7] But Thoreau revised the line, so that now Love said: "Surely, thou art not able to love" (229).

The accusation is a touching one, the more so in that Thoreau was obliged to violate the translator's oath of fidelity in order to make it. It is, however, quite strikingly peculiar that neither on its appearance in *The Dial*, nor in its reprinting in the *Week*, did any of his friends, so far as I am aware, object to or comment on this quite blatant misrepresentation of a classic text to make a personal statement.

Following the Anacreon selections, "Tuesday" runs down rather aimlessly with some emphasis on the wildness of the country as the brothers proceed north. It concludes with their camping that night in what they took to be a retired location.

In the morning, the brothers' encampment proved to be directly in the path of some masons who were repairing the locks. This ironic shattering of their assumptions of security was not an occasion for humor, however, for privacy was a serious matter to Thoreau. "This was the only time that we were observed on our camping ground" (235). Thoreau's obsessive need for seclusion should be catalogued with his equal passion for secret observation. He once owned a suit of various shades of brown mixed with a little green that he thought virtually conferred invisibility on him. Its value to him was primarily that "I could glide across fields unperceived half a mile in front of a farmer's windows" (*J*, XIII, 230). Here on the Merrimack, Thoreau exulted that, save for this one occasion, the brothers "beheld the country privately, yet freely, and at our leisure." Thoreau desired intimacy without involvement. He felt most secure afloat with a broad margin of water between him and the dubious land world. For him, "the genius of the shore" was the smaller bittern, moping and probing at the mud, uncertain and "limping" in flight, an altogether "melancholy and contemplative" bird (235–236).

The Charles Cotton epigraph to "Wednesday" expresses the chapter's generally ambivalent tone and point of view: "Man is man's foe and destiny."[8] The chapter is faintly organized, but it does move from bitterness to a compensatory dream. Inserted in the midst of its virtually random observations is that problematic giant of an essay, "Friendship." Until it appears, Thoreau offers disconnected passages of a travelogue, some of them—"such thoughts as the muses grudgingly lent us"—on the edge of meditative extension (238). The imagination is pitted against discouraging realities. No wonder the presiding totem of the chapter is that smaller bittern, running along the shore "like a wrecker in his storm coat" (235).

Thoreau's inserted memories of his Staten Island venture in 1843 illustrate this psychological pattern. He recalls having watched approaching vessels "from an old ruined fort" until they arrived in the channel to be boarded by the health officer and a newsman. "And then I could imagine what momentous news was being imparted by the captain, which no American ear had ever heard, that Asia, Africa, Europe—were all sunk" (239). A joke, to be sure, but typical of the morbid bent of Thoreau's imagination. Having provided himself a slot into which anything might fit—"Asia, Africa, Europe were all . . ."—he unswervingly generated destruction.

He goes on to describe a "long procession of vessels" putting to sea, then comments that all them no doubt were "counting on lucky voyages," even though in fact some were "destined to go to Davy's locker" (239). This cool prediction of disaster is reenforced by an image of a "huge shadow and dark descending wall of rain" overtaking the ships in the bay. Next, "this dark veil" moved on out to sea, where "gleamed the sunny sails of those vessels which the storm had not yet reached" (240). The strongest image Thoreau's imagination could create to counter this dynamically pessimistic vision was of the moonlight on the ocean, creating "a field of trembling, silvery light." There, "sometimes," Thoreau would perceive "a dark speck in its midst . . . some fortunate vessel pursuing its happy voyage by night" (240). The situation is far from reassuring. A minute, meaningless, animated dot briefly enjoys prosperity, not through any effort on its part, let alone through the solicitous attention of a protective deity, but randomly, inadvertently. Thoreau signals a partial recognition of the meagreness of this optimism by reverting to his initial image: "We, too, were but dwellers on the shore, like the bittern of the morning, and our pursuit the wrecks of snails and cockles" (240–241).

The "Friendship" essay, inserted into a creative lull in the chapter, clarifies an important source of Thoreau's pessimism. He had composed the piece early in January 1848, after he had already submitted the completed manuscript of the *Week* to four publishers (Harding, *Days*, 245–246). The essay, or, as he then thought of it, the lecture, drew together numerous journal entries he had made over the years on this subject (*Corr.*, 204, 208). In consequence, it failed to hold together as a consistent piece of exposition. The ideas burst forth in a series of eloquent but incoherent explosions, to which seven full-length poems and some verse fragments were added. As Joseph Wood Krutch observed, "Few passages in his writings . . . are so misty, so paradoxical, and so self-contradictory."[9]

Friendship was the consuming ache at the center of Thoreau's being. It absorbed into itself love, sexual feeling, stand-offishness, moral judgment, social awkwardness—the whole stew of individual problems in which Thoreau had long been simmering. However, the essay was composed at a time of relative stability in Thoreau's social life. He had left Walden Pond early in September, preparatory to serving as the man in the Emerson household, or, as Edward Emerson put it, "living at the house as kindly protector and friend of Mrs. Emerson and the three young children, and attending to his absent friend's affairs in house, garden, and wood-lot."[10] Emerson had sailed for England in early October, leaving Thoreau in an ideal situation for him: as head of household, with numerous handyman chores of the sort he could manage particularly well; as male to Lidian's female; and as the playful and loving father to Emerson's children. The situation did indeed constitute the first of the "several more lives" Thoreau had to live after his Walden residence (*Walden*, 323).

It was during this same period that Thoreau received from one Sophia Foord, his first and, so far as is known, only marriage proposal. He reacted with extraordinary verbal violence. He had had, he told Emerson, a "tragic correspondence" with Miss ———— (*Corr.*, 190–191). He continued: "She did really wish to—I hesitate to write—marry me. That is the way they spell it" (*Corr.*, 191). Consider the depth of distaste that produced that rhetorical hesitation, whether sardonically intended or not. Emerson's response was terse with shared contempt. "You tell me in your letter one odious circumstance, which we will dismiss from remembrance henceforward" (*Corr.*, 195). The unconventionality of a forty-five-year-old spinster's proposing to a man fifteen years her junior may account for these powerful reactions. But Thoreau went on to give the circumstance a metaphorical force special to his sensibility. "I sent back as distinct a *no* as I have learned to pronounce after considerable practice, and I trust that this *no* has succeeded. Indeed, I wished that it might burst, like hollow shot, after it had struck and buried itself and made itself felt there. *There was no other way.* I really had anticipated no such foe as this in my career" (*Corr.*, 191).

The cruel emphasis on hurting here, though not characteristic of Thoreau at all times, does regularly appear in moments of stress. The source of the stress on this occasion being an absurd, aggressive female, Thoreau was obliged to react with emotional violence because he was not otherwise equipped to deal with such amorous directness. There is a later journal entry often associated with the Foord affair, because there is evidence that she either threatened or actually did attempt suicide. It is August 5, 1852: "Hearing that one with whom I was acquainted had committed suicide, I said I did not know when I had planted the seed of that fact that I should hear of it" (*J*, IV, 280). Whatever the stern demands of friendship that Thoreau on occasion accepted, he emphatically rejected those of common humanity here.

Thoreau thought he strongly desired an idealized relationship, but whenever it came to practice, failure inevitably awaited him. "No word is oftener on the lips of men than Friendship. . . . All men are dreaming of it, and its drama, which is always a tragedy, is enacted daily" (264).[11] Thoreau dwelt on the barriers of communication between friends. Actions and feelings may be misunderstood. Too much may be required to be articulated. Thoreau elevated his personal reserve into a general principle. From his point of view, we dream friendship and practice repulsion. "One goes forth prepared to say 'Sweet Friends!' and the salutation is, 'Damn your eyes!' " (265). The only way Thoreau could conceive of avoiding such candid disapproval would be by worshipping the higher self in a friend, "the fact in a fiction" (270). Friendship then would love not "something private and personal" that belongs to the individual but "something universal and worthy of love" (269). In such a state of mind, friends would communicate spiritually. They would never "profane one another by word or action, even by a thought." Then the characteristic extreme: "Between us, if necessary, let there be no acquaintance" (270).

But Thoreau had discovered that such austerity does not prosper. His friends "complain," he writes sourly, "as if they expected a vote of thanks for every fine thing which they uttered or did" (277, 278). He lived in a world of imperfect beings, where "I have never known one who could bear criticism, who could not be flattered" (282). Thoreau saw the problem: no one could measure up to his standards. "Perhaps there are none charitable, none disinterested, none wise, noble, and heroic enough, for a true and lasting Friendship" (277).

If friendship were understood to exist at Thoreau's level of perfection, this was manifestly true. His was an explicitly unforgiving, implacable conception. Yet there can be no doubt about the depth of his need for the regard of others. As a young man, he found solace in insisting on the inevitability of friendship. It required no effort. "I need not ask any man to be my friend," he wrote in his journal in 1839, "more than the sun the earth to be attracted by him. It is not his to give, nor mine to receive" (*J*, I, 107). In 1842, he described a friend as "my creation, I can do what I will with him. There is no possibility of being thwarted" (*J*, I, 340). But there was, and Thoreau had suffered the consequences. "Our life without love is like coke and ashes—like the cocoanut in which the milk is dried up" (*J*, I, 348).

This long essay on "Friendship" struggles to a conclusion that is touching both in its rare expression of tolerance and in its overt desire for closeness. "Ignorance and bungling with love are better than wisdom and skill without" (284). Thoreau addresses those whom he calls "our cis-Alpine and cis-Atlantic Friends" as well as "the large and respectable nation of Acquaintances, beyond the mountains;—Greeting" (286). He uses the occasion to speak directly to those people who felt distant from him because of his coolness, who felt perhaps even estranged from him, as well as to those acquaintances who might grow closer to him. His message is an invitation to cross to him, even though "the mountains which separate us are high, and covered with perpetual snow" (286). Do *any-thing* to reach him, Thoreau urges—"If need be, soften the rocks with vinegar." The effort will be worth it, for "here lie the verdant plains of Italy to receive you" (286). Following this surprisingly luxurious receptivity, Thoreau then resumes his more familiar guise by appealing to his audience to use him boldly, for he is no piece of crockery, but an "old fashioned wooden trencher" that "will bear rough usage" (286).

The whole section on friendship displays a Thoreau at his most emotionally vulnerable. It does not belong naturally to the "Wednesday" chapter. Rather, Thoreau seems to have had rather little material to work with at this point in the reminiscence and, at the same time, to have felt the powerful need, first to gather his ideas about friendship together, then to insert them in what was essentially an already completed book. I take it that his impassioned address to potential friends was his most important motivation and that, having revealed how deeply he wished to be used, he then prudently sealed the whole off with the poem, "Let such pure hate still underprop our love" (287–289).

As the day wound down, Thoreau focused on two ideas not easily brought into balance, but each important to him. The first concerned the power of the imagination to affect the world. "This world is but canvass to our imaginations" (292). Thoreau was emphatic about his assumption of the superiority of the mind—"certainly there is a life of the mind above the wants of the body and independent of it" (292). The constitution of the world, then, depends on one's imaginative disposition. "Packed in my mind lie all the clothes / Which outward nature wears" (294). On the other hand, alteration cannot be forced. Rather,

> In vain I look for change abroad,
>   And can no difference find,
> Till some new ray of peace uncalled
>   Illumes my inmost mind. (295)

The ray of peace comes unbidden. Recognizing the subjective nature of one's perception of the world, Thoreau could not assert that its identity can be controlled. This uneasy realization was then mitigated by a second set of ruminations, namely that, even if we are "hedged about . . . by accident and circumstance," nonetheless we somehow do manage to act. "I cannot change my clothes but when I do, and yet I do change them," Thoreau says, wonderingly, then adds a sober extension, "and soil the new ones" (293). If the rhetoric of his observations appears positive, it nonetheless conveys undertones of pessimism. It is at once celebratory and apprehensive. For example: "What risks we run!" Thoreau exclaims, "famine and fire and pestilence, and the thousand forms of a cruel fate,—" So far, he is building toward an expression of wonder at man's capacity for survival. But then he finishes the sentence with an ironic turn: "and yet every man lives till he—dies. How did he manage that?" (294).

When we examine Thoreau's reflections, we can see everywhere his sense of impending disaster. "So much only can I accomplish ere health and strength are gone," he remarks, enunciating the common fate. Then he adds the minimally solacing phrase, "and yet this suffices." Does it? The next sentence looks to life other than that of conscious man, to life where not the slightest ultimate hope is furnished, only a mindless serenity existing in precarious equipoise: "The bird now sits just out of gunshot" (293).

As "Wednesday" draws to a close, Thoreau inserts a dream he had experienced in 1841. The journal entry is more restrained than its revision for the Week. In his journal, Thoreau writes that even though he had been true to his "highest instinct," he had in some undefined way been disappointed, but that at last "complete justice" was rendered him in his sleep (J, I, 177). The Week version brings this illustration of divine compensation down to a more personal level. Thoreau says that he had had "a difference with a Friend" that had given him unceasing pain, even though he himself was guiltless of his friend's suspicions. But when compensation came to him in his dream, he found himself "unspeakably soothed," and he rejoiced because "this seemed to have the authority of a final judgment" (296–297).

The importation of this instance of moral self-gratification is more touching than it is functional. When Thoreau concluded that "in dreams we see ourselves naked and acting out our real characters," he spoke more truly than perhaps he knew. Placed just here, to conclude a long chapter dominated by a central essay on the trials of friendship, the dream resurrects undeserved pain long endured, then rewarded with superior relief. As always, Thoreau wished to convince himself that his suffering was worth it.[12] Even though he drew on years of journal entries to compose the *Week*, Thoreau's imaginative engagement in the book was waning. The more perplexed he became in the face of his perceptions and of those truths he had uncovered by dint of writing, the more he tried to counteract the somberness of his vision. But this resort to the authority of dreams to assert one's moral superiority was unmistakably a desperate one.

"Thursday" is formally but not actually the climax of the journey. It does represent the furthest penetration the voyagers made. Thoreau recognized the external aptness of their pausing in Concord, New Hampshire, when he remarked, "This would have been the proper place to conclude our voyage, uniting Concord with Concord" (303). In fact, a week of ground travel intervened, culminating in an ascent of Mount Washington. Thoreau tried to emphasize its symbolic import by reverting to its Indian name and by putting it in bold capitals—"we were enabled to reach the summit of AGIOCOCHOOK"—followed by a substantial white space (314). But the sentence leading to the summit is crippled and inconsequential. We remain unenlightened by an experience that only fidelity to the literal permitted into the book. Of course, by this time Thoreau had very likely taken the trip (September 1846) to the top of Mt. Katahdin also. The stunning effect of that ascent may well have sobered Thoreau's fancy, for "Thursday" is a muted, wet chapter. It starts in rain and ends in the sounds of the sucking, whirling river currents and the rustling wind. The rain at the beginning is described as "ominous," and at the end the river is "lapsing downward" (298, 332). The vigorous spirit of the "Saturday" opening has quite disappeared. In "Thursday" the mood is languid, with shadows of doubt on the imagery. It was "a cloudy and drizzling day, with occasional brightenings in the mist" (299–300), but, Thoreau insists, the rain was not in itself depressing or destructive. "We managed to keep our thoughts dry, however, and only our clothes were wet" (299). He boldly affirms the salutary pleasures of a drenching, then inserts his extension—the "luxury" of spending a summer's day up to one's chin in some retired swamp, "lulled by the minstrelsy of gnats and mosquitoes!" (300).[13]

To drive home the paradox, Thoreau ended the day with the mosquito as well, evoking the pleasures of its "evening chant" from "a thousand green chapels" (300). He of course knew better. For example, in June 1854: "The mosquitoes encircle my head and torment me" (*J*, VI, 339). Although Thoreau would describe the mosquito's sound as it passed through his Walden cabin at dawn as "Homer's requiem; itself an Iliad and Odyssey in the air, singing its own wrath and wanderings," this was mere extravagance (*Walden*, 89). He told his journal, "Gnats and mosquitoes are the original imps and demons," and in the Maine wilderness he had to put his head in the smoke of the campfire to escape them, even as on Mt. Washington the black flies "compelled me . . . to sit in the smoke, which I preferred to wearing a veil" (*CinC.*, 189; *MW*, 251; *J*, XI, 35).

As part of this celebration of the outdoors life, Thoreau included his sentimental poem, "My books I'd fain cast off, I cannot read" (301). But its pedestrian tone was quite out of place here, as Thoreau was thinking about the universal evidence of men being on the surface of this earth, and speaking therefore for the value of evasiveness. "We do not avoid evil by fleeing before it, but by rising above or diving below its plane; as the worm escapes drought and frost by boring a few inches deeper" (304). This is the Thoreau who repeatedly counsels ignoring evil—not contesting it, but merely washing one's hands of it. Then another Thoreau revives, the belligerent one, and without transition he elaborates a frontier image, arguing that although the frontier may seem gone, when a man fronts a fact, then does he find himself in "an unsettled wilderness . . . and save his scalp if he can" (304).

Scalps were very much on Thoreau's mind during the composition of "Thursday." Writing at about the same time on Thomas Carlyle, Thoreau grew increasingly intoxicated by his initial metaphor of Carlyle wrestling with his subject, until the trope and Thoreau's commitment to it broke free of critical meaning into imaginative exuberance: "Rolling his subject how many ways in his mind . . . tries the back stitch and side-hug with it, and downs it again—scalps it, draws and quarters it, hangs it in chains and leaves it to the winds and dogs" ("Thomas Carlyle and His Works," *EE*, 231). Later in "Thursday," Thoreau elected to characterize the capacity for spontaneous creation as "very dangerous,—the striking out the heart of life at a blow, as the Indian takes off a scalp" (329). Reverting to the history of the region, Thoreau then retold the well-known story of Hannah Dustan, captured by Indians along with a nurse and a boy.[14] The boy, having been instructed by his Indian captor how to kill and scalp an enemy, confirms his lesson on his mentor and the Indian family. A total of two men, two women, and six children are killed. After fleeing, Dustan, "fearing that her story would not be believed . . . returned to the silent wigwam, and taking off the scalps of the dead, put them into a bag as proofs of what they had done" (322).

Thoreau follows the details of the party's flight with sympathetic interest, but draws no moral. He does not even justify his inclusion of the story, save implicitly for its confrontation with reality, for, as the party flees, Thoreau describes the landscape as being exactly that in which he expects a man to confront reality: "On either side, the primeval forest stretches away uninterrupted to Canada, or to the 'South Sea;' to the white man a drear and howling wilderness" (323).[15]

The story of Hannah Dustan turns out happily—"as by a miracle"—but Thoreau chooses to conclude it on a macabre detail. The family is restored, all save an "infant whose brains were dashed out against the apple tree" (323–324). Then follows without interruption one of Thoreau's more peculiar juxtapositions: "and there have been many who in later times have lived to say that they have eaten of the fruit of that apple-tree" (324). The effect is to join dashed brains, apples, and eating in an act of historical cannibalism.[16] Although there is no doubt that the associations are available and pregnant with significance, they constitute an odd conclusion to this abruptly inserted episode, whose focus would seem to be Hannah Dustan with her clothes "stained with blood." A resolute pioneer, she overcomes a Gothic situation in which she is told that she will be "made to run the gauntlet naked" (322, 321). But Thoreau's imperfectly understood loyalties toward confrontational bravery, the wilderness, and the Indian all cause the terms of the story to remain unfocused. In it, for example, the forest is doubly characterized: to the white man it is "a drear and howling wilderness," whereas to the Indian it is what Thoreau hoped it was to him, "a home, adapted to his nature, and cheerful as the smile of the Great Spirit" (323). And yet the Indian, that spontaneous devotee of nature, was murdered in his sleep by his pupil: "The English boy struck the Indian who had given him the information on the temple, as he had been directed" (321). It is a kind of harmony, but not of the sort Thoreau ever learned to advocate openly.

On "Friday," the last day of their trip, the brothers awakened into autumn and departed in yet another fog. Later in the day, the water turned from its earlier yellow to "a greyer hue" (335). The cattle were restless, "as if in apprehension of the withering of the grass and of the approach of winter" (336). The air of uneasiness that permeates the start of this chapter is temporarily countered by a hearty reminiscence of the annual Concord Cattle-Show. In this set-piece, Thoreau was appreciative of the gathering of farmers. Blown like leaves, they crowded to the fair in obedience to "the same ancient law" that made the bees swarm, to feed "heartily on coarse and succulent pleasures" (338). Thoreau's conclusion, which hardly seems complimentary, was: "How cheap must be the material of which so many men are made!" (339).

A general imagery of decline obtains in this chapter. Even the poet was not exempt from Thoreau's withering attention. Initially, he argues that because obstacles test the rarest genius, they will prove the poet to be "the toughest son of earth and of Heaven" (340). Independent, the poet writes "for his peers alone," yet finally gains popular acceptance (341). When "most inspired," however, the poet "is no longer a poet." The gods "encompass and sustain him with their breath." This would seem an affirmative view of the creative mind uplifted and mingling with the universe, but almost instantly comes an unexpected turn, as Thoreau shifts to the imagery of contempt: "When the poetic frenzy seizes us, we run and scratch with our pen, intent only on worms, calling our mates around us, like the cock, and delighting in the dust we make" (341, 342).

This grotesque "poetic frenzy" would seem to be the equivalent of inspiration. The mood in this particular paragraph is Chanticleerian—mocking, delighting in the overlap of "scratching" with a pen and with a chicken's nails in the barnyard dust—and for what? "Intent only on worms" Thoreau concludes his dismissive description by saying that we delight in the dust we make, but still "do not detect where the jewel lies, which, perhaps, we have in the mean time cast to a distance, or quite covered up again" (342). An ignoble activity attempting to be creative may in fact fling "the jewel" further away or cover it up. This scratching we call creation is very likely no more than mindless, unproductive display.

In an otherwise laudatory context, this skeptical view of the poet is disconcerting, unless one supposes Thoreau to be mocking merely the conventional poet. That was undoubtedly part of his satiric purpose, but Thoreau's perception turns out to be even larger. By irregular stages he was trying to establish the superiority of what *he* was: a better writer of prose than of verse; a better liver of life than its prose chronicler. Hence: "Great prose, of equal elevation, commands our respect more than great verse, since it implies a more permanent and level height." Thoreau regarded the poet as flighty, as but momentarily ejaculatory. "The poet often only makes an irruption, like a Parthian, and is off again," whereas "the prose writer has conquered like a Roman, and settled colonies" (342).

To conclude these peculiar ruminations on the poet, Thoreau makes one final extension. True art is embodied, not in any medium, but in the artist. "Not how the idea is expressed in stone, or on canvass or paper, is the question, but how far it has obtained form and expression in the life of the artist" (343). He summarizes his argument in a justly famous couplet:

My life has been the poem I would have writ,
But I could not both live and utter it. (343)

The couplet defends Thoreau's own career: not much of a poet and, from the point of view of editors, at best an indifferent prose writer, but already a man committed to an independent existence, dedicated to *being* an inspired poem.

Having provided the *Week* with a defense of its insufficiencies, Thoreau followed that defense with the poignancy of "The Poet's Delay," the poem that confesses that in a world of "boundless wealth" the poet remains poor within. Coming as it does from an earlier period (March 8, 1840—see

Bode, *Poems*, 301, and *J*, I, 127–128), this undefended confession of sterility seems quite out of place here, save that, provident as ever, Thoreau was determined to insert it somewhere and this evidently seemed as good a place as any. It was not, however. Thoreau had just finished arguing the superiority of the fully developed man, living his inspired life like a god, with no time for composition. To follow that assertion with this pitiful admission of artistic impotence was rhetorically unwise, however close it may bring us to the full complexity of the man.

By this point, Thoreau had pretty much lost his sense of the development of the *Week*. What better proof than that he now inserted the "Ossian" portion of a lecture he had first read before the Concord Lyceum on November 29, 1843? Again, the transitional seam was awkward and not to the point. Immediately after the rueful "Poet's Delay," Thoreau says that the "raw and gusty day" reminded the voyagers of "northern climes" rather than Greece and the Aegean (343). Then, following the Ossian segment, Thoreau offers a series of barely connected reflections, most of them affirmative and quite beautiful in their confidence. But eventually Thoreau concludes his long, mottled meditations by noting that "some have thought" that the "natural and original fragrance of the land" has been lost, for the "sweet-scented grasses and medicinal herbs" have been destroyed by grazing cattle and rooting swine, until the earth has been "converted into a stye and hot-bed, where men for profit increase the ordinary decay of nature" (355). No matter what the scene, nor how strong Thoreau's desire to ameliorate the distress forced on him by observation and extended thought, the terminus is almost invariably revulsion of this kind, and the sense of destructive loss.[17]

After a blank space breaks the narrative, Thoreau turns his attention to an apple tree on a Tyngsborough farm, following which the subject wanders, but always with the apple tree in the picture: first a record high flooding of the river, then a murdered Indian whose grave, dug close by the tree, sank beneath the weight of the water and disappeared forever. Although this is close to automatic writing, again one can see that when all other matters are quiescent, violent imagery takes a central place in Thoreau's imagination. For example, shortly a charmingly exhilarated paragraph follows, in which the brothers are driven down the river by a lively wind. Thoreau captures the tonic of "plowing homeward with our brisk and willing team, wind and stream, pulling together," and yet for all the light-hearted cheer, he cannot forbear concluding that their speed was such that, had they hit the shore, they would surely have stuck fast (360–361).

Such apprehensive turns of thought being so common with Thoreau, it comes as no surprise that, in the course of arguing that men acquire true knowledge only by direct experience, he should turn to Newton's law of gravitation as an example, then laconically chant:

We see the *planet* fall,
And that is all. (365)

And although he was (apparently) criticizing men's literalness, his illustration typically involved a destructive nihilism. We see the apple fall and draw no larger conclusion. We even see the planet fall and yet do not react. Thoreau's imagination was doom-laden.

Such truth inspired a lyric of declination, "I am the autumnal sun," in which he asked when his hazel tree would put forth its flowers or when his grapevine would ripen. Again, the poem was essentially a confession of depletion: "The winter is lurking within my moods" (378—the poem's date is October 7, 1842; Bode, *Poems*, 302). Against that weariness of a twenty-five-year-old, Thoreau erected a counterstatement in which he claimed that he was not prepared to concede hopelessness. The fields may be shorn, but they still possess "an inward verdure." Further, "under the sod, there lurks a ripe fruit, which the reapers have not gathered" (378).

And yet, who shall harvest it? In truth, only the imagined beings of Thoreau's imagination were potent, either those of former days and places or those he posited when he remarked that "this earth was made for more mysterious and nobler inhabitants than men and women" (377). But however much he might desire their existence, even to the extent of conjuring them up out of darkness, they inevitably proved illusory. "When we come down into the distant village, visible from the mountain top, the nobler inhabitants with whom we peopled it have departed and left only vermin in its desolate streets" (379). Thoreau needed to fill in the conceptual space between his poles of imagined aristocrats and vermin. He realized that he had to locate his ideal in that ground-level village or, as a compromise, in its environs, for, as he declared: "Here or nowhere is our heaven." The solution was an amalgam, "a *purely* sensuous life" in which one's eyes would "behold beauty now invisible. May we not *see* God?" (380, 382). But still Thoreau wondered, with understandable concern, "Where is the instructed teacher" who will develop our senses? (382).

Just here he inserts "Sic Vita," that poetic conceit of himself, earlier examined, as a bunch of violets and sorrel tied loosely with a straw, that "parcel of vain strivings" that, while it droops listlessly in its vase, imagines its sacrifice will bring future improvement. Although the poem's pretense of ultimate justice to come is unconvincing, the lament of ineffectuality is quite in place here. Over and over again Thoreau asserted that he had had glimpses of a higher truth, a greater beauty, a nobler life than that which he lived and observed, while at the same time he confessed his misery and feelings of creative impotence. In this portion of the concluding pages of the *Week*, Thoreau composed some of his most extraordinary statements on the limitations as well as the possibilities of human life. Their burden was that we exist on the margin of life only. "This world has many rings, like Saturn, and we live now on the outmost of them all" (384). Thoreau's wish to believe in the beyond was so strong that he emphasized it with capitalization—"those faint revelations of the Real" signal the presence of "that OTHER WORLD which the instinct of mankind has so long predicted" (385). Yet Thoreau's anticipation of success was muted and qualified. "I am not without hope that we may, even here and now, obtain some accurate information" (385). He realized that only rarely did a liberating perception break from "the common train of my thoughts," from which he concluded that this was "a sense which is not common, but rare in the wisest man's experience" (386).

Now, as the sun set, two herons passed overhead, going, Thoreau speculated, not to a marsh on the earth's surface, but "perchance" to alight "on the other side of our atmosphere, a symbol for the ages to study" (390). But in his actual imagery the herons disappeared behind the clouds and were succeeded by "dense flocks of blackbirds" (390). Although Thoreau imagined the blackbirds to be on a short pilgrimage or to be celebrating the fairness of the sunset, the fact is that their dark cloud remained, and, as the light disappeared, he remembered that he and his brother "rowed silently along with our backs toward home through the darkness" (390). The description is plausibly precise and there is something poignantly revealing about this voyage home, lost in thought and moving backwards, reluctantly returning through the gloom to the world of vermin.

The *Week*'s last set-piece is an apostrophe to silence. Silence was the infinite and, more specifically, seemed to Thoreau the final escape—"our inviolable asylum, where no indignity can assail, no personality disturb us" (392). The infinity of this silence becomes finally a boundless gulf that accepts the plunging man: "when he at length dives into her, so vast is the disproportion of the told to the untold, that the former will seem but the bubble on the surface where he disappeared" (393). The absoluteness of the engulfment is unmistakable. It is annihilation. "Nevertheless, we will go on," Thoreau adds, using those words that customarily succeed the recognition of an overwhelmingly hopeless situation (and do here as well), "like those Chinese cliff swallows, feathering our nests with the froth, which may one day be the bread of life to such as dwell by the seashore" (393). The imagistic problems of this passage are multiple and severe, but Thoreau's positing of a future nourishment was a desperate attempt to recover from that suicidal dive he had imagined. It defied, however, being transformed into affirmation.

The turmoil of Thoreau's imagery reflected the conflicting impulses in his mind. The deeper set opted for pessimism, felt contempt for his neighbors and the ostensibly civilized world, and therefore yearned for translation elsewhere, or extinction. The other part of him felt and formally believed in the necessity of asserting that a higher purpose to life existed than that which he was actually experiencing.

There is one more paragraph to the *Week*, and it too reflects ambivalence. For once, I quote in full. One should remember that this comes at the conclusion of a supposedly pleasurable voyage.

> We had made about fifty miles this day with sail and oar, and now, far in the evening, our boat was grating against the bulrushes of its native port, and its keel recognized the Concord mud, where some semblance of its outline was still preserved in the flattened flags which had scarce yet erected themselves since our departure; and we leaped gladly on shore, drawing it up, and fastening it to the wild apple-tree, whose stem still bore the mark which its chain had worn in the chafing of the spring freshets. (393).

"Gladly" is the one concession made to the surface myth of the *Week*. The rest of the language—"far in the evening," the boat "grating against the bulrushes," "the Concord mud," "the flattened flags," the wild apple tree with its trunk still bearing "the mark" worn by "the chain" during the "chafing" of the spring floods—is negative, suggesting the future to follow: grounded in the Concord mud.

Supposing one agrees that this is a peculiarly somber imagery for the conclusion of a celebratory book, one might still argue on behalf of its perceptive subtlety, even if, like many portions of the *Week*, it quite inadvertently reflects the underlying reservations Thoreau felt about the trip, about his life, and here, specifically, about the village to which he had returned. Those reservations would be more explicitly documented in *Walden*.

Earth Down at Last: *Walden*

We soon get through with Nature. She excites
an expectation which she cannot satisfy.
Journal, VI, 293

IF NO CONSISTENT DEVELOPMENT in Thoreau's life is reflected in
his writing, there are waves and cycles of change or, at the very
least, differing emphases in it. This is especially true of *Walden*, begun in the spring of 1846 but not completed until the
spring of 1854, with new materials and rephrasings being
introduced as late as Thoreau's reading of the page proofs.

The first draft of *Walden*, composed between March 1846
and September 1847 (but incorporating journal materials
written earlier), has been established by J. Lyndon Shanley and
separately printed in *The Making of Walden*. For this discussion I shall work centrally with that first version, taking note of
additions and changes appearing in the final version and,
where subjects of significance appear, discussing their other
manifestations in Thoreau's journal, correspondence, and
interim drafts. I do not intend to offer a full reading of *Walden*,
since its positive features have been commented on exhaus-

tively in the past. However, if I focus on certain passages, it is with the expectation that my conclusions about them will affect one's reception of the whole.

Like the *Week*, *Walden* is exceptionally uneven because of its long period of composition. Although philosophically Thoreau's most ambitious and rhetorically his most eloquent book, *Walden* paradoxically suffers from an insufficiency of depth and a confusion of attitudes. In some regards, it is a triumph of assertiveness. Thoreau has powerful negative arguments to make, and when they are coupled with a fresh and forceful rhetoric the result can be momentarily quite overwhelming. Nonetheless, the difficulties remain. I do not mean to condemn Thoreau with niggling accusations of inconsistency, but I am prepared to claim that his presentation will often puzzle and disconcert the attentive reader.[1]

"Economy" is a remarkable statement on behalf of devoting oneself to what one cares to do and against the accumulation of detritus in one's life. It is not enough to say, however, as Thoreau and his advocates do, that he is not prescribing a particular way of life for everyone, but rather that it is a principle of economy he espouses. Since Thoreau offers his own experience as proof that one can so live, that experience must in itself furnish a plausible example.[2] And of course on the whole it does not. Even Thoreau is rather defensive about his experience, explaining why, even though he was living on Emerson's land, he felt that he had enhanced its value; and why it was generous for him to have borrowed the axe he used initially to cut down the pines for his house frame; and why it was sheer neighborliness—not necessity—on his part to have called on some of his acquaintances to help raise that frame; and why, if he hired a team and a man to plough his field, still "I held the plough myself" (64, 41, 45, 55). His original version had been, "I held the plough for the most part myself."[3] I take the elimination of the qualifying phrase as additional evidence that Thoreau felt beleaguered by skeptical critics and was therefore anxious to anticipate the objections of those whom he tried to dismiss as "inveterate cavillers" (61).

This defensiveness is manifest in Thoreau's keeping of his accounts to the minutest detail, down to the quarter cent.[4] Such detail has been explained as a parody of the Franklinian businessman, who, in his preoccupation with the material minute, allows the philosophic hour to slip away. To a degree, Thoreau's ledgers *are* satiric, but there is also an unmistakable earnestness in his insistence that his accounting included all of his expenses—"pecuniary outgoes"—and all of his income, for he wished to prove it literally possible to live comfortably at little cost (60).

Strange that, groaning at the prospect, Emerson should embark on lecture tours to secure an income, or that, even when at home, he should engage in intricate correspondence with his brother William concerning the family's stock holdings. Had not Thoreau pointed out that a large house was not proportionally more expensive than a small one? (71). To be sure, it was Emerson who had purchased the wood-lot on which Thoreau built his cabin, but Thoreau had an answer for that: "If I were not permitted still to squat, I might purchase one acre at the same price" (64). Why then did Emerson distress himself needlessly? He, of course, had a wife and children and house-guests and hired help (sometimes Thoreau himself); he had a library; and he was given to planting trees— apple, pear, plum, peach, pine, hemlock, maple, elm, chestnut, and oak—not to speak of paying his dues to the Tree Society.[5] So Thoreau shifted his target uneasily: "I do not mean to prescribe rules to strong and valiant natures. . . . I do not speak to those who are well employed . . . but mainly to the mass of men who are discontented, and idly complaining of the hardness of their lot" (16).

That might seem to exempt such as Emerson, yet Thoreau criticized those with comfortable houses and all their civilized appurtenances—"clean paint and paper, Rumford fireplace, back plastering, Venetian blinds, copper pump, spring lock, a commodious cellar" (31). These advantages were purchased at a terrible cost, Thoreau argued. In confirmation, Ralph Rusk tells us that Emerson's "income from all sources was hardly more than enough to turn the wheels of the domestic machinery that Lidian quickly built up" (Rusk, *Emerson*, 251). Thoreau knew this household intimately; in fact, profited from it, living there before and after his stay at Walden Pond and, during it, customarily eating at the Emersons on Sundays.[6] In "Economy," though, Thoreau centered on the burden of houses and what they contain. A man must spend more than half his lifetime earning his house, "even if he is not encumbered with a family" (31). The latter verb accurately captured Thoreau's attitude toward the responsibilities that a family entailed. Otherwise, there are numerous reports of his congeniality in company among the Thoreaus and the Emersons. But in order to adhere to his principle that "the man who goes alone can start today," Thoreau had to evade the impediments represented by familial commitments. When responding to criticism—"But all this is very selfish, I have heard some of my townsmen say"—he skillfully relocated the selfishness. It was not in his divesting himself of human responsibilities, but in his failure to practice social charity (72). Thoreau's attacks on philanthropy are amusingly telling, but, more important, they successfully divert the argument that claims that because of its peculiar uniqueness Thoreau's "experiment" proves much less than he supposed.

But Thoreau, strong in dreams, regrets, and criticism, was never an exemplar of rationality. In "Economy," for example, one of his more extravagant propositions was that the poor would do well to live in railroad boxes. These were six feet by three in size and "many a man is harassed to death to pay the rent of a larger and more luxurious box who would not have frozen to death in such a box as this." To which Thoreau added, "I am far from jesting" (29). Quite so. Had he not improvised himself such a box with wooden boards on top of Saddleback Mountain? Yet only a little further on he attacked "the degraded poor" for living in "shanties which every where border our railroads," for they struck him as no better than "human beings living in sties" (34, 35). And whereas his proposed box-dweller needed only to bore a few holes to admit air, *these* creatures, Thoreau discovered, left the door open all winter "for the sake of light," with the result that "the forms of both old and young are permanently contracted by the long habit of shrinking from cold and misery" (35). Thoreau gave no indication of awareness of the relationship between his proposed box and the observed shanty.

In nature was where Thoreau wished to find his truth, and when it was less cooperative than he might have hoped, he twisted it into obedience. In *Walden*, he told of going to the pond and seeing a striped snake "run into the water," where it "lay on the bottom . . . as long as I staid there" (41). Thoreau conjectured that the snake's stillness was "perhaps because he had not yet fairly come out of the torpid state," which then allowed him to propose that "men remain in their present low and primitive condition" for the same reason, but that if they felt "the spring of springs arousing them, they would of necessity rise to a higher and more ethereal life" (41). From the example Thoreau provided, one might deduce rather that living creatures are often forced to flee danger but do not necessarily hide themselves in a secure place. On the other hand, should one accept Thoreau's moral lesson, then one would have to accept a mechanistic conception of man, in which spiritual torpidity is relieved, not through any effort, but only by responding to a stimulus sufficient—"of necessity"—to rouse them.

Still, in the opening pages of "Economy" Thoreau insisted on the superiority of his mode of behavior. He thought his balance sheet established that he "was doing better than any farmer in Concord did that year" and, furthermore, that he "was more independent than any farmer in Concord" (55, 56).

This assurance of preeminence was complemented by his ridicule of his fellow men and, deeper still, by the violence of his imagination. Significantly, almost all the instances of anger and metaphorical destructiveness were added after the initial version of *Walden* was composed. That is, Thoreau began fashioning an account of his life at the pond with the hope of finding peace for himself as well as of providing a model for others, but over the years, especially after he left the pond, his inner fury built up pressures that were eventually relieved in images generated during the writing of later drafts of the book.

Thoreau's aggressiveness was unmistakable from the outset. His contemptuous characterization of the "mean and sneaking lives" that the many lead appeared in his first version. It was then sourly amplified in a later draft by "my sight has been whetted by experience" (108/6).[7] His cruel dismissal of the old came later too. They have no advice to give, they have told him nothing, "their lives have been such miserable failures" (9). Those village Lears deserved not an iota of sympathy; since their lives were played out, they had best fall to their prayers. Thoreau's warmth was for eternity: "The stars are the apexes of what wonderful triangles!" (10). To free himself, he had to dismiss his elders and his neighbors. "One generation abandons the enterprises of another like stranded vessels" (11). The uncertain, lonely young man enlarged his own isolation into a trope of independence.

But his resentment still showed itself, still tore through the fabric of civilization. What shall we do about men's infatuation with fashion? Because the "monkeys in America" imitate "the head monkey in Paris," send them through a powerful press, "squeeze their old notions out of them" and make sure they are incapacitated for some time, so "that they would not soon get upon their legs again" (25). The original journal entry of January 14, 1854, was even more savage in its notion of what might be done to Fashion: "Oh, with what delight I could thrust a spear through her vitals or squash her under my heel!" (*J*, VI, 70). Similarly, the vanity of a pharoah having built a pyramid seemed sufficiently criminal to Thoreau for him to argue that the pharaoh should have been "drowned in the Nile" and his body "given . . . to the dogs" (58). Thoreau acknowledged that he might have been able to find an excuse for the royal ambition or for the acquiescence of the populace in his grandiose project, "but I have no time for it" (58).

It is true that the nineteenth century was in some respects less squeamish toward physical suffering and mutilation than its modern counterparts, presumably because the trapping of wild animals and the slaughtering of domestic ones were a more common part of one's daily experience. This would perhaps account for Thoreau's cool, even faintly amused phrasing of the fate of the James Collins's cat. After Thoreau had purchased the Collins's shanty for its boards, the family departed with everything except the cat in a single bundle (an admirable instance of simplicity that failed to inspire Thoreau's admiration, since Collins was only "an Irishman" or, as Thoreau first put it, "James Collins Irishman") (43/124). As for the cat, it "took to the woods and became a wild cat, and, as I learned afterward, trod in a trap set for woodchucks, and so became a dead cat at last" (44).

Reflecting on the imagery of *Walden* in conjunction with the subjects Thoreau chose to discuss and his attitudes towards them, one cannot miss the telling combinations: a contempt for what surrounded him coupled with a longing for escape, and an insistence on staying more or less in place, along with the assertion that *his* world was untainted by the corruption that threatened him. "I imagined that my house had its site actually in such a withdrawn, but forever new and unprophaned part of the universe," he originally wrote. Then he changed the operative verb to the more positive, "I *discovered* that . . ." (139/88, italics added). However, it was Thoreau's imagination alone that created the "auroral character" of his house. It reminded him of "the house of a sawmiller on the Kanterskill mountains" where he had once lodged, although, in keeping with the clean abstraction he had in mind, he eliminated the sawmiller in his revision (138/85). He brought the heavens down to reflect in the pond by selecting just the exact, rare time when such a phenomenon occurred—"in the intervals of a gentle rain storm in August" (86). He stood on tiptoe to catch sight of the mountain peaks off to the northwest (87). He imagined himself on an island by reminding himself that portions of the earth floated on water, then added to that yet another unusual occasion, when during a time of flood, "perhaps by a mirage," "all the earth beyond the pond" seemed to float (87). Seen in just the right light, his domicile was a celestial wonder, fit to "entertain a travelling god" (138/85). When such conditions did not obtain, then Thoreau relied on reminding himself that beyond the opposite shore lay "the prairies of the West and the steppes of Tartary" (139/87). The force of Thoreau's will was creating his environment, until "I seemed to dwell nearer to those parts of the globe, and to those eras in history which attracted me." In revision, this became an accomplished fact. "I seemed to dwell nearer" became "I dwelt nearer," and the scope widened until "the globe" became "the universe" (87).[8] Yet, for all of this local sublimity, undercurrents of hostility still flowed. Even though "God himself culminates in the present moment," still a mad dog was killed, and a steamboat blew up, a sleepwalker was run over by a train, and along the Wachito River a man had his eyes gouged out (97, 94, 92, 93).

The shape of "Where I Lived, and What I Lived For" displays this ambivalent mixture. The early portion is all mountain freshness, dawn, and bathing; yet there is a serpent in this rhetorical Eden. "That man who does not believe that each day contains an earlier, more sacred, and auroral hour than he has yet profaned . . ." Thoreau begins. Notice that Thoreau's assumptions are two: first, that man's normal activities profane existence, and second, that he must nonetheless believe that he will ever be provided a fresh tablet on which to write. Should one fail to believe this, Thoreau says, then that man "has despaired of life, and is pursuing a descending and darkening way" (89). There is considerable evidence that this man was Thoreau, in spite of his frantic efforts to brake his descent.

Thoreau's position was high Puritan. If the problem was that the nation was "ruined by luxury and heedless expense," then "the only cure" Thoreau could conceive was "a rigid economy," "a stern and more than Spartan simplicity of life," together with an "elevation of purpose" (92). This was a program not of joy but of zeal. To be fair to Thoreau, this moment was not fully characteristic of his thinking, although it was an important part of the whole man—a part he had to suppress or rechannel into more acceptable paths, transforming such judgmental narrowness into a dedicated belief in himself, or fashioning it into a hammer for his attack on slavery.

The famous paragraph beginning "I went to the woods because I wished to live deliberately" expressed Thoreau's doubts more vigorously than elsewhere in the past. Now he would "front" the essential facts of life, he would "suck out all the marrow of life," he would "put to rout all that was not life," he would "cut a broad swath," he would "shave close," and he would "drive life into a corner, and reduce it to its lowest terms" (90–91). This aggressive determination to force a crisis, to put the unnecessary to flight and break through to the core of the real, is remarkable. The discovery Thoreau then posited was over-balanced on the negative side: "if it [life] proved to be mean, why then to get the whole and genuine meanness of it, and publish its meanness to the world." Originally, Thoreau had added defiantly, "and throw it in the teeth of the gods," but he later eliminated that resentful bravado (91/141). As for the possibility of the world's *not* being mean at heart, Thoreau described that possibility in subdued terms—"or if it were sublime, to know it by experience, and be able to give a true account of it in my next excursion" (91).

The equally well known second portion of the chapter's

penultimate paragraph accords closely with Thoreau's central idea: there is mud everywhere, through which we must work down to reality. In fact, as his burrowing instinct asserted itself, Thoreau's imagination was truly taking "a descending and darkening way." That animalistic urge to dig down out of sight attracted him, for it was a secretive and protected action, yet one in search of something: namely, that "hard bottom and rocks in place, which we can call *reality*, and say, This is, and no mistake" (89, 98). Probing down to a hard reality was comparable to driving life into a corner. Both actions involved extreme exertion and persistence to reach a demonstrable solidity, whatever it might be, and supposing that it existed.

In contrast to that imagined solidity, freshets were an obsession for Thoreau at this time. Those sudden, unexpected overflows of streams that came at the time of thaw or during downpours were threatening to him. The world bore the marks of freshets, when things let go and poured over their confining banks. This uncontrolled expression of emotion being a threat, once the hard bottom was attained, one could establish one's position "below freshet and frost and fire." There Thoreau would place his "Realometer": to establish just "how deep a freshet of shams and appearances had gathered from time to time" (98). The intensity of Thoreau's desire to be in touch with unchanging truth was expressed in his poem, "He knows no change who knows the true," which in one version of the manuscript was inserted at this point in *Walden* (Stern 229, fn. 67). Ultimately the poem was excised, and in its place Thoreau welded one of his ecstatic passages, that which said that a true encounter with a fact will kill you, happily. It is an extraordinary sentence, quite saintlike in its vision of a reality that transports one beyond mortality: "If you stand right fronting and face to face to a fact [the tautology and alliteration were perhaps necessary accompaniments of strong feeling], you will see the sun glimmer on both its surfaces, as if it were a cimeter, and feel its sweet edge dividing you through the heart and marrow, and so you will happily conclude your mortal career" (98). That was a termination Thoreau could enthusiastically conceive, for the idea of settling things once and for all was compelling to him. If life proves mean, then let us get the whole and genuine meanness of it and publish it to the world. Now here: "If we are really dying, let us hear the rattle in our throats and feel cold in the extremities." In both instances, the hypothesized positive experience is rendered with equal laconicism: "if it were sublime, to know it by experience," and "if we are alive, let us go about our business" (91, 98).

In the concluding paragraph of "Where I Lived, and What I Lived For" the heavens do not descend to mingle with the pond, conferring divinity on it, but rather, earthly time proves to be merely a shallow stream, compared to the sky's oceanic eternity where Thoreau would drink and fish. Later, though, in "The Ponds," Thoreau presented another kind of experience, one that showed how hard it was to keep one's mind fixed on eternity. The setting was midnight, with Thoreau drifting on the moonlit pond, idly fishing, while at the same time his thoughts "wandered to vast and cosmogonal themes in other spheres" (187/175). Then, feeling "a slight vibration" on his line, he would slowly raise "some horned pout squeaking and squirming to the upper air" (175).

As phrased, it was an odd and even rather repellent moment. Thoreau had initially established himself as harmoniously immersed in nature, "serenaded by owls and foxes" and "surrounded sometimes by thousands of small perch and shiners, dimpling the surface with their tails in the moonlight" (174, 175). In short, the occasion commenced as a lyrical union with the natural world. But then, up into this harmony Thoreau drew a particularly unattractive fish, the very components of whose name, the horned pout (a kind of catfish), have negative connotations. Consider how the equation would have changed had Thoreau's catch been a fiercely resistant bass, or one of his revered pickerel, rather than an unattractive fish seemingly suffering, even though Thoreau described it, not only without sympathy, but with a degree of implied disgust at its reaction to being hooked—"squeaking and squirming."

Thoreau suggested a meaning for this incident. It was "very queer," he said, to have this "faint jerk" "interrupt your dreams and link you to Nature again." The emblematic quality of the occasion is clear. It is related to Melville's young Platonist dreaming on the masthead until with a shriek he falls into the very real ocean waters below. But more is revealed in the emblem than is overtly articulated by Thoreau. A creature "of dull uncertain blundering purpose" interrupts Thoreau's lyrical dreams, forcing him to admit the actual world again. Thoreau refuses to draw that larger conclusion. Rather, he tries to redeem the occasion: "It seemed as if I might next cast my line upward into the air, as well as downward into this element, which was scarcely more dense" (175). "I *would* drink deeper; fish in the sky . . ." he had said at the end of "Where I Lived" (98; italics added), And here, "It *seemed as if I might* next cast my line upward" (italics added). Thoreau forced his aspirations upward, but that was the wrong way. For him, paradise was to be found on earth in moments of absorption in nature, whereas he tormented his understanding with hopes of transcendence that when denied, he tried to simulate verbally. He ended the fishing incident: "Thus I caught two fishes as it were with one hook" (175). But he had not. That was mere fanciful assertion.

The antithesis of sky-fishing dominates the balance of the last paragraph of "Where I Lived." If one direction of Thoreau's desire was to soar off to an airy mountain cabin, or into the empyrean, the other was to dig, to burrow down into the secret of things. So, using his head—"I do not wish to be any more busy with my hands than is necessary"—he began to mine (98). But that mining activity turned out to be no more than "Reading," the title of the next chapter of *Walden*. Although dismissive toward books, Thoreau was nonetheless an avid reader. He tells us that he read "one or two shallow books

of travel in the intervals of my work, till that employment
made me ashamed of myself," but John Aldrich Christie can
identify "a minimum of one hundred and seventy-two separate
travel accounts read by Thoreau." In particular, Christie reports that in "the decade of the 1850s, we find him averaging
between twelve and thirteen new travel works a year" (100).[9]
Thoreau's zest even for "shallow" reading is evident. His
chapter on the subject makes clear how jealously he reserved
for himself the capacity of reading truly.

Concord culture failed to meet his standards. "With a
very few exceptions," no one in the town had a taste "for the
best or for very good books even in English literature" (106).
He had already dismissed the sensibilities of the majority of
men. They were no more than "the mob" and "the crowd" or,
as he originally designated them, "the herd" (102/148). Even
in ancient days, when the whole populace automatically knew
the classical languages, they "were not entitled . . . to *read* the
works of genius" (101). Books being "the fit inheritance of
generations and nations," Thoreau reserved them for an intellectual elite. He argued for "reading as a noble intellectual
exercise," but then used the concept as a cudgel (102, 104).

At the same time that Thoreau expressed his contempt at
men's failure to read that superior literature he reserved for
superior men, he doubted their capacity to change, especially
that of the brutes who jostled him on all sides. In the essay
"Walking," he describes a two-tiered world in which "the
majority, like dogs and sheep, are tame by inherited disposition." That certainly sounds like a conception based on
biological determinism, especially since the aristocratic
minority also have apparently inherited rather than acquired
their independent natures, for Thoreau goes on: "this is no
reason why the others should have their natures broken that
they may be reduced to the same level" (*W*, V, 235). And, not
much further on in *Walden*, Thoreau remains openly dubious
about the possibility of men's altering their characters: "I
confess, that practically speaking, when I have learned a man's
real disposition, I have no hopes of changing it for the better or

worse in this state of existence" (120–121). Then, citing certain "Orientals" who had commented on the impossibility of straightening a cur's tail, Thoreau, with characteristic brusqueness, provides a solution for such tails: "make glue of them" (121).

For all of his criticism of Concord's cultural limitations, Thoreau was equally vulnerable. His own reading was severely limited in its scope. He knew little of modern continental literature, and despite his friendship with Hawthorne he never seriously thought about the place of fiction in a man's learning, but merely revealed complacently in the *Week* that "I never read a novel, they have so little real life and thought in them" (71). He prescribed for the village of Concord that it do what "the nobleman of cultivated taste" does—surround itself with "genius—learning—wit—books—paintings—statuary—music—philosophical instruments, and the like" (109–110). But one would look long to discover Thoreau's musical interests transcending the pathetic song "Tom Bowling" or simple melodies on the flute, let alone for some evidence of his interest in either painting or sculpture. Thoreau was quite as narrowly preoccupied with his own interests as his neighbors were with theirs.

The chapter "Sounds" opens in sunny mellowness. Thoreau's account of sitting in revery on a summer's morning is utterly convincing, precisely because it was a passive situation in which, for a brief period, he felt neither critical nor defensive, but merely drifted through the day. "It was morning, and lo! it is now evening, and nothing memorable is accomplished," he wrote in his first draft, then added, perceptively, "Yet my nature is almost content with this" (152). Almost. He possessed a center that was not finally content with "the language which all things and events speak without metaphor" (111). "Sounds," then, has little to do with that common language, for square in its center sits the railroad and, by extension, the commerce it represents.

Only later in the afternoon does Thoreau begin to record sounds attentively. His characterizations are initially brief and conventional—bells make "faint, sweet, and, as it were, natural melody"; the cow's lowing is "cheap and natural music"; the whippoorwills chant vespers (123). Only with the coming of night and the owls does Thoreau's attention become heightened. "I love to hear their wailing, their doleful responses." He interprets them at length. They represent "low spirits and melancholy forebodings," so that his translation of their sounds is psychologically precise for him: *"Oh-o-o-o-o that I never had been bor-r-r-r-n!"* (124–125). The sound of a hooting owl represented to Thoreau "the dying moans of a human being,—some poor weak relic of mortality who has left hope behind" (125). He tried both to reveal the power of the owls' cries and to neutralize them. "I rejoice that there are owls. Let them do the idiotic and maniacal hooting for men" (125). As we follow the ensuing interpretation, though, Thoreau failed to corroborate that dismissive reference, which says by implication that there is no legitimate reason to utter these dismal sounds; therefore, it is preferable that wild creatures give vent to them rather than man. For, as Thoreau continued, these sounds became genuine expressions of life, suggesting "a vast and undeveloped nature which men have not recognized" (125). If, however, the cries of the owls accurately suggested some Alaska of mankind, why should they be designated "idiotic and maniacal"? To judge by Thoreau's next sentence, he was not referring to some lamentably undeveloped capacity of men. The owl cries "represent the stark twilight and unsatisfied thoughts which all have" (125). In short, those dismal sounds do reflect an aspect of human existence, although Thoreau obviously does not believe that one's pain should be expressed. Men do not cry—they let the owls do it for them. Night is the owl's kingdom, when "a more dismal and fitting day dawns, and a different race of creatures awakes to express the meaning of Nature there" (125–126). Note that the melancholy setting is called "more . . . fitting," and that

Thoreau does not say that some diabolic race of creatures issues forth from Hell to traduce God's sunny reality, but merely that these creatures are different and express "the meaning of Nature there." Yet Thoreau could not examine the dimensions of the possible negativity—perhaps even depravity—of the world, nor say what the language of sounds meant to him, other than "O, that I never had been born!"

He could, however, indulge in another fantasy of absorption by yet another manifestation of nature. Having dismissed the sounds of the domestic world, Thoreau imagines a benign invasion by "unfenced Nature" when a young forest grows up under his windows, when sumach and blackberry shrubs break through into his cellar, when pitch pines rub against the shingles while their roots reach "quite under the house" (128). Then, exulting, Thoreau crowned the conditions as affording "no path to the civilized world!" (161/128—the exclamation mark was a later addition). The idea of such isolated absorption grew increasingly attractive to him. It was the attic, the mountaintop, the pond, enhanced.

Thoreau wished to convince his readers that at Walden Pond he enjoyed an abundance of space. To be sure, when he asked "for what reason have I this vast range and circuit, some square miles of unfrequented forest for my privacy, abandoned to me by men?" one impolite answer would be: you have it because Emerson purchased this forest tract to keep it from being cut by lumbermen; not "abandoned by men," it was provided for you out of his good will (130). Thoreau made slight revisions to enhance the impression of his isolation. The forest, which was first "a square mile and more," became "some square miles," and the village fishermen who originally came to fish "occasionally" turned up in revision "at long intervals" (163/130, 164/130).

Although Thoreau was anxious to establish that "it is as solitary where I live as on the prairies," that was far from the case (130). To speak of Walden Pond as if it furnished a frontier experience would be to betray the actual lives of prairie settlers. Walden Pond was not even comparable to the Maine wilderness, the granitic indifference of which shook Thoreau's provincial complacency when he finally saw it. His claims, then, about the benignity of nature are suspect. When once he felt oppressed by the solitude of Walden, he tells us that he was quickly made sensible of the "sweet and beneficient society in Nature. . . . Every little pine needle expanded and swelled with sympathy and befriended me" (132). The occasion so inspired him that he even denied a fundamental perception achieved on Mt. Katahdin. Here in *Walden* he says that he was "distinctly made aware of the presence of something kindred to me, even in scenes which we are accustomed to call wild and dreary" (132). But in the Maine wilderness he had drawn back on finding the surroundings "vast, and drear and, inhuman," realizing that "Man was not to be associated with it" (*MW*, 70).

It is true that the assurance that "the most sweet and tender, the most innocent and encouraging society may be found in every natural object" was set down in *Walden*'s first draft, and so may well have been written before the Katahdin trip (164). (Thoreau evidently started planning that first draft before March 13, 1846, although Shanley says the actual writing did not begin until late 1846 or early 1847) (18, 24). But since one of the received truths about Thoreau is that he was a painstaking reviser, one might have expected this passage to undergo revision, if not to be excised altogether. But Thoreau seemed to think compartmentally. In any case, here he sought to create the impression of genuine isolation, whereas in fact he was like a child camping overnight in a tent in the backyard. From that perspective, his reported triumph over the "slight insanity" of a temporary melancholy was an insignificant victory (165/131). There is no doubt that solitude appealed to Thoreau. He was a man who generally found company painful and who preferred to fill his hours reading, writing, and in nature. He had no difficulty in saying so directly: "To be in company, even with the best, is soon wearisome and dissipating. I love to be alone" (135). But when he attempted to account for and explain away feelings of gloom in such a condition, or when he tried to elevate that solitude into a higher state of company, then his resources failed him.

The failure of those resources is most evident in "Visitors," a chapter dominated by Thoreau's irritable characterization of those villagers who came to the pond to trouble him, and by his enthusiastic celebration of the French-Canadian woodchopper, Alex Therien.

Therien's attraction for Thoreau is clear. Independent, knowledgeable in the ways of the forest, good-natured, manly, Therien was precisely Thoreau's age, a child-like, nonintellectual version of himself. He lived at ease in the woods, working only as much as he chose, unapologetically indifferent to society's expectations. Thoreau enjoyed Therien's company, even though he found his thinking "primitive and immersed in his animal life" (150). After trying to shift Therien to "the spiritual view of things," Thoreau doubted he would ever change (150).

Thoreau wrote equally positively (if callously) about visits from "half-witted men from the almshouse and elsewhere" (151). It amused him to listen to them "make their confessions to me," or at least, in his usual accountant's language, he found himself "compensated" by their discourse (151). One in particular who "expressed a wish to live as I did" he found memorable (151). The simplicity, sincerity, and truthfulness of this man impressed Thoreau so strongly that when he transferred his journal entry to the *Walden* manuscript he added the observation: "He was a metaphysical puzzle to me" (*J*, III, 198–199; 151). But Thoreau never pursued the significance of such simplicity as Therien and "the poor weak-headed pauper" represented (151). He could feel condescendingly superior to such men, while at the same time using them as easy weapons against a society he detested. He designated, for example, some of the "half-witted men" as "wiser than the so called *overseers* of the poor" (151). And, in order to sustain the image of the good-natured Therien, Thoreau excised one aspect of his childishness from the printed text. Therien, it seems, amused himself "all day" by shooting a pistol. He liked to frighten his dog by pointing the pistol at him and "firing powder only." He also "would occasionally steal up behind my house and fire a stout charge—& laugh loudly at my surprise" (Shanley, 172).

In his conclusion, Thoreau noted that "girls and boys and young women generally seemed glad to be in the woods." Originally, some Whitmanesque "healthy and sturdy working men" also appeared, who, Thoreau said, began to look upon him as one of their kin (Shanley, 173). One in particular, "a handsome younger man, a sailor-like, Greek-like man," told Thoreau that he liked his notions and expected to live so himself, but preferably in wilder surroundings (J, I, 366). These men "came in troops on Sundays in clean shirts, with washed hands & faces, and fresh twigs in their hands" (Shanley, 173). In the published version, all that remained was the phrase, "railroad men taking a Sunday morning walk in clean shirts" (154). Why the "troops" of working men were eliminated we do not know.

We do know that Thoreau claimed "I love society as much as most" and that he was "ready enough to fasten myself like a bloodsucker . . . to any full-blooded man that comes in my way" (140). His metaphors for discourse were equally aggressive. One needs room to talk, he said; otherwise, the bullet of one's thought "may plough out again through the side" of the hearer's head (141). He devoted a page to maintaining one's distance, for humans repelled Thoreau as much by their physical presence as by their moral failings. Whereas the "merely loquacious" might stand "cheek by jowl and feel each other's breath," the thoughtful want to give "all animal heat and moisture . . . a chance to evaporate" (141). On the other hand, many houses seemed excessively large to Thoreau, making their inhabitants seem mere "vermin which infest them" (140). (All these negative observations were added in later revisions.)

As Thoreau's ruminations on visitors continued, the vermin multiplied. His list of irritating types is noteworthy in its detail. He contemptuously satirized those who appeal for help but will not help themselves; those who stay too long on a visit; those with one idea and those with a thousand; businessmen; ministers; prying housekeepers; the old, the infirm, the timid; and, bringing up the rear of this ungenerous procession, "the self-styled reformers, the greatest bores of all" (152–154). Most curious in this strongly negative list is the mention of two categories of runaway slaves—"runaway slaves with plantation manners" and "one real runaway slave" (152). The meaning of "plantation manners" goes unexplained. Thoreau might have meant that these were house-slaves who had absorbed some of the elaborate courtesies associated with plantation life; or he might have meant the converse, ironically suggesting that these were field hands brutalized by life on the plantation. In any case, these slaves "listened from time to time, like the fox in the fable, as if they heard the hounds a-baying on their track, and looked at me beseechingly, as much to say,—'O Christian, will you send me back?' " (152). The turn the paragraph now takes is disconcerting: "One real runaway slave, among the rest, whom I helped to forward toward the northstar." Real? If we cannot account confidently for Thoreau's distinction, we can identify the man as probably Henry Williams, whom Thoreau mentions helping in a journal entry for October 5, 1851, since in that entry he also discusses the black fugitives' reliance on the north star for guidance (J, III, 37–38). But there is nothing to distinguish Williams as "real" in contrast with the other slaves, unless it be that he was "an intelligent and very well-behaved man, a mulatto" (J, III, 38) or unless it was the case that blacks frequently abused the confidence of their northern friends by pretending to be runaways. The most that we can assert from this paragraph is that Thoreau mentions runaway slaves in the general context of unwelcome visitors; that he is not complimentary about them; and that, insofar as his words are clear, they involve, in the first instance, the slaves' fear that they will be returned to servitude and, in the second, Thoreau's reference to having helped one on his way to freedom. But, as I shall suggest in my discussion of "Civil Disobedience," it may be that Thoreau was less exercised about slavery as a condition affecting a specific race than he was indignant at the idea of any abridgement of freedom, since implicitly it represented community pressure on him to conform.

"The Bean-Field" is a curious chapter that percolates along, happily engaged in describing the pleasures of gardening—"I came to love my rows"—of being absorbed in a productive outdoors activity (155). But periodically the serene mood is broken by sarcasm or downright condemnation of that ever-threatening presence, the village of Concord.

Thoreau was especially determined to make it clear that in his gardening he used no manure, for he seems to have been countering practical criticism from more orthodox farmers. He mentioned one "hard-featured farmer" who stopped to ask what Thoreau was up to, since he saw no fertilizer in his furrows (157). To the recommendation of "a little chip dirt, or any little waste stuff, or it may be ashes or plaster," Thoreau responded that he was only cultivating two and a half acres, and moreover lacked a cart to transport the "chip dirt," which was "far away" (157–158).

On three other occasions he addressed the same subject. It appeared to rankle in his mind as an accusation. Back in "Economy" he was at his most defiant, saying that he did not fertilize the soil at all because he didn't own the land but was merely a squatter, and anyway didn't expect to cultivate so much in the future (54).[10] At the outset of "The Bean-Field" he repeated that he gave his garden no manure, then went on to say that the arrowheads he turned up suggested that Indians previously dwelling there had to some extent already exhausted this soil (156). The logic of this assertion is unfathomable, but, beyond that, the assertion itself is unexpected and can be reasonably accounted for only by supposing that Thoreau's neighbors had criticized him for taking nutrients from the soil without giving any back. His rejoinder then was that someone had done it before he had. Thoreau addressed the issue once more in "The Bean-Field," again acknowledging that he gave his beans no fertilizer, but insisting that he did hoe them vigorously, an activity that Evelyn attested was much superior to the application of compost (162). As Thoreau devoted a good deal of space to a question hardly deserving it and provided diverse and unrelated explanations for his practice, one can only assume that, like his burning of the woods, his refusal to use fertilizer was an especially vexed subject for him.

Thoreau also erected an implicit defense of himself by reproducing in detail his budget, which resulted in a profit for the year of $8.71½. In "Economy" he had provided an equally detailed cost accounting of the expenditures for his house and food (49, 59–60). Thoreau was genuinely proud of the soundness of his financial dealings. Not only did he keep careful accounts of his own professional activities as a surveyor but, more important, his exposition is threaded through with economic idioms, of which the most common is his saying that something was "worth the while" to do (45, 88, 113, 127). Of keeping a journal, he remarked that "I got only my labor for my pains," but that "my pains were their own reward" (18). Or he commented that "it is worth the expense" to learn a classical language, or that rain was "of far more worth" than his hoeing (100, 131). Which is to say that, whether he liked it or not, he himself was permeated by the idioms of profit and loss.

Yet he felt himself impinged on by the representatives of

that commercial system. One can detect the irritation and contempt increasing over the years during which the book expanded. Thoreau diminished the village by placing its cele- brations on the distant horizon, so that they were no more than trivialities on the margin of his consciousness. The crowd hummed like swarming bees, and he felt as if an itching, an eruption of a disease, were impending (160). Such occasions so reassured him, Thoreau remarked sarcastically, that he felt inspired to "spit a Mexican with a good relish," and, lacking one, he "looked round for a woodchuck or a skunk to exercise my chivalry upon" (161).

Toward the end of the chapter, he renewed his attack, this time against the perversion of husbandry. Thoreau thought that farming was no longer a sacred art, that it simply treated land as property. Such materialism caused the farmer to lead "the meanest of lives. He knows Nature but as a robber" (165–166). (This from the man who refused to fertilize his soil.) The causes of such behavior were "avarice and selfish- ness, and a grovelling habit." To that analysis, Thoreau later added the rare concession, "from which none of us is free" (165).

Thoreau did sometimes hint publicly of failure, as in the following conceit. After a summer's experience of industrious farming, he decided that he would next plant "such seeds, if the seed is not lost, as sincerity, truth, simplicity, faith, inno- cence and the like" (164). Consider the components of that list. Numbing and overlapping abstractions, originally set down in no coherent sequence in his journal, they help explain Thoreau's difficulties in establishing a coherent conception of the world (*J*, I, 382). When he transferred this 1845 journal entry to the first draft of *Walden*, he dropped "trust" from his original list, but we cannot tell if that was deliberate, or an inadvertance, or a temporary sourness about the trustworthi- ness of others (Shanley, 182). At any rate, the omission of "trust" was not likely to be of momentous significance in Thoreau's thinking. Still, there is evidence that at some point

Thoreau turned his attention to the list again, for in the final printed version of *Walden* he added to it the phrase "and the like," but that only increased the metaphorical blur (164).

Thoreau continued: "and see if they will not grow in this soil, even with less toil and manurance, and sustain me" (182/164). The original journal entry proposed seeing if the virtues would grow "with such manure as I have." The "less toil and manurance" came later. In the printed version, this simple enough idea received a rueful appendage. Thoreau now supposed that surely this soil "has not been exhausted for these crops," but he has nonetheless been disappointed. It is not clear whether the virtues failed to develop in himself or in others, or both. Nor is it clear why the virtues failed to germinate: "Alas! I said this to myself; but now another summer is gone, and another, and another, and I am obliged to say to you, Reader, that the seeds which I planted if indeed they *were* the seeds of those virtues, were wormeaten or had lost their vitality, and so did not come up" (164).

This passage exemplifies how Thoreau offered suggestive analogies from the physical world for the moral one, but failed to think them through carefully. If one opts to be a moralist, then it is of some moment to discover why one's prescriptions go awry. It is not sufficient merely to posit that the seeds planted were improper or without vitality, or that their environment failed to nourish them, or that pests destroyed them. But since Thoreau could locate neither the source of his unhappiness nor a satisfactory model for emulation, he really could go no further.

He was confident, however, that the answer did not lie in "The Village." Accordingly, the chapter devoted to it is the shortest in *Walden*. In his first draft, Thoreau could produce but five paragraphs on the subject. These were reasonably equable, but when he augmented those early observations, quite different moods emerged, giving the chapter as a whole a curiously inconsistent surface.

It seems that originally Thoreau meant to compose a brief, good-natured mockery of the village with its propensity for gossip and for seducing the visitor with its material goods. But eventually he came to regard the village as a separate social entity, at best trivial in its vaunting self-importance, at worst a corrupt microcosm of an oppressive national government. The movement began in the amused condescension with which Thoreau looked in one direction from his house to "a colony of muskrats," then in the opposite to the village, which seemed "as curious to me as if they had been prairie dogs" (167). This same exercise in diminution Thoreau had employed in "The Bean-Field" when he mocked the village's martial exercises. Both instances of ridicule were later additions.

Next Thoreau offered the village as a gauntlet. What was a miniature curiosity at a distance became, close up, a trial. Thoreau provided a quite extraordinarily paranoic description, one in which he tried to sustain his superior perspective but in which, nonetheless, his assumption that as he entered the village "every man, woman, and child" was out to "get a lick at him" is clearly amplified self-consciousness. So too, if the tavern, the dry-goods store, and the barber-shop were allurements, invitations to houses became out-and-out "dangers" (168–169).

But even when captured in a house, Thoreau eventually "escaped to the woods again" (169). Here followed a lyric interlude on the pleasures of making one's way home through the woods on tempestuous nights. Thoreau knew his path so well that he could make the trip without any conscious effort. Against this, he placed the experience of numerous villagers, lost and wandering through the night because they had not learned to steer by their feet rather than their eyes (170). One instance Thoreau cited, though, seemed to contradict this principle of trusting the body: "gentlemen and ladies making a call have gone half a mile out of their way, feeling the sidewalk only with their feet, and not knowing when they turned" (170). Since this is a description of people failing as they

steered by the feet, the motivation for including it could only
be to show that others were less adept than Thoreau at ma-
neuvering through the dark. But Thoreau was also flirting with
the notion that, if one trusts one's unconscious, it will guide
one safely. He recognized, however, that one can easily become lost, especially if "we go beyond our usual course" (171;
originally *J*, V, 62–64). At such a moment, we may still be
steering unconsciously by some familiar landmark. This
seemed to be a concession on Thoreau's part to the difficulty
of adapting to a new environment. Nonetheless, he staunchly
asserted the value of being lost, for only then "do we appreciate the vastness and strangeness of Nature" (171).

The philosophic thoughtfulness of this sequence of ideas
is abruptly broken by Thoreau's indignant account of his having been jailed for failing to pay his poll tax. At this point, the
previous conception of society as lying in wait for him erupted
into that of society as actively malevolent: "wherever a man
goes, men will pursue and paw him with their dirty institutions" (171). Thoreau's feeling of having been violated was
strong, and to judge by what followed and concluded the
chapter, such a violation could only take place in the village.

Still, "I was never molested by any person but those who
represented the state" (172). Perhaps, but the representative
of the state in question was only Sam Staples, who remained
Thoreau's friend until his death. But Thoreau wished to make
a point: namely, that he was protected by his purity. Everyone
respected his belongings at the pond, even though his cabin
went unlatched, and even though he was away for as long as a
fortnight in Maine. Was this because people were generally
honest? No. It was because of Thoreau's mode of living: "if all
men were to live as simply as I then did, thieving and robbery
would be unknown" (172). Confucius supplied the moral:
"Love virtue, and the people will be virtuous" (172). This is
not, of course, what we learned in "The Bean-Field," where
the seeds of virtue failed to germinate. But it does convey
Thoreau's strong feelings about organized society. It is that

entity that flails away at and imprisons one, a venomous, seductive, gossiping community of prairie dogs against whom the individual in nature stands.

In comparing the first draft of *Walden* with its final version, one is repeatedly struck by two features of the revisions. First, they tend to be more somber and irritable, and second, they are often badly written or badly placed. For example, "The Ponds" opens with the observation that when Thoreau tired of village life, he set off into the hills to make his supper on berries. That minor pastoral note was subsequently elaborated to make the point that city people are benighted fools if they imagine that they can ever have this experience. "It is a vulgar error to suppose that you have tasted huckleberries who never plucked them. A huckleberry never reaches Boston" (173). However, this initial paragraph has nothing whatsoever to do with the long appreciative chapter on ponds that it introduces. The chapter itself provides overwhelming proof of Thoreau's intimacy with Walden Pond and his reverence for it. It is a successful mosaic, bringing together numerous journal entries and statistical facts about the pond that served so centrally as a focus for Thoreau's thoughts for two years.

In fact, the pond is at once Thoreau's creation and Thoreau himself. Midway in the chapter, he referred to "that ancient settler whom I have mentioned" (182). This is apparently the mythological creature invoked back in "Solitude": "an old settler and original proprietor, who is reported to have dug Walden Pond, and stoned it, and fringed it with pine woods" (137).[11] Thoreau provided an account of how this old settler picked the spot for Walden. He "remembers so well when he first came here with his divining rod, saw a thin vapor rising from the sward, and the hazel pointed steadily downward, and he concluded to dig a well here" (182). The imagery is familiar because it had appeared earlier in "Where I Lived, and What I Lived For." "I think that the richest vein is somewhere hereabouts; so by the divining rod and thin rising vapors I judge; and here I will begin to mine" (98). We cannot be certain how conscious Thoreau was of using virtually identical wording, but the two activities of digging for water and digging for truth were demonstrably related in his mind.

Further, the identity between Thoreau and his pond is equally close in attributes. Walden is notable, Thoreau points out, for having no "visible inlet or outlet" (175). It is related to other bodies of water, yet separated from them, which contributes to its extraordinary immaculateness. It is "remarkable for its depth and purity" (175). Hence, Thoreau declared, "It is no dream of mine . . . / I am its stony shore, / And the breeze that passes o'er; / In the hollow of my hand / Are its water and its sand" (193). In the prose immediately preceding this little verse, Thoreau had said, "It is the work of a brave man surely, in whom there was no guile! He rounded this water with his hand, deepened and clarified it in his thought, and in his will bequeathed it to Concord" (193). So a specific group of images clustered around the pond and its creation—an old settler, the divining rod, digging, burrowing, cupping it in the hand. And the components of the pond and of its celebrant are analagous: "by living thus reserved and austere, like a hermit in the woods, so long, it has acquired such wonderful purity" (194).

The extreme contrast was Flint's Pond. "Comparatively shallow, and not remarkably pure," it was discussed idly as the largest of the neighborhood lakes, until suddenly Thoreau erupted into extraordinary vituperation, initiated by italics and an exclamation mark—*"Flint's Pond!"* (194, 195). The violence of Thoreau's language was markedly incongruous. He first constructed an incredible, melodramatic villain, a "skin-flint" with "fingers grown into crooked and horny talons," who, in Thoreau's imaginative expansion of him, exploited the pond and, given the opportunity, "would have drained and sold it for the mud at its bottom" (195, 196).

Thoreau harangued this creature for growing no crops but dollars. Then, increasingly agitated by his own language, Thoreau finally exploded in sensuous disgust. "A model farm! where the house stands like a fungus in a muck-heap, chambers for men, horses, oxen, and swine, cleansed and uncleansed, all contiguous to one another! Stocked with men! A great grease-spot, redolent of manures and buttermilk!" (196).

It is an astonishing outburst. There is nothing else like it in *Walden*. It is, quite literally, as if a friend were to begin to fume, then to talk faster and louder, and finally to shout imprecations at what would seem to be inconsequentialities. Flint as a man does not exist in Thoreau's journals, and every entry in his journal concerning Flint's Pond is merely descriptive. There is no clue in Thoreau's writing as to what sparked this outburst. We are familiar, to be sure, with Thoreau's animus toward farmers who moved beyond subsistence farming to profit (even though he himself proudly did so). Flint, says Thoreau indignantly, "would carry the landscape . . . to market" if he thought he could sell it (196). Yet Thoreau tells us that *he* used to visit White Pond "to collect the sand by cart-loads, to make sand-paper with" (197). The terms of Thoreau's indictment are therefore perplexing. We do see that certain kinds of dirt that particularly agitated him culminated the diatribe against Flint—muck, grease, manure.[12] But when we look at Thoreau's bill of particulars, we find only (1) that Flint would have profaned the pond, could he have managed it, (2) that Flint was a prosperous farmer who sold crops at market, and (3) that Flint's farmhouse was evidently contiguous to his livestock barn, a practice altogether common in New England. The condemnation was so irrational that one is obliged to suppose that the source of Thoreau's rancor was a much more personal one. A plausible explanation offered by Walter Harding is that "the Flints who owned the land" around the pond had refused permission to Thoreau in 1841 to build a cabin on its shores, such as the one Stearns Wheeler (with whom Thoreau had spent six weeks in the summer of 1837) had constructed (*Days*, 123, 49).

The opportunity of living quietly in a kind of dreamy passiveness, antithetical to anything a Flintian businessman-farmer might stand for, was what Thoreau sought. A central image for this was floating in his rowboat, in a charmed state, with the clouds or moon reflected in the water, and the passing fish seeming like flocks of birds flying beneath his balloon (174, 189). Best of all were those summer mornings, spent daydreaming on the pond "until I was aroused by the boat touching the sand" (191). We can see that there is no difficulty in understanding the pleasures of such pensive idleness. Thoreau could render the strong positive with convincing clarity. And for Thoreau the pond was an ideal presence. It had no leeches nor snapping turtles, and no one drowned in it. It was all eye and no mouth, all nostrum and no poison. Its fish were "much cleaner, handsomer, and firmer fleshed than those in the river and most other ponds," and even its frogs and tortoises were "a clean race" (184).

This enthusiastic idealization concluded the chapter as Thoreau made White and Walden Ponds equivalent to that nature that humans, living in towns, failed to experience, let alone appreciate. "She flourishes most alone," Thoreau asserted, then directed toward the villagers one last scornful exclamation: "Talk of heaven! ye disgrace earth" (200).

The ponds have an equivalent in the trees of the neighborhood, which Thoreau said he visited regularly as shrines. The long descriptive paragraph opening the chapter "Baker Farm" mentions a variety of trees. The enumeration contains an equally variegated religious vocabulary—temple, pagoda, Valhalla, "wild forbidden fruits"—no doubt conceived to irritate conventional church-goers. It is not otherwise an impressive paragraph.[13] Like the opening huckleberry paragraph of "The Ponds," it is unconnected with the rest of the chapter. Moreover, even though the passage is clearly dominated by sacramental imagery, the first sentence blurs the focus by describing pine groves "standing like temples, or like fleets at sea, full-rigged." The second simile is an acceptable comparison, but one that steers the reader away from the central point, which is that trees in nature constitute places for worship. Toward the end of the paragraph, Thoreau was reduced to mere mechanical enumeration—"the bass; the hornbeam; the *Celtis occidentalis*, or false elm, of which we have but one well-grown." The whole ends on the vaguest of notes: "and many others I could mention" (201–202).

In general, "Baker Farm" is a disturbing chapter, for it seems to reveal a bigotry and a megalomania in Thoreau that are difficult to credit. Built around a single anecdote, the encounter with John Field and his family, it is bracketed by revelatory rainbows. Thoreau recalls once standing at the base of a rainbow—"in the very abutment"—and, as his own pot of gold, being dazzled by this "lake of rainbow light" (202). Then, without transition, he speculated on the fact that his shadow had a "halo of light" around it. What might that mean? Anticipating his encounter with John Field, Thoreau reports that a visitor had once declared that "the shadows of some Irishmen had no halo about them, that it was only natives that were so distinguished," an ironic sentiment worthy of the Know-Nothing Party, which was just then gathering its forces against the Irish immigrants. As for Thoreau, he "would fain fancy myself one of the elect," although he realized that there might be a natural explanation for it. For "are they not indeed distinguished who are conscious that they are regarded at all?" (202–203).

Once Thoreau had established himself as a man who had stood under a rainbow's arch and whose shadow had a halo, he was ready to recount a fishing expedition that was interrupted by a thunderstorm, so that he was obliged to seek shelter in a previously uninhabited hut. There he found the John Field family. Thoreau's description of its members is one of amused yet contemptuous hauteur, from the "broad-faced boy" to the wife with her "round greasy face and bare breast" to the baby, a "wrinkled, sibyl-like, cone-headed infant," whom Thoreau also refers to as "John Field's poor starveling brat" (204).[14]

Learning that Field worked very hard spading up meadows, Thoreau decided "to help him with my experience," a priggish decision, fortunately not put into practice in the actual incident (205; *J*, I, 383–384). Thoreau's imaginary exhortation made no more impress on Field than others like it had on Thoreau's Anglo-Saxon neighbors. However, Thoreau chose to ascribe Field's obtuseness to his race. "But alas! the culture of an Irishman is an enterprise to be undertaken with a sort of moral bog hoe" (205–206). Concluding therefore that the situation was hopeless, Thoreau with a "rainbow over my shoulder" departed to fish again, reminding himself to adapt to the weather. "Let the thunder rumble; what if it threatens ruin to the farmers' crops? that is not its errand to thee. Take shelter under the cloud, while they flee to carts and sheds" (207). These sentiments sit rather poorly with the earlier scene, when, routed by the thunderstorm, Thoreau "made haste for shelter to the nearest hut" (203).

Reaching the pond, Thoreau was shortly joined by Field, but even as a fisherman the Irishman could not please Thoreau. His sense of efficiency offended, Thoreau made much of the fact that Field caught shiners with worms, then used them as bait for perch (206, 208). But later, in "The Pond in Winter," Thoreau would approvingly describe fishermen who were "wise in natural lore," one of whom used worms to catch perch, which in turn he used as bait for pickerel (283). "Such a man has some right to fish, and I love to see Nature carried out in him" was Thoreau's comment in that instance (283–284). But Field was Irish, so inevitably failed to equal Thoreau's catch. It is no wonder that Leon Edel characterized this incident as being "as cruel as it is sanctimonious."[15] At best, defendants of Thoreau in this matter have pointed out that, in time, Thoreau's attitude toward the Irish changed.[16]

One reason for the change may well be Thoreau's preoccupation with Johnny Riordan. He was a young Irish boy: Thoreau describes him as four years old at one point and, a year later, as three. (*J*, II, 117 and *J*, III, 149). We first encounter him in a journal entry of November 28, 1850, when Thoreau was so impressed by the Dickensian misery of this child crying from the cold as he makes his way to school through the snow that he composed a piece of doggerel, "I am the little Irish boy" (*J*, II, 117–118; see also *Poems*, 177–178). On December 21, 1851, it was pointed out to the shocked Thoreau that this child had but a ragged cloth for a coat and holes in his shoes. This belated knowledge exercised him: "This little mass of humanity, this tender gobbet for the fates, cast into a cold world with a torn lichen leaf wrapped about him . . . I shudder when I think of the fate of innocency" (*J*, III, 241–242). Finally, on February 8, 1852, Thoreau acted: "Carried a new cloak to Johnny Riordan." Furthermore, having gained entrance to the Riordan shanty, Thoreau learned that "the shanty was warmed by the simple social relations of the Irish. . . .What if there is less fire on the hearth, if there is more in the heart!" (*J*, III, 289).

Since this revelation that the Irish have an admirable social warmth and that "these Irish are not succeeding so ill after all" came to Thoreau well before *Walden* was published, and since he was revising the book up to the last minute before publication, how is it that he did not revise his several contemptuous assessments of the Irish (*J*, III, 289)? Furthermore, had he utterly forgotten the sentiments expressed back in 1843 when he was in temporary exile on Staten Island? Emerson had written him, "Now the humanity of the town suffers with the poor Irish, who receives but sixty, or even fifty cents, for working from dark till dark, with a strain and a following up that reminds one of negro-driving" (*Corr.*, 137). On October 17, Thoreau responded: "The sturdy Irish arms that do the work are of more worth than oak or maple. Methinks I could look with equanimity upon a long street of

Irish cabins and pigs and children revelling in the genial Concord dirt, and I should still find my Walden wood and Fair Haven in their tanned and happy faces" (*Corr.*, 146). Whatever the explanation for these variant positions, it is the case that Thoreau's pronouncements on the Irish were in general negative, even though he was quite capable of positive responses to an individual, especially to a vulnerable young boy.

"Higher Laws" takes Thoreau more centrally into the wilderness of contradictions that existed in his mind than does any other chapter in *Walden*. Accordingly, it has received much critical attention, generally dedicated to smoothing matters out by tracing a continuous development in Thoreau from the thoughtless savage youth to the reflective adult naturalist. In fact, the confusions of the chapter accurately represent the conflicts in Thoreau caused by the clash of his perceptions with his ideals. Manliness, curiosity, coldness, sympathy, and prudery were all at contest within him.

The chapter opens with memorable verve. Returning home from another fishing expedition, Thoreau said, he saw a woodchuck "and felt a strange thrill of savage delight, and was strongly tempted to seize and devour him raw; not that I was hungry then, except for that wildness which he represented" (210). This passage is heightened from the original journal entry (*J*, I, 385). The "strange thrill of savage delight" was added, as was the "strongly" that qualifies "tempted." And, giving the woodchuck more identity, its pronoun was changed from "it" to "him." Finally, to "devour him," Thoreau added "raw." And although he had originally commented, "The wildest, most desolate scenes are strangely familiar to me," he prudently excised "most desolate" for publication. Thoreau was not aiming for self-revelation, then, but rather was building an argument on behalf of a wildness of the sort that has proved to be particularly compelling to the urban reader. So elemental is the action of devouring a woodchuck raw, it creates a certain intellectual *frisson*. At the same time, it is obviously not to be understood literally, although neither is it a metaphorical act. Rather it is a kind of creative exaggeration, since Thoreau was not talking of a desire to devour a woodchuck raw, but rather of freeing himself of civilized constraints by ingesting the beast's wildness. "Once or twice" while living at the pond, Thoreau remarked, "I found myself ranging the woods, like a half-starved hound, with a strange abandonment, seeking some kind of venison which I might devour" (210).[17]

If Thoreau was preoccupied with carnivorousness, he only practiced imaginary assimilation. In person, his tastes were quite delicate and he abstemious, especially concerning flesh. In the *Week*, one recalls, he and his brother could not bring themselves to eat the squirrels they had killed, so revolted were they by their skinned bodies (*Week*, 224). The idea of hunting had its attractions for Thoreau, but its actualities disturbed him. Muskrat hunting in particular gave him numerous shocks: "Yesterday I met Goodwin shooting muskrats and saw the form and blood stains of two through his game-bag. . . . I saw one poor rat lying on the edge of the ice reddened with its blood" (*J*, VII, 132). Or: "There lies the red carcass of one whose pelt he has taken on the spot, flat on the bloody ice" (*J*, XIII, 53). Or: "We see Goodwin skinning the muskrats he killed . . . leaving their red and mutilated carcasses behind. . . . See the red and black bodies . . . which the crows have already attacked" (*J*, VIII, 256–257). Throughout his life, the vision of the immediate effects of hunting was understandably repulsive to Thoreau. "What a pitiful business is the fur trade," he told his journal in 1858. "When we see men and boys spend their time shooting and trapping musquash and mink, we cannot but have a poorer opinion of them, unless we thought meanly of them before" (*J*, XII, 120–121). Years before, in "Paradise (To Be) Regained," he had declared: "We slander the hyena; man is the fiercest and cruelest animal" (*RP*, 22). If he could not bring himself to cook a skinned squirrel, it was unthinkable that he could literally devour a woodchuck raw.

Yet there were aspects of hunting involving masculine competence that appealed to Thoreau. That is what caused the internal debate in "Higher Laws." Even the hunter whom Thoreau observed year after year slaughtering muskrats and littering the ice with their skinned bodies led Thoreau to observe one day: "Goodwin cannot be a very bad man, he is so cheery" (*J*, XI, 351). That same winter (1858–1859), Thoreau wrote of the hunters' guns: "I must confess they are to me a springlike and exhilarating sound, like the cock-crowing, though each one may report the death of a musquash" (*J*, XI, 424). He expanded this idea in revealing ways. "The energy and excitement of the musquash-hunter even, not despairing of life, but keeping the same rank and savage hold on it that his predecessors have for so many generations, while so many are sick and despairing, even this is inspiriting to me" (*J*, XI, 422–423).

One can see the attraction of hunting for Thoreau: the primitive expression of self in the act of mastery, it is equivalent to life, to energy, to action. Opposed to it is bookish despair, the disease of civilization, of those who live indoors. Thoreau could even find inspiration in the annual slaughter of muskrats because "these deeds of death are . . . evidences of life, for life will still prevail in spite of all accidents" (*J*, XI, 423). The directness of a Fortinbras had its attractions, especially if one were not directly confronted with the results of a "rank and savage hold" on life.

Like the more obvious "savage," the word "rank" had a powerful attraction for Thoreau as a counter to desolation. It represented several coarse powers, a weedy profusion superior to cultivation and mortality. The very strength of odor associated with something "rank" suggested indomitable existence to Thoreau. So he told his journal, "I love the rank smells of the swamp, its decaying leaves" (*J*, IV, 305). And in

The Maine Woods he specified that a fresh, moist, swampy odor possessed for him "that sort of vigor and perennialness . . . that toad-stools suggest" (20). The same association of rankness and life appeared when he said, "I am not offended by the odor of the skunk. . . . I am invigorated rather. It is a reminiscence of immortality" (*J*, II, 5).

On occasion, Thoreau did revert to a more conventional, even literary, use of "rank." Speaking of the odor in summertime from the village slaughterhouse, he observed, "Our offense is rank, it smells to heaven" (*J*, I, 480). Still, "rank" normally had positive connotations for Thoreau. Whereas in his journal he originally wrote, "I find an instinct in me conducting to a mystic spiritual life, and also another to a primitive savage life," in "Higher Laws" the latter condition became "a primitive rank and savage one." To this version he further added, "I like sometimes to take rank hold on life and spend my day more as the animals do" (*J*, I, 384; 210).

Hunting had its attractions as well. The same man who could avow that the young man goes to the forest "first as a hunter and fisher, until at last, if he has the seeds of a better life in him, he distinguishes his proper objects, as a poet or naturalist it may be, and leaves the gun and fish-pole behind," *this* man, without any sense of contradiction, could enter this statement in his journal in 1857: "If, as a poet or naturalist, you wish to explore a given neighborhood, go and live in it, *i.e.* get your living in it. Fish in its streams, hunt in its forests" (213; *J*, X, 146). In 1856, Thoreau had made yet another extended justification of hunting, as opposed to mere appreciation of nature. "From the brook in which one lover of nature has never during all his lifetime detected anything larger than a minnow, another extracts a trout that weighs three pounds, or an otter four feet long. How much more game he will see who carries a gun, *i.e.* who goes to see it! Though you roam the woods all your days, you will never see by chance what he sees who goes on purpose to see it. One gets his living by shooting woodcocks; most never see one in their lives" (*J*, VIII, 192).

This might seem a remarkable position for someone to hold who would spend hours seated in a clearing to observe its wild life. But there was always a Thoreau who sympathized with the male mastery connected with hunting. In "Higher Laws," since he was moving toward an argument on behalf of purification of being, Thoreau chose to identify hunting as a stage in one's growth to manhood. As for boys—"*make* them hunters," he counseled, for "we cannot but pity the boy who has never fired a gun" (212). His own youthful callousness was evident in his 1836 review of *The Book of the Seasons*. There, he specified May as "the pleasantest month of the 12," for now "commences the harvest of death." Thoreau then described in a language of comic elevation the young hunters going forth to shoot, until at last a bird was brought down, leaving its fledglings unattended in the nest, or as Thoreau put it: "The victim is finally transmitted to the hands of the executioner as completely bare and destitute of feathers, as the callow young who are piping anything but melody in the deserted nest" (*EE*, 31–32). Similarly, in writing his "Natural History of Massachusetts" (1842), Thoreau described the local fur trade with a certain proprietary pride. One trapper, he said, "takes from one hundred and fifty to two hundred muskrats in a year, and even thirty-six have been shot by one man in a day" (*W*, V, 115). A decade later, in 1853, he made a similar statistical entry in his journal. "In Brooks's barn I saw twenty-two gray squirrel skins freshly tacked up. He said that as many as one hundred and fifty had been killed this fall within a mile of his barn. . . . His brother killed sixteen in one day a month ago" (*J*, VI, 18). Thoreau could object strongly to such killing, but the two opposed selves were never permitted to confront one another. He kept his mind protectively compartmentalized, for in the next year (May 28, 1854) he asked himself: "Do we live *inhumanely*, toward man or beast, in thought or act? To be serene and successful we must be at one with the universe. The least conscious and heedless injury inflicted on any creature is to its extent a suicide. What peace—or life—can a murderer have?" (*J*, VI, 310–311).

Yet the capacity to observe and record slaughter without reaction remained with Thoreau. In 1856, he described a young man who, after the water was drained from a mill-pond, killed "a number of pouts and eels and suckers with a shovel," then impaled still more on a spear. Thoreau himself held on to a snapping turtle when a larger "seized the one I had by the head and they braced and struggled awhile" (*J*, VIII, 326–328). Elsewhere, the mayhem mounted. He told of a turtle being decapitated with a cleaver; of cats being struck by trains—"they found her head on the track separated from her body"; of tortoises also run over by trains—"they lie just under the rail, and put their heads out upon the rail to see what is coming, and so their heads are crushed"; and the passage continues with inexorable placidity, "Also he had seen snakes cut in two. The men on the road told him that small birds were frequently run over." When a new paragraph begins, the grisly toll goes on: "Jacob Farmer brought me the head of a mink tonight and took tea here" (*J*, VIII, 40).

To Thoreau, there was sufficient significance in these morbid collisions, deliberate and inadvertent, between men and living creatures for him to record them, but he was not inclined to see through them to a comprehension that might well challenge his assumptions about the benignity of the universe, even though, ironically, such truth might have brought his own private doubts and eccentric impulses into harmony with a more accurate way of conceiving the world. At times, he seemed to have sensed the limitations of his practice. "Man cannot afford to be a naturalist, to look at Nature directly, but only with the side of his eye. He must look through and beyond her. To look at her is as fatal as to look at the head of Medusa. It turns the man of science to stone" (*J*, V, 45). Thoreau's hardness in the face of pervasive natural misery is in part a reaction to this Medusa, but to look beyond her would be to adopt something like a Christian view that this world was a harsh one, dominated by suffering. But, in rejecting his neighbors, Thoreau was also rejecting their religion and so could hardly locate the transcendent positive in an afterworld. He was committed to *this* world, but his dilemma was that his accumulated experience had darkened his consciousness since that halcyon time when, as a young man, he wrote Mrs. Lucy Brown that "sometimes, in a fluttering leaf, one may hear all your Christianity preached" (*Corr.*, 45). Too much evidence afforded by this world said that it was not only unsatisfactory but downright voraciously cruel. Others— Balzac, Baudelaire, Melville, and Dostoevsky—were making a variety of adaptations to this possibility, but such were largely beyond Thoreau. He was too disorganized because too skittish. He could not even say what Emerson could: "We must see that the world is rough and surly, and will not mind drowning a man or a woman, but swallows your ship like a grain of dust."[18]

Still, Thoreau did have moments of compunction about killing, even if it was for study. Having just dispatched a box tortoise, he was temporarily racked with a fit of guilt. "I cannot excuse myself for this murder, and see that such actions are inconsistent with the poetic perception, however they may serve science, and will affect the quality of my observations. I pray that I may walk more innocently and serenely through nature." But even this expression of piety could not still the incident. It continued to agitate him. "No reasoning whatever reconciles me to this act. It affects my day injuriously. I have lost some self-respect. I have murderer's experience in a degree" (*J*, VI, 452). One might suppose that such an extreme reaction would have a lasting effect. But less than a year later, June 2, 1855, a moth emerged from a cocoon that Thoreau had brought home and pinned to his window sash. He described its unfolding in the most admiring terms: "It was wonderful how it waxed and grew, revealing some new beauty every fifteen minutes. . . . It looked like a young emperor just donning the most splendid ermine robes that ever emperor wore." This extravagant appreciation concluded: "at dusk, when apparently it was waving its wings preparatory to its evening flight I gave it ether and so saved it in a perfect state" (*J*, VII, 402). The man had no memory. Two years later, he commented, "I have the same objection to killing a snake that I have to the killing of any other animal" (*J*, IX, 343).

In 1861, on his last trip to Minnesota with the enthusiastic seventeen-year-old naturalist Horace Mann, Thoreau, perhaps from the weakness caused by his developing tuberculosis, perhaps from a subsiding of tender scruples, put up with a plenitude of scientific killing, apparently without protest. Mann, for example, wrote his mother: "I shot two birds, Rosebreasted Grosbeaks, of which I had shot three before, two chipmunks and a gopher, and I would have shot a cart load more if my arm had not been so sore from the old gun kicking." Mann sent his kill back to Concord in a five-gallon keg of alcohol.[19]

In "Higher Laws," Thoreau tells us that he long ago gave up hunting and even now feels twinges of doubt about fishing. But you will not find him telling you explicitly why either act might constitute unacceptable activity. He does observe that "no humane being, past the thoughtless age of boyhood, will wantonly murder any creature. . . . The hare in its extremity cries like a child" (212). A good deal depends on how "wantonly" is defined. It does not seem that the intrinsic act of killing troubled Thoreau much. He tells us, "I did not pity the fishes nor the worms" (211). Rather, he believed that there were activities to pursue that were superior. Thoreau flirted with Christian analogies. "Mothers should at last try to make their sons "hunters as well as fishers of men," but what that cleverness might have meant to him is impossible to determine (212).

What really bothered Thoreau was a subject that he abruptly broached in the middle of a paragraph. "Beside, there is something essentially unclean about this diet and all flesh"

(214). The statement is revealing, especially in the extension "and all flesh," for such ascetic revulsion was generally consistent with Thoreau's character. He continued in the same vein: "The practical objection to animal food in my case was its uncleanness" (214). And he went on to speak with disgust of "animal food," of "flesh and fat," as grossness and filth, profoundly offensive to his imagination (214–215). At one point, eating itself seemed repugnant to him. "The indecent haste and grossness with which our food is swallowed have cast a disgrace on the very act of eating itself" (*J*, I, 372).

Occasional signs of tenderness did appear in the midst of this fastidiousness, as when Thoreau remarked that man lives largely by preying on animals, "but this is a miserable way,—as any one who will go to snaring rabbits, or slaughtering lambs, may learn" (216). The choice of examples is interesting, since rabbits and lambs are particularly attractive and defenseless creatures whose killing any but the most callous might acknowledge was a disagreeable task. Thoreau therefore spoke on behalf of a diet of "a little bread or a few potatoes" and speculated that it was man's destiny to give up eating animals (214, 216).

His sense of abnegation was radical, he realized: "If one listens to the faintest but constant suggestions of his genius [to the original formulation, Thoreau here added the next, intensifying phrase] which are certainly true, he sees not to what extremes, or even insanity, it may lead him; and yet that way, as he grows more resolute and faithful, his road lies" (216). That is as fine and bold an assertion of independence as Thoreau ever made. At a moment such as this, Thoreau truly made himself vulnerable to the cynics of Concord, who were already contemptuous of the dietary faddists and other idealists who had invaded their community. But Thoreau was right to feel that he was, here, following his genius, for such scrupulosity in eating was everywhere evident in his writing, and Thoreau did well to recognize it. As he reflected on his position, though, he recognized the evanescence and doubtfulness of such perceptions. "The greatest gains and values are farthest from being appreciated. We easily come to doubt if they exist. We soon forget them. They are the highest reality" (216). This psychological observation may explain Thoreau's lamentation over the crime of killing a tortoise for science, followed a year later by his emotionless anesthetizing of a moth. In any case, he realized that the logic of his argument might lead to an extreme that would be definable as "insanity."

To temper the vulnerability of his idealism, Thoreau interjected: "Yet, for my part, I was never unusually squeamish; I could sometimes eat a fried rat with a good relish, if it were necessary" (217).[20] Perhaps, although one always feels such moments partake of imaginative bravado. Thoreau was certainly more ironic here than the young man who wrote Mrs. Brown: "I grow savager and savager every day, as if fed on raw meat" (*Corr.*, 45). But he still possessed an ascetic nature. No coffee, no tea, no wine. Only water.

That ascetic inclination joined with the increased coarseness and indifference that Thoreau discovered with some regret in himself (*J*, IV, 417; *Walden* 217). In 1851 he had observed in his journal: "We are more careless about our diet and our chastity." "But," he concluded, "we should be fastidious to the extreme of sanity"—an injunction that finally found a place in "Life Without Principle" (*J*, II, 463; *RP*, 167). Again, there was the note suggesting that fidelity to one's instincts could lead to madness.

This alternation between revulsion with animal life and an assertion of a personal coarseness capable of enjoying such dietary infamies as fried rat and raw woodchuck was visible throughout the chapter "Higher Laws," although, toward the end, Thoreau moved to a crescendo of confused abnegation. The problem for him was animal life. One was defiled by consuming animal flesh, one was defiled by behaving animalistically. "Gross," "gross," Thoreau chanted, "sensual," "sensual," "worms . . . possess us," "worms . . . occupy our bodies." Revolted by this "reptile and sensual" life, he emphasized its lowness by opposing it to the universal music of the "zephyr." "The wonder is how they, how you and I, can live this slimy beastly life, eating and drinking" (218, 219; cf. *J*, II, 9). Thoreau was obviously anxious to overcome that side of animal life in him that was fundamentally slimy. As we shall see further on, it was ineradicably associated in his mind with bowels, which in turn suggested the hypocritical compassion displayed by preachers, undertakers, and their kind.

In the course of arguing the power of spirit over "the grossest sensuality," Thoreau asserted that "the generative energy, which, when we are loose, dissipates and makes us unclean, when we are continent, invigorates and inspires us" (219). With this passage, the haunting shadow of sex falls over the chapter. In one of the passages ultimately omitted from *Walden*, Thoreau complains of women that, regarding indulgences of diet, "I am struck with the fact that in these respects she is rarely a reformer, and is intolerant of reform" (Stern, 346).[21] Similarly, the observation that "we may be well, yet not pure" takes on a somewhat different appearance when restored to the original context, which was later pruned by Thoreau: "I do not know how it is with other men, but I find it very difficult to be chaste. Methinks I can be chaste in my relation[s] to persons, and yet I do not find myself clean. I have frequent cause to be ashamed of myself. I am well, but I am not pure" (Stern, 347; HM924, V, 104). Here and elsewhere, there is an oscillating ambiguity between an idealized version of what Thoreau intended by "pure" and "chaste" and nocturnal emissions or masturbation. It is perhaps important to remind oneself that at this point Thoreau was in his mid-thirties and to all evidence had never been sexually involved with anyone. And, though much of his "generative energy" may indeed have been expended in physical activity and in writing (he was twenty-eight in 1845, the year he completed the *Week* and started *Walden*), Thoreau seems to have been concerned by the sexual unruliness of his physical self, which he insisted on subsuming under the general problem of sensuality. "All sensuality is one, though it takes many forms" (220). Still, he circled around sex, managing to touch on it in two lists. "It is the same whether a man eat, or drink, or cohabit, or sleep sensually. They are but one appetite" (220). Cohabitation (which scarcely tempted him) he would invoke once more, but "sleeping sensually" (which he could not control) disappeared into the vagueness at the end of this list of things that the "Hindoo lawgiver" teaches: "how to eat, drink, cohabit, void excrement and urine, and the like" (221).

Because this is a crucial chapter in *Walden* and because this is a crucial juncture in this chapter, the discussion must balloon out here to consider afresh Thoreau's attitudes toward sexuality, which when last reviewed were visible as sublimated, exalted versions of friendship. But by his late twenties, Thoreau was no longer the romantic boy, although he was still a singularly naive adult who, though sexually mature physically, was far from psychologically perceptive. My argument here has been that much of Thoreau's twisting obscurity was due to his inability to come to terms with the quite powerful feelings that were tormenting him; that he tended to associate the soft, wet, and messy with moralists, slaughtered animals, and women, and to experience revulsion when confronting them; and that although Thoreau's suppressed and confused sexual feelings sometimes discovered an outlet, more often they did not, whereupon they turned to animus; and finally that Thoreau's inability to reconcile these feelings in turn bore on his conception of the world, producing aggressiveness sometimes, sometimes melancholy.

So here the transformation of "generative energy" was elevated into a positive prescription. Continence will inspire us, or, in Thoreau's familiar paradox: "Chastity is the flowering of man" (219–220). The issue was urgent for him. Perfection required earnest effort, since "sensuality is a sluggish habit of mind. An unclean person is universally a slothful one" (220–221). Self-purification, then, demanded action. It may seem very odd to hear Thoreau say grimly, "Nature is hard to be overcome, but she must be overcome," but the issue was of paramount concern for him (221).

Why not marry rather than burn? The subject is a familiar one for Thoreau's critics.[22] He was fairly consistent in his dismissal of women. In the early 1850s he made no effort to conceal his contempt for them. Females "have but little brains" (*J*, III, 258). Even Thoreau's appreciation of the peculiar Mary Moody Emerson was expressed in terms of her essential masculinity. "In short, she is a genius, as woman seldom is, reminding you less often of her sex than any woman whom I know" (*J*, III, 114). Female society, specifically that of young women, he thought "the most unprofitable I have ever tried," "so light and flighty" were these creatures (*J*, III, 116). They were the true sensualists of the human species. Although people "commonly concede a somewhat finer and more sibyl-line nature" to women, in Thoreau's experience they were more subservient "to their animal instincts" than were men (*J*, II, 116).

Thoreau also thought that men degraded themselves by their irreverence toward sex. "I know a man who never speaks of the sexual relation but jestingly," he observed disapprovingly one day (*J*, IV, 185). The subject had galled him in 1852 as well. "We do not respect the mind that can jest on this subject," that being "the sexual relation" (*J*, III, 335). In comparison, Thoreau felt himself "unaccountably better than they" (*J*, II, 186). A Galahad trapped in a bawdy world—"I think that none of my acquaintances has a greater love and admiration for chastity than I have"—Thoreau appointed himself the champion of decency, even though his fitness for the role struck him as questionable, inasmuch as to himself he appeared "irrevocably impure." He did not know whether his impurity was caused "by constitution or by education" (*J*, II, 186).

In consequence, those extraordinary enclosures "Love" and "Chastity & Sensuality" that Thoreau dispatched to H. G. O. Blake in September 1852 were sent "with diffidence and shame," for Thoreau confessed he was not certain "how far I speak to the condition of men generally, or how far I betray my peculiar defects" (*Corr.*, 288). As in *Walden*, Thoreau argued that "the subject of copulation" should not be "so often avoided from shame" nor out of reverential feelings "winked out of sight, and hinted at only." But how should we manage it, then? Thoreau's response was that copulation should be "treated naturally and simply." Just as he would seem to have achieved a Whitmanesque candor, he reversed his direction; perhaps it should be "simply avoided, like the kindred mysteries" (*EE*, 274). Such seesawing helps to explain Thoreau's mixed response to *Leaves of Grass* in an 1856 letter, also to Blake: "There are 2 or 3 pieces in the book which are disagreeable to say the least, simply sensual. He does not celebrate love at all. It is as if the beasts spoke" (*Corr.*, 444). There was the man who sought to rise above the slime of the flesh. "As for its sensuality . . . I do not so much wish that those parts were not written, as that men & women were so pure that they could read them without harm, that is, without understanding them." And yet Thoreau was invigorated by Whitman's heartiness, which he was certain would appall Whitman's neighbors. "How they must shudder when they read him!" In this respect, because Whitman had overcome genteel niceties, Thoreau could appreciate him—"He is awefully good" (*Corr.*, 445).

Thoreau could think abstractly of marriage when it was removed from the tiresomeness of women and the grossness of the sexual connection. "To be married at least should be the one poetical act of a man's life." But most men failed in this respect. "The marriage which the mass of men comprehend is little better than the marriage of the beasts" (*J*, V, 369). For himself, he continued to imagine a state of elevation: "Love tends to purify and sublime itself. It mortifies and triumphs over the flesh, and the bond of its union is holiness" (*J*, VI, 75). It is difficult to read this as a reconciliation with realities. Unable to achieve a union, Thoreau conceived of exalted relationships at a distance, as with Lidian Emerson, or at a psychic distance, as with Ellery Channing and other men, all the time choosing to regard his celibacy as a sacred state of being. His accommodation was, by and large, attractive to him. "I must make my life more moral, more pure and innocent. The problem is as precise and simple as a mathematical one. I must not live loosely, but more and more continently" (*J*, V, 517).

Thoreau's anxious idealizing is what makes the anecdote of John Farmer with which he concludes "Higher Laws" so poignantly special for this man to whom denial was natural. Although some effort has been expended to identify this "John Farmer," he seems a clear embodiment of Thoreau's own preoccupations.[23] The story is a simple one. John Farmer put in a hard day's work, then bathed. He now sat at his door, trying to turn his mind away from his labors to intellectual matters. As he tried to compose his mind, which kept reverting to the day's work, he heard someone playing a flute. Its music, seemingly from a different sphere, assisted him in realizing that there was more important work to be done. But then a crucial interchange takes place. A voice asks Farmer, "Why do you stay here and live this mean moiling life, when a glorious existence is possible for you?" Farmer ponders how he might manage such a welcome change, but his imagination remains barren. "All that he could think of was to practice some new austerity, to let his mind descend into his body and redeem it, and treat himself with ever increasing respect" (222). The anecdote and the chapter end on this note of puzzled dissatisfaction.

It is not clear why the life that John Farmer leads is a "mean moiling" one, since, given his generic name and no other contradictory evidence, we assume that his work is farming and attendant matters. His occupation obviously presents some concern to his mind, which cannot readily detach itself from that concern. Aside from that, however, it is not obvious why farming is a life of drudgery, nor why the prescription for negative brooding is to "migrate thither," that is, to ascend into the realm of the flute.

Supposing, though, that there *is* a superior realm, where chastity flowers, where nature is overcome and spirit reigns, transmuting "the grossest sensuality into purity and devotion," how shall one gain access to it? (219). By meditation and prayer? By conscious effort to refine one's character? By willed engagement in activities associated with it? Thoreau's answer was gloomily revealing. It begins with an idiom that confesses insufficiency and the expectation of failure. That is, the idiom "all that he could think of" is customarily used where the possibilities are limited. The problem was that Thoreau had posed his dissatisfaction and had indicated his presumption that there was another realm of being, but then he needed a practical plan of action to achieve it. The only one to occur to Farmer/Thoreau was one distressing in its imaginative poverty: the practice of some new austerity. It did not seem to matter what austerity, for the feeling of the passage is that it would not succeed anyway. It just happened to be all that occurred to him. The mechanical bleakness and resignation of this solution is notable. Although frequently criticized for its reserved tone, Emerson's elegy for Thoreau captured this aspect of his character precisely. "Few lives contain so many renunciations," Emerson observed. "It cost him nothing to say No."[24]

If "Higher Laws" concluded that an aspiring man will give up the hunting and eating of flesh, the following chapter, "Brute Neighbors," considered the activities of some of the wild life in the vicinity of Walden Pond. The chapter shows virtually no awareness of what preceded it, and, being a patchwork of various journal entries ranging from 1845 to 1852, it lacks an imperative order. It opens in a mood of unusually good humor, with a little dialogue between the Hermit and the Poet. The Hermit is found in a meditative state, pondering why "men worry themselves so? He that does not eat need not work" (223). The Hermit seems to be living the life of philosophic austerity that John Farmer had posited as the necessary prelude to migration into a "glorious existence." But this interim state is broken by the rustling of leaves, which the Hermit first supposes might be "some ill-fed village hound," then a "lost pig" (223). These comically unflattering conjectures introduce the Poet, who has come to take the Hermit fishing. The Hermit, wishing to conclude his meditation, sends the Poet off to dig worms, then reverts to his thoughts. "I was," he remarks, "as near being resolved into the essence of things as ever I was in my life" (224). In fact, this had not been the case. The Hermit's soliloquy had opened on a note of distraction: "I wonder what the world is doing now" (223). He now finds that he cannot reenter the earlier state, but can only manage an impression of it: "It was a very hazy day" (224). In an effort to recapture the mood, the Hermit decides to "try these three sentences of Con-fut-see." But they prove ineffective. The Hermit does not even know if his previous meditations had been "the dumps or a budding ecstacy" (224, 225). Consequently, as the Poet returns with the worms, the Hermit makes the best of it by drawing a practical moral: "There never is but one opportunity of a kind" (225).

The playful balance of this opening was rare for Thoreau. It suggests that philosophizing and poetizing are important, perhaps, but that they must yield to companionable activities like fishing with a friend. Underneath the amiability are more serious revelations about philosophy. Its practice might constitute "a very hazy day," and out of it Thoreau cannot promise what might develop, "the dumps" or "ecstacy." He reminds himself, however, of the stern truth that "there is never but one opportunity of a kind," an observation that at one point in the writing of *Walden* was even more emphatic: "They never give us but one chance—though we may think there will be another. There never is but one opportunity of a kind" (HM924, IX, 36).

As for those three sentences of Confucius, they have never been identified. Thoreau had printed a set of "Sayings of Confucius" in *The Dial* of April 1843, but none of these seem obvious candidates for the three. On the other hand, if we consider the form of the chapter to follow, we can see that it falls pretty clearly into three parts: animals and birds carrying out their normal domestic activities, with the mother and her brood featured; then the ant-war follows this peaceful pageant; and the last portion of the chapter rings with the mocking laughter of the elusive loon. Nature domestic, nature bellicose, nature playful. By extension, they might be regarded as the main activities of the human animal as well, although the relationship is so understated that we are not encouraged to go much further with it. Still, thus far is sanctioned, for Thoreau begins the main body of the chapter with the phenomenological question: "Why do precisely these objects which we behold make a world?" (225). His answer is that animals are "all beasts of burden, in a sense, made to carry some portion of our thoughts" (225).

That provocative assertion was faithful to a transcendentalist interpretation of the world, and yet again Thoreau would not follow his observations through to their more general significance. For example, he reflected at length on the fact that partridge chicks have an instinct to stay still when in danger, while the mother hen seeks to divert the potential menace by pretending that she is crippled. The results of this strategy were not, however, always successful. A man might step on a chick because it has failed to run; or the mother might be shot, leaving the young immobile and helpless under a leaf; or the chicks, on being hatched, might instantly disperse in alarm and never respond to their mother's call. These are all Thoreau's examples, but although he outlined a variety of possible disasters, he did not specify what portion of his thoughts these chicks, ironically doomed by their very instincts of preservation, were meant to carry.

When he did turn to "events of a less peaceful nature," the

descriptions proved to be markedly grisly (228). The ant-war is frequently excerpted and, ugly as it is, presumably admired. Thoreau's facetious tone was thoroughly unfeeling in its account of the contesting ants. He dwelt with a distasteful zest on the slow mutilations of the combatants, this one gnawing on a foreleg, that one's breast "all torn away, exposing what vitals he had there to the jaws of the black warrior," which soldier finally managed to sever the heads from his antagonists' bodies (231). It is an odd episode, with reactions insufficiently pondered. What was the point of this extended and gruesome description? To show that ants share behavior with humans? To show that human endeavors were finally as inconsequential as those of ants? I doubt that Thoreau himself knew—and, by transferring the episode virtually without revision from his journal (III, 209–212), he showed that he was as unwilling to think through its significance as he was to weigh the meaning of the partridge chicks betrayed by their instincts for preservation.

Thoreau concluded his description by avowing that he had felt "for the rest of that day as if I had had my feelings excited and harrowed by witnessing the struggle, the ferocity and carnage, of a human battle before my door" (231). But harrowing is certainly not the impression that Thoreau's amused account gives. Rather, he was provided an entertaining, miniaturized spectacle to enliven his day. "I was myself excited somewhat even as if they had been men," he observed. "The more you think of it, the less the difference" (230). All the more troubling, then, is Thoreau's close, enthusiastic scrutiny of the mutilations. One group in particular he puts under a tumbler on the windowsill, then watches through a magnifying glass. When the battle is won by a disabled black ant, Thoreau raises the tumbler "and he went off over the window-sill in that crippled state" (231). Thoreau's musings are cold as ice and dominated by an economic measure. "Whether he finally survived that combat, and spent the remainder of his days in some Hotel des Invalides, I do not know; but I thought his industry would not be worth much thereafter" (231).

The chapter's ending centers on the derisive laughter of a loon, circling Thoreau's boat, then diving out of sight when Thoreau approached, then surfacing where least expected, again to mock Thoreau's efforts to reach him. Yet the impression given of the loon was not so much of playfulness as of a malevolent wildness. The words associated with the bird are "cunningly," "coolly," "unweariable," "unearthly," and its sounds are characterized as a "demoniac laughter" and "a long-drawn unearthly howl" (234–236). The loon certainly embodied an elusive aspect of the natural world; its capacity to tease and mock Thoreau in his efforts to join it were underlined. Thoreau could not accept human society, but the untamed natural world adamantly refused to accept *him*. Once, Thoreau tells us, the loon gave a long howl as if calling on the god of loons, whereupon a misty rain instantly filled the air. The incident impressed Thoreau. He felt "as if it were the prayer of the loon answered," and worse, as if "his god was angry with me" (236). This sense of otherness in respect to nature constituted an important frustration for Thoreau. It blocked access to a domain that he knew well but that remained mockingly alien to him. The young partridges? They were stepped on. The ants? They tore one another to pieces. The loon? It contemptuously called down the rain upon him. There was no brotherhood in Thoreau's brute neighbors.

"House-warming" and its adjacent chapters were for the most part composed late and exhibit a certain structural looseness. For example, Thoreau remarked that "only one or two of my guests were ever bold enough to stay and eat a hasty-pudding with me"; "but when they saw that crisis approaching they beat a hasty retreat rather, as if it would shake the house to its foundations" (245). It is clear that "they" refers to the majority of Thoreau's guests who chose *not* to eat his pudding, even though syntactically the antecedent of the two "theys" is "one or two of my guests." Although not a serious matter in itself, this exemplifies the periodic breakdown of Thoreau's prose. "House-warming" affords another example in "Light-winged Smoke, Icarian bird," one of Thoreau's most admired lyrics. F. O. Matthiessen contributed a particularly strained reading of the poem in *American Renaissance*, where, although determined to find excellence in the poem, even if obliged to praise "the succession of predominantly high-pitched vowels in the opening two lines," he was finally forced to concede that his interpretation fully "emerges only through the poem's context in *Walden*."[25] A poem with reassuringly classical features and apparently free from the crippling subjectivity of many of Thoreau's lyrics, it was likely to attract relieved attention despite its problems.

> Light-winged Smoke, Icarian bird,
> Melting thy pinions in thy upward flight,
> Lark without song, and messenger of dawn,
> Circling above the hamlets as thy nest;
> Or else, departing dream, and shadowy form
> Of midnight vision, gathering up thy skirts;
> By night star-veiling, and by day
> Darkening the light and blotting out the sun;
> Go thou my incense upward from this hearth,
> And ask the gods to pardon this clear flame. (252)

The comparison to Icarus is tenable only superficially: both the smoke and the wax of Icarus' wings first rise, then melt. But of course the Icarus story centers in the pride of undertaking an unnatural action and in the resulting fall—neither of which has anything to do with the smoke. Similarly, in the second quatrain, the notion of the smoke gathering up its skirts is apparently cued by the fact that smoke rises, even though the image is dubious at best. The next two lines tell us something about the fire-making habits of Concordians or of Thoreau himself, for the wood must have been either green or

wet for the smoke from a mere fireplace to veil the stars,
darken the light, and blot out the sun. Even though Thoreau
said that he preferred "hard green wood just cut" for his fire,
the volume of smoke would seem excessive (253). Moreover,
it clashes with the concluding prayer that this incense shall rise
and "ask the gods to pardon this clear flame." A "clear flame"
when its smoke is sufficient to obscure the sun?[26]

Truly, appreciation of this modest verse can only be
accounted for by supposing that it has seemed to critics to have
a certain dignity in comparison to those peculiar and oblique
sentiments that Thoreau too often set to jingling rhyme, such
as these lines that open his poem "The Hero":

> What doth he ask?
> Some worthy task.
> Never to run
> Till that be done,
> that never done
> Under the sun.
> (*Poems*, 161)

Or here is a complete poem, the quatrain "Expectation":

> No sound from my forge
> Has been heard in the gorge,
> But as a brittle cup
> I've held the hammer up.
> (*Poems*, 188)

Compared to such work, "Light-winged Smoke" offers an
accomplished and traditional surface that might well gain it
appreciation. Otherwise, it is difficult to discern any unusual
merit in it.

That Thoreau felt the need to seek forgiveness from the
gods is, however, perhaps significant. The chapter "House-
warming" has moments revealing Thoreau's feelings about the
insecure tenure men have on life. Writing of the cold and its

relief through the protection of a house and fire, Thoreau
observed how easily mankind "may at last be destroyed." Just a
little deeper snow or greater cold "would put a period to man's
existence on the globe" (254). Meanwhile, the natural world
nibbled away at his sustenance. There were weevils in his peas
and moles in his potato cellar, and his newly acquired cooking
stove now hid the companionable fire that formerly could
purify the laborer's thoughts "of the dross and earthiness
which they have accumulated during the day" (243, 253, 254).
Inconsequential as the chapter is, it has an elegiac note to it.
Something has been lost or is going, and to Thoreau the loss
seemed deserved.

The tone does not change appreciably in the succeeding
chapter, "Former Inhabitants; and Winter Visitors," one that
was also assembled late and awkwardly.[27] For example, the
account of Thoreau and the Connecticut philosopher (Bronson Alcott) whittling on pumpkinpine "during my last winter
at the pond" in fact came from a journal entry of May 9, 1853
(J, V, 130–131). The semicolon in the chapter title is virtually
all that holds its materials together. The dismal memorials in
the first half of the chapter to now dead inhabitants of the
woods might have been brought into accord with Thoreau's
celebration of a handful of superior guests, but they were not.
The chapter is split in two, its parts connected by a passage on
walking through the snow and another on watching a barred
owl.

Winter was especially attractive to Thoreau, so that he
exclaimed, "The Great Snow! How cheerful it is to hear of!"
(265). Part of the attraction of a particularly heavy snowfall
was that it left him isolated, "snug as a meadow mouse," and
even when he ventured forth there was no one else about—or
so he claimed. There were moments when Thoreau would
seem to have been describing a genuinely isolated cabin—
"when the snow lay deepest no wanderer ventured near my

house for a week or fortnight at a time" (264). Yet Horace
Hosmer, while arguing that Thoreau's cabin would not have
been a safe place for a "station" on the Underground Railroad,
writes: "For one hundred years, certain, Walden has been
visited at all seasons of the year by hunters, sportsmen, boys,
wood choppers, and land owners . . . and parties go every
winter to fish through the ice on the rivers and ponds and have
needed no guide to Walden." Hosmer's conclusion then was
unqualified: "Thoreau had no privacy."[28] The evidence of
activity at Walden Pond that Thoreau offers in the chapter
"The Pond in Winter" certainly corroborates Hosmer's con-
tention. But we know that the *idea* of being fenced off from
intrusion was powerfully seductive to Thoreau.

Still, the lives of those "former inhabitants" of the Walden woods whom Thoreau memorialized failed to provide
superior alternatives to civilization. The inhabitants' stories
and Thoreau's reflections on them prove to be persistently
bleak. Disaster and misery, drunkenness, destruction, and
graves predominate. What is our fate? Zilpha is heard to
mutter "over her gurgling pot,—'Ye are all bones, bones!' "
(257).[29] Cato Ingraham lost his walnut grove to a younger
white speculator, but it did not matter—he now inhabited a
"narrow house" in the ground. When fire consumed Zilpha's
house, her cat, dog, and chickens were destroyed along with it.
Brister Freeman? One knew indirectly of his existence
through his epitaph: "with staring emphasis" it revealed when
he died (258). Given this rather disconnected but consistently
moody series of reflections on the fate of local blacks, it is
perhaps understandable that Thoreau should say of Brister's
wife, Fenda, that she "told fortunes, yet pleasantly" (258). (In
the journal: "Fenda, his hospitable, pleasant wife, large, round
black, who told fortunes . . ." [*J*, I, 429]). A soothing presentation of the misery sure to come would be welcome.

Breed's Hut? It stood where "New-England Rum" played
its tricks, coming as it did "in the guise of a friend or hired
man" who then "robs and murders the whole family" (258).

Hosmer remembered that there were three large taverns in the center of Concord and that "all the stores sold liquor by the gallon or quart."[30] But after his initial temperance moralizing, Thoreau remarked that it was too early to "tell the tragedies enacted here; let time intervene in some measure to assuage and lend an azure tint to them" (258; *J*, I, 424). Why someone convinced of the inimical powers of alcohol should wish to suppress its tragedies is hard to understand, especially since Thoreau would shortly turn at length to the fate of the drunken Hugh Quoil. In any case, one night Breed's Hut was burned down by "mischievous boys," and the next night, on one of his nocturnal rambles, Thoreau came across Breed's son on his stomach, looking at the still-smouldering cellar and muttering to himself like some Faulknerian half-witted survivor (259–260). There is no reason for this long account of a relatively trivial occurence (Breed's house was about the size of Thoreau's), unless one posits some underlying preoccupation with misery not directly expressed by Thoreau. And it is clear enough that the Breed story centers on rum, fire, and eccentric survival, so that in those respects, although dispro-portionately extended in treatment, it does contribute to the general subject of afflicted humanity. Only Wyman the potter appears to have been a partial exception to this chronicle of disaster, and even he was an indigent squatter, regularly har-assed by the sheriff in search of back taxes.

Of Hugh Quoil, Thoreau wrote: "All I know of him is tragic" (262). Possibly, Quoil was an ex-soldier; his ostensible occupation around Concord was as a ditcher. But drink domi-nated his life. His face was "carmine," he suffered "terrible shaking fits," and he died in the road (262). Visiting his house before it was pulled down, Thoreau found old clothes, a broken pipe, soiled and scattered playing cards, a single black chicken "awaiting Reynard," and an untended garden "over-run with Roman wormwood and beggar-ticks" (262). The details are somber, although somewhat reduced in their transfer from the long journal entry (*J*, I, 414–418). There,

Thoreau directly reported Quoil's addiction to rum, and explained his title "Colonel Quoil" with the mordant observation, "I believe that he had killed a colonel and ridden off his horse." He said that Quoil's cheek was so bright, it would have burnt one's finger to touch it, but this, like the extraordinary details of that abandoned black chicken, was excised. In the journal, the chicken went "stepping silent over the floor, frightened by the sound of its own wings, black as night and as silent too, not even croaking; awaiting Reynard, its god actually dead." That powerful analogy to modern existence failed to survive translation into the book in full.

In his revisions, Thoreau tended not to rewrite much (despite some examples Shanley offers) but to change a word here and there, not necessarily for the better, and to eliminate phrases and sentences until his original version was weakened or beclouded. In the present instance, I would argue that Thoreau drew together these essentially inconsequential sketches of the outcasts of Concord because their cumulative fates, invariably miserable as they were, felt right to him, although in ways far from clear to him, and that when they were too powerful he muted them, even though the truth was there to be seen, could he only face it. One's god might be a drunken ditcher, now dead, so that one stepped silent and frightened through the inky rooms, awaiting the arrival of the fox.

Cellar dents, the graves of houses and of human aspirations, were all that remained "where once were the stir and bustle of human life" (263). Had these histories any meaning? Thoreau posited that all these people "in some form and dialect or other" had discussed philosophic questions, but that their conclusions came only to this: "Cato and Brister pulled wool." That, Thoreau observed, was "about as edifying as the history of more famous schools of philosophy" (263). The cynicism of that observation was altogether consistent with Thoreau's mood. Whatever the phrase "Cato and Brister pulled wool" is taken to mean, it must represent a homely task

of little consequence, but equivalent in value to any speculation ever done about the significance of human life. No wonder he remarked, "Alas! how little does the memory of these
human inhabitants enhance the beauty of the landscape!"
(264).

Against this gloomy account of former inhabitants of the
Walden woods, Thoreau then offered a set of positive, although somewhat abstract, figures, identified with reasonable
certainty as Alek Therien, Edmund Hosmer, Ellery Channing,
Bronson Alcott, and Emerson. Therien hardly existed there,
except in the signs of his visit—a pile of shavings and the
lingering odor of his pipe. Emerson was merely "one other"
with whom Thoreau remembered having had memorable
periods at his village house, and who "looked in upon me from
time to time" (270). The middle three, however, seem
emblematic. With Hosmer, the "long-headed farmer,"
Thoreau talked of "rude and simple times" (267). With his
poet he shared "boisterous mirth," and his philosopher, "the
sanest man," opened vistas of improvement to Thoreau (268,
269). The simple, cheerful sanity of these visitors seems intended to counteract the somberness of the first half of the
chapter, although the lack of specificity in their descriptions
finally makes them a good deal less real than the earlier
sketches of the doomed poor.

And "the Visitor who never comes," whom Thoreau said
he "sometimes expected," never came (270). If the Hindu
notion of remaining in readiness to exercise one's hospitality
was a humane one, it was also fruitless. On that idealistic
conception, shaded with negativity, the chapter ended.

"Winter Animals" is a brief and mildly interesting but
finally inconsequential essay. Although it features sketches of
squirrels and chickadees that diverted Thoreau, still much
destructiveness underlies it, extending even to the mice he
claimed girdled scores of pines during a particularly hard

winter, with the result that after another winter, "such were without exception dead" (280). The chapter offers foxes barking "raggedly and demoniacally" and crests in fox-hunting and skinning, supplemented by recollections of skinned bears, wildcats, and deer (273, 277–279). The whole ends by invoking the fecund presence of partridges and rabbits in the countryside. Their trails were everywhere beset with snares (281).

The chapter does contain indications of Thoreau's groping toward an accurate conception of his environment. He described the hooting of an owl as a "forlorn but melodious note" that struck him as "the very *lingua vernacula* of Walden Wood" (271–272). Given the destructive world Thoreau inhabited, where hounds pursued the fox even without human inducement, where "cow-boys" snared the unsuspecting rabbit, where even Walden Pond would whoop through the medium of its ice, as if it "were troubled with flatulency and bad dreams" (originally: "it was hypsy, and nervous and did not sleep well" [Shanley, 193–194]), the owl's hooting might well establish the minor key of nature's song (281, 272).

Even more impressive was "the most harsh and tremendous voice" of a cat-owl that Thoreau described as offering "thrilling discords" when set against the honking of a goose that was purposefully leading his formation south (272). Thoreau not only felt the force of this powerful owl-voice but avowed that, to a discriminating ear, it had "the elements of a concord such as these plains never saw nor heard" (272). It seems reasonably clear that here the "commodore" goose honking "with a regular beat" represented the world of organized affairs, which is challenged by the woods-dwelling owl (272).

In the next chapter, Thoreau pursued this contrast at a more generalized level. There, in trying to formulate some regularity in the relationships existing among the dimensions of the various ponds, he argued that man's problems are caused by an ignorance of all the necessary laws, *not* by "any confusion or irregularity in Nature" (290). Thoreau was hypothesizing a coherence in nature that should be present in himself as well. Often he could not see or feel it, but here, as with the owl's voice, he wrote: "Our notions of law and harmony are commonly confined to those instances which we detect; but the harmony which results from a far greater number of seemingly conflicting, but really concurring, laws, which we have not detected, is still more wonderful" (290). Thoreau wished to be able to rely on the assumption that this was an ordered world, although he knew that that order differed from the mechanical observation of schedules by his Concord neighbors. What he could not directly formulate was some version of Darwinian struggle, of such destruction, waste, and suffering as would encompass the partridge chicks, the chicken that survived Hugh Quoil, and, for that matter, Hugh Quoil himself. Thoreau could reflect that it was remarkable that a single mouse "should thus be allowed" to bring down a pine, but he could not free himself from the notion of an overseeing will that permitted all action in the world. Furthermore, he could not consciously or directly entertain the possibility that such a will was anything but benevolent. So, in the case of the pines brought down through girdling, "perhaps it is necessary in order to thin these trees, which are wont to grow up densely" (280). But even if Thoreau could not free himself from these assumptions of a positive order, he could feel otherwise. The "thrilling discord" of the owl he translated as: "Boo-hoo, boo-hoo, boo-hoo!" (272).

"The Pond in Winter" opens on Thoreau's admiration for a nature that exists, untormented by such problems as he unwillingly entertained. He had the impression on awakening that he had been trying "in vain" to answer some question put to him (282). But with the coming of morning, Thoreau perceived that nature was complete and serene unto herself, which inspired him to accept its fullness, at least for that day.

It was a *winter* day that proved unreservedly satisfying to

Thoreau from beginning to end. The chapter has an unusual, appreciative calm to it, for winter possessed a stability and purity that Thoreau very much esteemed. The squirming, oozing, rotting world of other seasons achieved a dignified firmness in winter. Thoreau inquired, "Why it is that a bucket of water soon becomes putrid, but frozen remains sweet forever?" then added with a deceptive casualness: "It is commonly said that this is the difference between the affections and the intellect" (297). It was a peculiar context in which to make that contrast, but consistent for the Thoreau who now gazed down into the "quiet parlor of the fishes" through the window he had cut in the ice to see "a perennial waveless serenity" reigning there, "corresponding to the cool and even temper of the inhabitants" (283). The model offered by the ice-water world was compelling to him.

In his journal, Thoreau elaborated on such seasonal distinctions. He noted that "the alert and energetic man leads a more intellectual life in winter than in summer. . . . In winter cold reason and not warm passion has her sway; he lives in thought and reflection; he lives a more spiritual, a less sensual, life" (*J*, III, 70). This was October 1851. By the following April, though, he was restless with the austerity of the long winter and his idealized commitment to the cool life. He had been severely buffeted emotionally during that winter, to the point that in April he observed parenthetically, "I hear the sound of the piano below as I write this, and feel as if the winter in me were at length beginning to thaw, for my spring has been ever more backward than nature's. For a month past life has been a thing incredible to me. None but the kind gods can make me sane. If only they will let their south winds blow on me! I ask to be melted" (*J*, III, 398; see also *J*, III, 259, 262, 270). Yet the melted state was even less acceptable to him. Thoreau's ruminations show us the pain he suffered from too permanent psychological withdrawal, and yet the other extreme, that of trembling, uncontrolled existence, was intolerable to him. So, in his public self, Thoreau always opted for control, for austerity, for winter. "How wholesome winter is seen far or near," he wrote H. G. O. Blake concerning Mt. Washington, "how good above all mere sentimental warm-blooded—short-lived, soft-hearted *moral* goodness, commonly so-called." Then he moved to a comfortable public formulation of a paradox of the sort that often vexed his friends. "Whatever beauty we behold, the more it is distant, serene, and cold, the purer & more durable it is. It is better to warm ourselves with ice than with fire" (*Corr.*, 598).

Thoreau's enthusiasm for the pickerel of Walden centers precisely on their jewel-like stillness in the freezing air. One of their attractions for him was that they died "easily, with a few convulsive quirks" (285). Their "rare beauty" surprised him "when I see them lying on the ice, or in the well which the fisherman cuts in the ice" (284). There, they displayed "a quite dazzling and transcendent beauty." Walden's ice also stimulated Thoreau's reverent appreciation, seeming when cut a "solidified azure" and, elsewhere, great blocks of emerald (294, 297).

As Horace Hosmer claimed, there was a lot of activity at the pond in winter, to which, strangely enough, Thoreau did not object. The fishermen he chose to designate as "wild men" in order to distinguish them from the artificial, bookish townsmen (283). Much more surprising was Thoreau's placid acceptance of the arrival during "the winter of '46–7" of "a hundred Irishmen, with Yankee overseers," come to cut and to market Walden's ice (294, 295). One might have expected him to object strenuously to the very interruption of his peaceful hermitage and, further, to resent the commercial rape of his beloved pond by, of all people, Irish laborers. But he accepted the activity with equanimity, even finding their work proceeding "in admirable order," and, when they had stacked the cakes of ice and covered them with hay and boards, Thoreau manifestly admired the resulting structure. It initially resembled "a vast blue fort or Valhalla," then later "a venerable moss-grown and hoary ruin" that lasted through the summer of 1848 (294, 296).

If Thoreau was not incensed by this activity, it was because it proved a welcome diversion, carried on by competent workers who also were "a merry race, full of jest and sport" (294). Further, the notion that Walden's water would go in the form of ice as far as India stimulated his imagination. The inhabitants of Calcutta drank his water as he drank of the *Bhagvat Geeta* (298). During winter, then, the pond afforded Thoreau the pleasures he most admired: to study Walden's contours; to appreciate the jewel-like pickerel and frosted ice-castle; and to reflect on those activities, such as Walden's ice being carried round the world, that were amenable to attractive philosophic extension. Spring, although it might also have been expected to yield useful analogies, proved rather more troublesome because it aroused hidden resistances in him.

As a season, spring produced an odd mixture of the conventional and the equivocal in Thoreau. On April 4, 1853, for example, he went forth on a long and generally affirmative walk in the awakening outdoors. Then: "Saw a sucker washed to the shore at Lee's Bridge, its tail gone, large fins standing out, purplish on top of head and snout. Reminds me of spring, spearing, and gulls" (*J*, V, 91). In short, in spring the killing recommenced.

The melting of the ice was Thoreau's initial preoccupation in "Spring." This action he conceived as both an opening, a breaking up, and a dissolving, a rotting. The pond yawned and stretched after its long nap, then boomed and thundered. The action of thawing was subtle, subversive even, as when the ice was honeycombed with air-bubbles, but also it was violent, cracking "with a startling whoop as loud as artillery" (303). It was a tumultuous birth, as when "the alligator comes out of the mud with quakings of the earth"; yet the ice grating against the shore seemed resentful and dangerous, and it made "a sullen rush and roar" "as if it would have a universal and memorable ending" (303, 304). Thoreau's accumulation of imagery around spring as a phenomenon both welcomed and resisted suggests some of the tension he felt at the onset of this generative season.

It was during the troubled dark year of 1851–1852 that Thoreau had a long dream that began with him out riding, but then "the horses bit each other and occasioned endless trouble and anxiety, and it was my employment to hold their heads apart" (*J*, III, 80). This need to control intractably opposed forces in his life was a persistent strain for Thoreau, in October as in March. As the dream ended he had managed to conceive of himself as a musical instrument through which a melodious note had been sounded (although that note was now dying out). Still, the sensation of having once been "the thoroughfare of glorious and world-stirring inspirations" made him infinitely regret his awakening. He now found himself no longer a musical instrument; rather, "a scuttle full of dirt" (*J*, III, 81–82).

One must approach spring's regeneration, and specifically the famously thawing sand bank of *Walden*, with the memory of Thoreau's feeling of having been that scuttle of dirt, for it constituted a central and deeply troubling portion of his humanness. A string of interconnected images surrounded it in his mind: slime, hypocritical sentimentality, womannishness, filth. At the same time, creative warmth, blood, the womb, and sex were all confusedly mingled with the images of revulsion. For example, in November 1851 Thoreau attributed "a certain softness" he detected in himself to having been obliged to remain indoors for several days. This "loosened" (not "opened") "the gates . . . to some emotions." For the moment he had become sufficiently vulnerable to find that he "cried while reading a pathetic story." But when he had recovered his spirits, that display of sentiment made him laugh, for "what is my softness good for?" He then dismissed the whole episode. That "expression of my sympathy" he now characterized as "something mean," "merely a phenomenon of the bowels," which, were it discovered, would shame him (*J*, III, 106).

Thoreau then attempted in his journal to locate just the right moment when spring became acceptable to him. It was somewhere between frozen rigidity and ooze. "The poet's creative moment is when frost is coming out in the spring . . ." but "if the weather is too warm and rainy or long continued, it becomes mere diarrhoea, mud and clay relaxed" (*J*, III, 165). Already the metaphor was getting out of hand, but for the moment Thoreau persevered, feeling he had something imperative to say: "The poet must not have something pass his bowels merely; that is women's poetry. He must have something pass his brain and heart and bowels too, it may be, all together. So he gets delivered" (*J*, III, 165). The figures of speech having become totally confused by this time, Thoreau ultimately excised this material in his final version of *Walden*. But one can see his wish somehow to locate an organic principle of true creativity in this spontaneous, earthy flow without, however, allying himself with slop.

The worst associations Thoreau ever had of bowels were generated by several "ultra-reformers" who came to stay briefly at the Thoreaus in June 1853. Two were ministers of sorts, a profession about which Thoreau was strongly dubious, as when, arriving in Montreal in 1850 for the first time and observing many priests in the street, he had remarked that "like clergymen generally, with or without the gown, they made on us the impression of effeminacy" (*Yankee*, 15). Thoreau's loathing of the clergymen boarders was intense, expressed in terms of grease, slime, and sweat. One of them obviously was much too familiar—"addressed me as 'Henry' within one minute." This clergyman spoke with a "drawling, sultry sympathy" and, having written a book called *A Kiss for a Blow*, "was bent on giving me the kiss." Such men, Thoreau wrote, "lay their sweaty hand on your shoulder, or your knee, to magnetize you." They "rubbed you continually with the greasy cheeks of their kindness. They would not keep their distance, but cuddle up and lie spoon-fashion with you, no matter how hot the weather nor how narrow the bed." Although it is not clear whether the Thoreau boarding-house was sufficiently crowded to make this a literal complaint, Thoreau's revulsion at intimacy is manifest. He conceived of the whole experience as involving varieties of seductive gestures: touching, kissing, lying spoon-fashion, licking.

The central figure of Thoreau's disgust, though, is the bowels. His images are again somewhat chaotic. His initial notion of how the reformers menaced him seemed to derive from some action like that of a starfish, extruding its stomach to swallow its prey. "It was difficult to keep clear of his slimy benignity, with which he sought to cover you before he swallowed you and took you fairly into his bowels." And finally, "I do not like the men who come so near me with their bowels. . . Men's bowels are far more slimy than their brains" (*J*, V, 263–265). Now, Thoreau's attitude toward the physical reality of bowels as well as toward the encroachment of the overly attentive is certainly a common one, although it was here raised to a higher level of revulsion than one normally encounters.[31] That being the case, Thoreau had a troubling set of images to deal with when he turned to the thawing sand bank of the Deep Cut.

The Deep Cut itself was the nexus of equally complicated but related images. Ellery Channing reported that in his last days Thoreau had a dream "of being a railroad cut, where they were digging through and laying down the rails,—the place being in his lungs" (*Thoreau*, 322). But that was far from his usual response to the cut. Originally created by the Fitchburg Railroad project, on the whole it garnered positive responses from him. The railroad workers themselves interested him, the daily passage of the train diverted him, and the railroad causeway itself afforded him a handy path for walking to and fro from the village (115). Most of all, the changing features of the Deep Cut regularly attracted Thoreau's attention. As when the ice was stripped from Walden's surface, one might have expected Thoreau to fulminate against this violation of nature, but not at all. The Cut enchanted him, and no more so than when it flowed. That occurrence was far from a phenomenon uniquely associated with spring. For example, "the Deep Cut is sometimes excited to productiveness by a rain in midsummer" (*J*, II, 70). And on December 31, 1851, Thoreau noted that he was "too late, perhaps, to see the sand foliage in the Deep Cut. . . . it is now too wet and soft" (*J*, III, 164). Some of his observations from that December day were ultimately included in the "Spring" chapter.

Although Thoreau had several long descriptive and reflective passages on the Deep Cut to work from in his journal, translating them coherently into the text was not easy for him. Of the sand bank descriptions, Philip Van Doren Stern points out that "Thoreau had a great deal of trouble with the phrasing, for this is one of the most heavily revised sections in the entire manuscript" (423, fn. 10). Some of the revealing emotional and imagistic force of the original journal entries was suppressed. For example, the redness of the flow disappeared. January 28, 1852: "I have come to see the clay and sand in the Cut. A reddish tinge in the earth, stains. An Indian hue is singularly agreeable, even exciting, to the eye. Here the whole bank is sliding. Even the color of the subsoil excites me, as if I were already getting near to life and vegetation. This clay is faecal in its color also" (*J*, III, 248). Then, March 9, 1852: "The sand is flowing in Deep Cut. I am affected by the sight of the moist red sand or subsoil under the edge of the sandy bank" (*J*, II, 342).

These ambiguous expressions of excitement edge towards sexuality, yet are susceptible to yielding both to associations of the passing of excrement and to fantasies of wounding. As an example of the latter, in *A Yankee in Canada*, Thoreau took note of "the woodbine . . . for the most part on dead trees, draping them like a red scarf. It was a little exciting, suggesting bloodshed, or at least a military life, like an epaulet or sash, as if it were dyed with the blood of the trees whose wounds it was inadequate to stanch" (*W*, V, 3). A year and a half later, he exclaimed, "I love that the rocks should appear to have some spots of blood on them, Indian blood at least; to be convinced that the earth has been crowded with men, living, enjoying, suffering, that races passed away have stained the rocks with their blood." These were not likely to be common reactions to rocks that only appeared to be bloodstained, but Thoreau was quite emphatic about the odd sense of community they gave him: "I am the more at home. I farm the dust of my ancestors" (*J*, III, 334).

The final, synthesized description of the sand bank in *Walden* begins by expressing the "delight" that the thawing sand and clay gave Thoreau. It is hard, however, to locate the explicit source of that delight. The reddishness virtually disappears, the brownishness dominates. Further, the descriptive comparisons that Thoreau utilized between his fanciful linguistic and organic speculations are far from attractive. The cut suffered a "sandy rupture," it was "the slag of a furnace," it was "like lava," it was "brains or lungs or bowels, and excrements of all kinds" (306, 308, 305, 305). That is, Thoreau's central impression of this flowing mass was that it had burst forth like a rupture, or was the expelled excrement of earth—"I know of nothing more purgative of winter fumes and indigestions"—or was a revelation of the earth inside: "The whole cut impressed me as if it were a cave with its stalactites laid open to the light." That was the sectioning metaphor. Then there was the unnatural reversal: "there is no end to the heaps of liver lights and bowels, as if the globe were turned wrong side outward" (308, 305, 308).

All of these versions of the mechanics by which the clay and sand emerged are, I would submit, reasonably unattractive. The earth has burst or been cut open or been turned inside out. And what it revealed was "somewhat excrementitious in character" (308).

Still, critics have been willing to countenance Thoreau's intense preoccupation with the sand bank as if it did represent the positive aspects of spring. But from the images thus far discussed, one feels that something violent had been done to nature, as in fact it had, by the crews who first cleared the Deep Cut to accommodate the Fitchburg tracks. As for Thoreau's association of the sand flow with the growth of vegetation and of man, here one must deal with truly grotesque speculations. "What is man but a mass of thawing clay? The ball of the human finger is but a drop congealed. The fingers and toes flow to their extent from the thawing mass of the body" (307). The metaphor here is neither that of the superior hand shaping the clay nor of organic growth, but rather of a gravity-dominated diffusion: "The nose is a manifest congealed drop or stalactite. The chin is a still larger drop, the confluent dripping of the face" (308). Thoreau was driven by his obsession into these and other dubious imaginative exercises: "The radicals of lobe are *lb*, the soft mass of the *b* (single lobed, or B, doubled lobed,) with a liquid *l* behind it pressing it forward" (306).[32] And when he sought to establish all this movement as being more positively organic, as representing, for example, the formation of blood vessels, he betrayed his own observations. In *Walden*: "You here see perchance how blood vessels are formed" (307). But in the journal: "I have not observed any cylindrical canals this year. Did I ever?" (*J*, III, 344).

Thoreau's situation drove him from one contradiction to another. In many ways he enjoyed the icy firmness of winter and was comfortable in his habitual modes of self-expression. Nonetheless, such bleakness eventually told on him, so that the released energies of spring were welcome—except that he was most powerfully impressed by one whose flowing forth had certain connotations that he emphasized. The reddish stain, the exciting moist redness—the female associations—largely gave way to the excremental. Still, Thoreau was able finally to posit a higher and finer extension for this activity. Initially caught in the mechanics of his own associations, he felt obliged to emphasize the congealed drops of the nose and chin. But by thinking of the relationship of leaves to feathers, Thoreau could escape with a "Thus, also, you pass from the lumpish grub in the earth to the airy and fluttering butterfly. The very globe continually transcends and translates itself" (306). Were it only true! The image of man as thawing clay was too distinctive to permit overt optimism. The best even Thoreau could manage was the question: "Who knows what the human body would expand and flow out to under a more genial heaven?" (307). But was this heaven not sufficiently genial? What after all caused the flowing but a thaw? What caused the thaw but heat? Why then was a May day not a more genial heaven than one in February? And were one to follow this line of deliberation far enough, what of the paradox that more heat dries and again, like freezing, halts motion?

We may be impressed by Thoreau's long involvement with the sand bank in the Deep Cut, and we can certainly locate throughout his life a desire to be diffused and spiritualized, but what we cannot discover in these pages is a triumphantly imaginative reconstitution of the world, comparable to spring. Although Thoreau tried to see this flowing pulpy mass as positive, he rendered its excremental features. Even in his most all-encompassing vision in this section, that of the world as a plant—"rivers are still vaster leaves whose pulp is intervening earth"—he still could not keep his deepest feelings from expression. That vision concludes: "and towns and cities are the ova of insects in their axils" (307). Never mind "axils." It is but the botanical term for the upper angle between a branch and a stem. Consider rather those insect eggs.

In Thoreau's imagery, man fulfilled his destiny by flowing out of his human form into an unimaginable liquefaction or perhaps, ultimately, vaporization. His imagery of the sand bank was not of birth, not even of birth amidst or out of bowels. Rather, it was as if mother earth had ruptured herself violently in her labor, so that the abdominal walls were breached and filth poured out. And that sequence was redeemable only through an imaginative transfer of attention to leaves and thence to inauthentic fantasies of transcendental refinement.

Further verification of this description is available in the balance of the chapter. Following the long sand bank meditations, Thoreau's first apostrophe is on winter weeds. In their durable refinement, the weeds strike him as having a "stately beauty." They are "graceful" and like "many of the phenomena of Winter are suggestive of an inexpressible tenderness and fragile delicacy" (309, 310). By contrast, spring was gross, messy, and unbalanced. Thoreau recalled that "at the approach of spring the red-squirrels got under my house, two at a time." There they made the "queerest" sounds Thoreau had ever heard—"chuckling," "chirruping," "vocal pirouetting and gurgling"—and they could not be stopped, "as if past all fear and respect in their mad pranks." Nonetheless, in order to interrupt what would seem to have been unmistakable reproductive activities, Thoreau persisted in stamping his feet, until at last the squirrels "fell into a strain of invective that was irresistible" (310).

Thoreau's most enthusiastic commitment to springtime was in response to the brooks filling, the grass flowing up the hillsides "like a spring fire," and above all the birds, all flying "with song and glancing plumage," symbols of elevation and freedom (310, 313). Through them he could celebrate the blessedness of spring, its capacity to forgive all men's sins. Yet none can miss Thoreau's evocation of a hawk, "very slight and graceful," sporting "with proud reliance in the fields of air" (316). Genuinely affected by the sand bank, Thoreau had tried to transform it into a sacrament of earth; but in vain, for as both titles of his published books attest, he was a man of water and of air. Hence his hawk, unlike the lascivious red squirrels under his floorboards, "appeared to have no companion in the universe,—sporting there alone,—and to need none" (206/317). If any relationship existed between the independence of the air and the grossness of the earth, it was one of aggression, for as spring moved past the sand bank, Thoreau described another hawk, "sailing low over the meadow . . . already seeking the first slimy life that awakes" (310).

In "Spring," Thoreau built to that celebration of destruction with which the book began. There is no doubt about the genuineness of Thoreau's attraction to wild, nonhuman nature, even if the experience of Mt. Katahdin qualified his excited assertion that "we can never have enough of Nature. We must be refreshed by the sight of inexhaustible vigor, vast and Titanic features" (318). Thoreau's preferred wilderness was the local one, "in marshes where the bittern and the meadow-hen lurk" (317). He knew wilderness took other forms and was mildly curious to explore them—sufficiently, at least, to go to the Maine woods, Cape Cod, and Minnesota. (It was Emerson, however, who visited Yosemite.) And he boldly and imaginatively spoke for the desirability of having our limits transgressed. He warmed to the task by lauding the stench of a dead horse, then gave a full-scale demonstration of violating limits by asserting that he loved to see nature so abounding with life that (like the bison and the passenger pigeon) "myriads can be afforded to be sacrificed and suffered to prey on one another." Whereupon, and with zest, Thoreau squashed, ran over, and gobbled up his various "tender organizations" (318). Why were living things created? For destruction—originally "like soft pulp," but then, in revision, "pulp" alone seemed sufficient (208/318). Spring? "Sometimes it has rained flesh and blood!" (318).

Thoreau's imagination was always well-stocked with violent imagery, often aggressive and punishing in nature. Thinking of the lack of depth among his fellow citizens, Thoreau envisaged fishing "for the pond itself" by "impaling the legislature for a bait" (213). Or, on August 8, 1854, the day before *Walden* was officially published, Thoreau found himself maddened by the noise of various people, among them an Irishman who "erects his sty, and gets drunk, and jabbers more and more under my eaves, and I am responsible for all that filth and folly." But he explained to H. G. O. Blake how he had silenced that "shallow din." He paddled up river into stillness where "the falling dews seemed to strain and purify the air." Then, as one sympathetically shares his relief, there comes an imaginative figure, typical for him, that is more difficult to sympathize with: "I got the world, as it were, by the nape of the neck, and held it under in the tide of its own events, till it was drowned, and then I let it go down stream like a dead dog" (*Corr.*, 330, 331).

Walden's "Conclusion" is one of those transcendental essays composed of numerous bits and pieces, arbitrarily fastened together. It neither coheres intrinsically nor does it emerge naturally from the book it purports to finish. It is surprising, perhaps, to discover that this culminating chapter in a book generally regarded as inspiriting should be marked throughout with morbid imagery such as "diseases of the skin," "a maggot in their heads," "brain-rot," and "the seven-years' itch" (320, 321, 325, 332). It is not just that these are Thoreau's scornful descriptions of what afflicts men. His images of self are troublesome too, and raise doubts as to the outcome of any optimistic venture. "Is not our own interior white [that is, as yet unexplored] on the chart? black though it may prove, like the coast, when dis-covered" (321). It is true that Thoreau tried to inspire his reader and himself with a courageous acceptance of reality. "However mean your life is, meet it and live it," he coun-seled, "do not shun it and call it hard names. It is not so bad as you are" (328). Thoreau ever maintained the suspicion that the essential self was unfathomably corrupt. One can hear his concessive candor when he says, "Any truth is better than make-believe" (a statement that is immediately followed by a wry anecdote concerning the last words of a tinker on the gallows) (327). The accumulating sense is that things all around are quite awful, although better to know it than to be deluded. "There is a solid bottom every where," but we may sink to our death in the swamp before we reach it (330). A whole series of phrases appear in the "Conclusion," each employed in the service of affirmation, yet each affording a gloomy representation of actuality. "I live in the angle of a leaden wall" (329). "If I were confined to a corner of a garret all my days, like a spider . . " (328). "I do not wish to go below now" (323). "A living dog is better than a dead lion" (325–326). "Love your life, poor as it is" (328).

The last pages of the book pass from a seventeen-year locust to an insect on the forest floor to a bug in an apple-tree table. The central image of "the insect crawling amid the pine needles on the forest floor, and endeavoring to conceal itself from my sight," was brought forth to illustrate how little we know, how superficial is our knowledge (332). Thoreau stood over this insect of unspecified identity and had god-like thoughts. I ask myself, Thoreau said, why the insect "will cherish those humble thoughts, and hide its head from me who might perhaps be its benefactor, and impart to its race some cheering information" (332). But when did a human being ever come to an insect as a benefactor? Thoreau was really not interested in anthropomorphizing the insect; rather, he wished to insectize man. So, he said that by this encounter "I am reminded of the greater Benefactor and Intelligence that stands over me the human insect" (332). The capitalized abstractions are clue enough that Thoreau's conception is dubious (for irony does not seem to be at work here). The equation that man is to insect as God is to man is a characteristically unsatisfactory one, from which it is particularly difficult to wring affirmation.

Suffering the contradictions of his nature and frustrated

by the disparity between what he sensed and what he could express verbally, Thoreau paused in his conclusion to deliver himself of his feelings. In so doing, he provided us a reason for examining his parables and images carefully. We may believe him when he writes, "I desire to speak somewhere *without* bounds" (324). But despite this much admired apostrophe to *"extra vagance,"* Thoreau could not cross many bounds, for the psychological ones were as forbidding as the verbal ones. This study is focusing on the numerous points at which Thoreau did strain against his limits, in order to see what those limits were, to understand how they sometimes distorted what he wished to say, and to honor his probing intelligence seeking deliverance from the solitary confinement that his independent aloofness had too often proved to be. His extravagance manifested itself in exaggeration and overstatement, in various surly dismissals of his fellow villagers, and in occasional misty evocations of some higher plane of existence. But I do not believe that Thoreau ever managed to write anything of liberating excess.

Thoreau's scorn for those who asked "that you shall speak so that they can understand you" was excessive, though. He characterized their demand as "ridiculous." But although there was an attractive force to his protest that one should not assume there is "but one order of understandings," in general it cannot be said that Thoreau offered another order that he comprehended. "We should live quite laxly and undefined in front, our outlines dim and misty," he argued. "The volatile truth of our words should continually betray the inadequacy of the residual statement" (324, 325). Thoreau's was a position well worth taking as a counter to materialistic positivism. But he was speaking neither for a polysemous truth nor for a truth beyond any conceived at that point. He thought he was advocating independence, whereas in fact he was contesting his own demons. "In proportion as he simplifies his life, the laws of the universe will appear less complex," he asserted, but his writings showed this was not true (324). Thoreau preferred to believe it, but the bewildering assault of the components of his world, with their testimony belying anything he then believed (such as the existence of a great Benefactor and Intelligence), mocked his certainties. Truly, "the universe is wider than our views of it" (320).

This will suggest why so many of Thoreau's analogies in the "Conclusion" twist toward negativity. One or two such moments could be credited to inadvertence, but when repeated they must be assigned to some motivation. For example, Thoreau said that men hunt in order to distract themselves. They hunt such things as snipe and woodcock and will even travel to Africa to hunt giraffe. But to him these were trivial prey: "I trust it would be nobler game to shoot one's self" (320). This startling proposition was immediately followed by the Habington quatrain, which assured us that Thoreau was being allegorical, that trips afield were really self-exploration, "home-cosmography" (320). But instantly Thoreau turned our attention to the map and the possibility that the present white blankness of our interiors might ultimately prove—black.

Thoreau's pessimism could expand to apocalyptic dimensions in his unaired imagination. No one has ever endeavored to explain the meaning of Thoreau's image of starting "on that farthest western way" that "leads on direct a tangent to this sphere." He had earlier dismissed other exploratory efforts as "only great-circle sailing," by which he apparently meant superficial and predictable (322, 320). His tangential voyaging, though, would be "summer and winter, day and night, sun down, moon down, and at last earth down too" (322). Whatever those verbal extensions may have been intended to mean, they cumulatively make, I think, a negative effect. Winter follows summer, night follows day and the sun, the brightest source of illumination goes down, followed by the other major source of light in the sky, the moon, until the overall impression made is one of doom, from warm season to cold, from light to darkness, with the light twice more extinguished until "at last earth down too" (322). This imagery could be interpreted as Thoreau's describing how an effort of sufficient determination will lead one beyond mundane cycles, but such an intepretation would ignore the cumulative effect of down, down, down. . . . The passage does not seem to have an explicit meaning, or, if it was intended to, the phrasing has obscured it. But it does create a feeling of impending annihilation, of traveling into a nothingness for which a pile of empty tins could well serve as a sign.

Only by selective reading, then, can the last pages of the "Conclusion" be interpreted as a springlike affirmation. For example, consider the locust. Thoreau began, "These may be but the spring months in the life of the race." The implication of this is that the best may be to come. But the next sentence reads: "If we have had the seven-years' itch, we have not seen the seventeen-year locust yet in Concord" (331–332). Insofar as the parallelism of the two sentences obtains, the itch would be comparable to the spring, the locust to the summer possibly to come; or, the mild irritation may yet be succeeded by a full-scale infestation. But perhaps Thoreau meant to refer only to the rare and marvelous appearance of the *Magicicada septendecim* after its years underground in its larval stage, for he also asked, "Who knows what sort of seventeen-year locust will next come out of the ground?" (332). If the rareness was intended, the connotations attached to the locust are at best equivocal. For Thoreau, on the evidence of a letter to his mother in 1843 from Staten Island, those connotations were negative: "Pray have you the Seventeen year locust in Concord? The air here is filled with their din. They come out of the ground at first in an imperfect state, and crawling up the shrubs and plants, the perfect insect burst[s] out through the bark. They are doing great damage to the fruit and forest trees" (*Corr.*, 121).

Thoreau repeatedly insisted on conceiving human possibilities in terms of insects, though—the locust, the human insect crawling at the feet of the greater Benefactor and Intelligence, and, finally, his most famous carrier of hope, "a strong and beautiful bug." The facts provided by Thoreau are that an egg had been "deposited in the living tree"; that after some time the tree was cut down and made into a table "which had stood in a farmer's kitchen for sixty years"; and that at last the bug began to gnaw its way out, "hatched perchance by the heat of an urn." At this point, Thoreau interjected, "Who does not feel his faith in a resurrection and immortality strengthened by hearing of this?" (333).

Some might not, for this is an unsatisfactory parable of regeneration. The terms have nothing to do with resurrection. No body was buried in the wood; an egg was. The tree served as receptacle and nourisher, like a womb. At best, the bug's history is a model of prolonged gestation. It was no more a miracle of resurrection that the insect emerged than it is for a foetus to quicken and eventually to emerge. Nor was this in any way a demonstration of "immortality." Thoreau spoke of the insect's emerging "to enjoy its perfect summer life at last," but that life had a distinct terminus to it, and perhaps not a normal one either. In the letter to his mother about the locusts, Thoreau ended the subject by noting: "Dogs, cats and chickens subsist mainly upon them in some places" (*Corr.*, 121).

When the same story was used by Melville in "The Apple-Tree Table: or Original Spiritual Manifestations," he took a decidedly mocking attitude toward the superstitious fearfulness that even educated people displayed in the face of the prolonged ticking that preceded the bug's emergence. The narrator's daughter Julia, being possessed "of a very nervous temperament," is the one who, after hearing a straightforward scientific explanation of the phenomenon, persists in advancing the Thoreauvian interpretation: "Say what you will, if this beauteous creature be not a spirit, it yet teaches a spiritual lesson. For if, after one hundred and fifty years' entombment, a mere insect comes forth at last into light, itself an effulgence, shall there be no glorified resurrection for the spirit of man?" Melville's narrator cools this enthusiasm with a dash of reality: "The mysterious insect did not long enjoy its radiant life; it expired the next day."[33]

In Thoreau's case, although he did not share Melville's skepticism, there is reason to suppose that his very uncertainty about the true constitution of a world that repeatedly betrayed his romantic assumptions contributed to his embodiment of spring hope in various insects, even as in spilling bowels. At times he turned away with loathing from the spectacle before him. "I do not think much of the actual," he confided to his journal in 1850. "It is something which we have long since done with. It is a sort of vomit in which the unclean love to wallow" (*J*, II, 44).

Given the uncertainties of the "Conclusion," it is not surprising that Sherman Paul should end his lengthy discussion of *Walden* by quoting in full the parable of the artist of Kouroo, nor that Charles Anderson, after analyzing the same parable, should comment: "One might prefer that *Walden* should end here."[34] Indeed, F. B. Sanborn's dubiousness about *Walden*'s ending was such that he proposed an alternative conclusion, drawn from the unpublished pages of Thoreau's manuscript. The lines accord much more closely with the actuality of the book as a whole:

We know not yet what we have done,—still less what we are doing. Wait till evening, and other parts of our day's work will shine than we had thought at noon; and we shall discover the real purport of our toil. As when the husbandman has reached the end of the furrow, and looks back, he can best tell where the pressed earth shines most.[35]

The organic necessities of adhering to a seasonal structure forced Thoreau to draw such regenerative conclusions at the end of *Walden* as he could not fundamentally believe. Insofar as Thoreau did react to spring, it was in a far more complicated and eccentric way than any conventional message of rebirth could convey. Sanborn's selection acknowledges the perplexities of our experience and makes a much more modest prophecy than that which controls the ending of *Walden* in print.

As everyone knows, Thoreau "left the woods for as good a reason as I went there. Perhaps it seemed to me that I had several more lives to live, and could not spare any more time for that one" (323). On January 22, 1852, though, Thoreau reflected on his decision and could not perceive that good reason: "But why I changed? why I left the woods? I do not think that I can tell. I have often wished myself back. I do not know any better how I ever came to go there" (*J*, III, 214). After another page of meditation on the matter, he reverted to his puzzlement: "I must say that I do not know what made me leave the pond. I left it as unaccountably as I went to it. To speak sincerely, I went there because I had got ready to go; I left it for the same reason" (*J*, III, 216). How forcefully direct Thoreau could be when not on the defensive. No mechanical puns nor tortured syntax mar the straightforwardness of that statement. The mystery of his coming to and going from Walden Pond is conveyed there with a rueful clarity.

At a sufficient distance, we can see that the Walden experiment was a simulated retreat, bounded at one end by severe local antagonisms exacerbated by Thoreau's careless burning of the Concord woods, and at the other by an invitation to head the Emerson household while its master was lecturing abroad. Long anticipated, the experience was then long sifted, expanded, and reshaped, until, when the book at last appeared, the man who had gone to the pond at twenty-eight and left it at thirty was now thirty-seven. By then Thoreau had traveled to the Maine woods, to Cape Cod, to

Fire Island, and to Canada. The parochial, hypersensitive, and immature young man had broadened his experience somewhat and, further, had managed to endure the abrasions of his peculiar and lonely life. But long gestation is no guarantor of favorable issue. The changes of a decade mark *Walden*. For all its assurances of speaking universal truths, it is a book of personal and even eccentric vision, in which Thoreau neither tried to reconcile his clashing views nor managed to rise sufficiently above them to acknowledge their clamorous contest.

The Voracious Beach:
Cape Cod

> Here is this vast, savage, howling mother of
> ours, Nature, lying all around, with such beauty,
> and such affection for her children, as the
> leopard . . . .
>
> "Walking"

IN COMPARING the first draft of *Walden,* written between ap-
proximately March 1846 and September 1847, with the final
printed version, one discovers that in general the revisions
move in the direction of pessimistic irritability. Thoreau had
several psychic disturbances to deal with in those years, especially after he had to yield the Emerson household to Waldo
toward the end of July 1848. We cannot determine this in
detail, since the journals for 1848, 1849, and part of 1850 are
apparently no longer extant, save for disparate sheets later
used in various of Thoreau's public writings.[1]

The period in Emerson's house had been a productive
one. Thoreau had enlarged the *Week*—"My book is swelling
again under my hands"—and after some frustrating negotia-

158

tions he was again actively engaged in seeking its publication (*Corr.*, 225). Referring in a letter to Emerson to his son Edward, Thoreau remarked exuberantly, "He is a good companion for me—& I am glad that we are all natives of Concord—It is *Young Concord*—Look out—World" (*Corr.*, 199–200). Thoreau had settled into the household comfortably and confidently. He told H. G. O. Blake, "I am at present living with Mrs. Emerson, whose house is an old home of mine, for company during Mr. Emerson's absence" (*Corr.*, 222). It is an odd way of putting the situation and suggests that Thoreau felt himself a surrogate husband. Wherever one looks, there was a covert competition with Emerson, probably barely recognized by Thoreau himself, as when, writing James Munroe and Co. about the manuscript of the *Week*, he mentioned parenthetically, "The book is about the size of one vol of Emerson's essays" (*Corr.*, 185).

After laborious efforts, Thoreau finally saw the *Week* in print. It was the same month, as it happens—May 1849—that his sister Helen died. Then, because sales of the *Week* were so negligible, his publishers refused to bring out *Walden.* A period ensued in which Thoreau was traveling, lecturing, and absorbing new experiences, especially in connection with the Atlantic coast. In October of 1849 he made his first trip to Cape Cod, in the company of Ellery Channing. The following June he made a second visit to the Cape. Soon after his return, he was requested by Emerson to go to Fire Island, where the *Elisabeth,* the ship on which Margaret Fuller Ossoli was returning to the United States with her husband and child, had run aground July 19th. On the 24th, Thoreau departed on his mission in search of her effects.[2]

The relationship between Thoreau and Fuller had been cautiously courteous. Despite her editorial reservations about his writing, Fuller at one time thought they might establish a friendship. In rejecting his poem "With frontier strength ye stand your ground" for *The Dial* in 1841, she remarked, "If intercourse should continue, perhaps a bridge may be made between two minds so widely apart, for I apprehended you in spirit, and you did not seem to mistake me as widely as most of your kind do" (Corr., 57). But that tentative suggestion of rapprochement did not take. They kept their distance, but also observed the amenities. In 1843, Thoreau took Fuller around Staten Island when she visited there, a tour she remembered "with great pleasure."[3] Thoreau's few written references to Fuller were respectfully non-committal. On November 13, 1851, after a visit to Mary Moody Emerson, whom he found "capable of a masculine appreciation of poetry and philosophy," Thoreau added: "Miss Fuller is the only woman I can think of in this connection, and of her rather from her fame than from any knowledge of her" (J, III, 114). That was evidently a compliment, directed to one now dead over a year.[4]

Now, in the summer of 1850, he found himself commissioned to search out what he could of Margaret Fuller, her possessions, and her works in the sands of Fire Island. It was a bizarre and grisly errand. Thoreau found little—some clothing, papers of little consequence, and a portion of a human skeleton, apparently not Fuller's. He remarked in his journal, "There was nothing at all remarkable about them. They were simply some bones lying on the beach" (J, II, 43, 44). And he repeated those sentiments in one of his stiff letters to H. G. O. Blake, written on his return to Concord: "Actual events . . . are truly visionary and insignificant,—all that we commonly call life and death,—and affect me less than my dreams" (Corr., 265).

Yet he carried in his pocket a button ripped from her husband's coat, as a talisman of something. And, shortly, he was preparing early versions of Cape Cod, for in February 1850 he had already begun to deliver lectures on the subject.[5]

Cape Cod is not often commented on, and, when it is, it is generally characterized as a cheerful travel book. Henry

Seidel Canby, for example, said that "those who find 'Walden' too much of a tract read 'Cape Cod' with more pleasure," for in it Thoreau displayed "an ease and fluency that is engaging." Joseph Wood Krutch even regretted the "journalistic jocosity" of the book," which he thought "too deliberately directed at a relatively vulgar audience."[6]

If these assessments are not off the mark, they do neglect to mention how permeated the book is with images of sickness, drowning, and mutilation, of whirling madness, of dwarfed trees, of lanced and grounded fish, all culminating in the awesome seashore, which Thoreau bluntly characterized as "a vast *morgue*" (186). The overwhelming character of this arm of Massachusetts, thrown up defensively in contest with an implacable ocean, joined with the trip in search of Fuller at Fire Island to quite powerfully affect Thoreau in ways he had not felt since his visit to the Katahdin wilderness. He later recognized the similarity of mountain and seashore in his journal, when, reflecting on a camping trip in 1858 to the summit of Mt. Monadnock, he wrote: "It often reminded me of my walks on the beach, and suggested how much both depend for their sublimity on solitude and dreariness. In both cases we feel the presence of some vast, titanic power" (*J*, X, 473).

Thoreau began the book by explaining that he had made his three trips to Cade Cod "wishing to get a better view than I yet had of the ocean." It was like another world, he went on. The ocean "covers more than two thirds of the globe," and yet "a man who lives a few miles inland" (like Thoreau) "may never see any trace . . ." (3). The trips proved illuminating for him but scarcely edifying. They were effectively summarized by the Boston handbill that diverted Thoreau and Ellery Channing from their anticipated steamer trip to Provincetown. Its headline read: "Death!"[7] Learning from the handbill that one hundred and forty-five lives had been lost off Cohasset, "we decided to go by way of Cohasset" (5). Not to help or to sympathize, but to observe. The victims were Irish, emigrating from Galway. Having inspected the horrors in detail, Thoreau summarized their effect on him: "On the whole, it was not so impressive a scene as I might have expected. . . . If this was the law of Nature, why waste any time in awe or pity" (11).

And yet, how carefully Thoreau recorded the grim facts—the large mass grave, freshly dug; the farm wagons bearing coffins; still other boxes awaiting transport "on a green hillside" (6). Then he came in closer for more grisly particulars, such as a girl "livid, swollen, and mangled," "gashed by the rocks or fishes, so that the bone and muscle were exposed . . . with wide-open and staring eyes" (6, 7). Thoreau further reported that a mother, having discovered the body of her sister in one of those coffins with her own child in that sister's arms, died within three days "from the effect of that sight" (7). He questioned one survivor, "but he seemed unwilling to talk about it, and soon walked away" (10). That comment reveals the extent of Thoreau's lost or severely atrophied awareness of others' feelings. At the same time, the careful recording of objective detail seems done in order to confront the worst, and to survive it.

Thoreau was particularly impressed by the collectors of sea weed (for fertilizer) who worked, as it were, among the bodies. He was anxious to make their professional composure as dramatic as possible: "they were often obliged to separate fragments of clothing from it, and they might at any moment have found a human body under it" (8). Contemplating one old man at work, Thoreau observed, "those bodies were to him but other weeds which the tide cast up, but which were of no use to him" (11).[8]

All of this is certainly an unexpected way of opening an amiable travel book. But the reason for it must be clear. The cool, objective tone was the means by which Thoreau mastered those appalling sights to which he hurried. This was not new behavior for him. He habitually recounted in his journal the grotesque and shocking detail, like the aftermath of the

powder mill explosion, or the improvised burial of Bill
Wheeler: "he was found dead among the brush over back of
the hill,—so far decomposed that his coffin was carried to his
body and it was put into it with pitchforks" (*J*, III, 197).

It is worth noting that Bill Wheeler was a cripple, a point
that Thoreau also made with excruciating explicitness. Having
evidently frozen his feet while drunk, Wheeler now "had two
clumps for feet," mutilations that Thoreau also called "stubs."
No sentimentalist in such matters, Thoreau joked that although somebody was said to have given Wheeler "his drink
for the few chores he could do," no reference was made to his
meat, "he had so sublimed his life" (*J*, III, 195). The passage of
reflections on Wheeler is a long one (the date is January 16,
1852), in which Wheeler becomes a version of Thoreau himself. Encountering him one day curled up asleep, Thoreau
"came away reflecting much on that man's life . . . how low he
lived, perhaps from a deep principle, that he might be some
mighty philosopher, greater than Socrates or Diogenes,
simplifying life, returning to nature, having turned his back on
towns; how many things he had put off,—luxuries, comforts,
human society, even his feet,—wrestling with his thoughts"
(*J*, III, 196). One can detect here an essential seriousness on
Thoreau's part as he pondered this exemplar of his own way of
life, but he offset it with a joke, and an insensitive one at that.
The sense of the extreme to which Wheeler could take
Thoreau's line of thought was as close as Thoreau could come
to the tragic potential of his own condition, even as in *Cape Cod*
his extensive contemplation of the Irish drowned was the
means of handling his own uneasiness at his life and its certain
resolution.

Thoreau continued in a mock-speculative vein for yet
another page in his journal, following the theme that perhaps
Wheeler was a philosopher beyond words, made dumb by his
"very vividness of perception." At last, though, Bill Wheeler
was pitched piece by piece into his coffin, following which
Thoreau said that he still had misgivings whether Wheeler

"died a Brahmin's death" and was "absorbed into the spirit of Brahm." Nonetheless, he went on, someone had since assured him that Wheeler "suffered from disappointed love" and that all the rest had followed from that—drinking, frozen feet, separation from society. Wheeler was, in short, "love-cracked,—than which can there be any nobler suffering, any fairer death, for a human creature?" (*J,* III, 197). So this long meditation concluded in a satirical-serious mode, aware of the agonies of love, aware of the injuries and withdrawals from society that result from it, and aware of the final outcome.

Rather than another day to dawn, that promised to be Thoreau's fate. One way that he dealt with a meaningless death was to describe it coldly. At other moments, Thoreau had a more commonplace reaction to such scenes of corpses as Bill Wheeler and the wreck of the *St. John* afforded. As a young man he had imposed a strong moralism on physical dissolution: "How may a man most cleanly and gracefully depart out of nature? At present his birth and death are offensive and unclean things. Disease kills him, and his carcass smells to heaven. It offends the bodily sense, only so much as his life offended the moral sense. It is the odor of sin" (*CinC,* 189). *Cape Cod* was a means of exorcising such issues, so that near the end Thoreau could write placidly of the beach: "The carcasses of men and beasts together lie stately up upon its shelf, rotting and bleaching in the sun and waves, and each tide turns them in their beds, and tucks fresh sand under them" (187).

If one means by which Thoreau managed "Death!" was to describe it without emotion, a second was afforded by the example of the seaweed collectors, who went about their business with a cool professionalism that proved "this ship-wreck had not produced a visible vibration in the fabric of society" (8). In them Thoreau found a stability superior to this dreadful disaster, even though that was not the only conclusion one might derive from the collectors' indifference to the corpses littering the beach.

Thoreau's last strategy for managing the terrible scene
that had drawn him out of his way was to minimize its importance. "If I had found one body cast upon the beach in
some lonely place, it would have affected me more. . . . I saw
that corpses might be multiplied, as on the field of battle, till
they no longer affected us in any degree as exceptions to the
common lot of humanity" (11). This psychologically perceptive idea that "it is the individual and private that demands our
sympathy" rapidly yielded, though, to a starker image and a
more exaggerated proposition (11). Some time after the
wreck, Thoreau tells us, "something white was seen floating
on the water." Examined more closely by boat, it proved to be
"the body of a woman, which had risen in an upright position."
The whiteness was her cap (12). Thoreau perceived a truth in
this as well—that such a sight would spoil the beach "for many
a lonely walker there" or at least it would until—"until he
could perceive, at last, how its beauty was enhanced by wrecks
like this, and it acquired thus a rarer and sublimer beauty still"
(12). We cannot escape noticing that all the particularized
dead in Thoreau's account were women: the girl swollen and
livid, the woman with her sister's child, the floating corpse
with its white cap. Thoreau did not attempt to explain *how* the
seashore's beauty was enhanced by such tragedies, nor what
constituted their special rarity and sublimity. Rather, he was
trying to conjure away the grisly bleakness of such scenes by
showing that they could not upset him, or by insisting without
warrant on their "beauty" while at the same time, perhaps,
gratifying a certain punishing streak in himself.

Thoreau forced the point in the next paragraph. "Why
care for these dead bodies? They really have no friends but the
worms or fishes" (12). Following this morbid observation, he
fashioned an antidote, the presumptive reality of some
superior existence following death. The cliches multiplied.
The emigrants "emigrated to a newer world than ever Columbus dreamed of, yet one of whose existence we believe that
there is far more universal and convincing evidence." Al-

though their "empty hulks" came shore, "they themselves, meanwhile, were cast upon some shore yet further west, toward which we are all tending" (12). And so on. The Reverend Mr. Foss could not better wind his greasy bowels about a congregation. Although Thoreau asserted there was universal evidence for immortality, he failed to suggest what it was, nor can it be found in his other writings, save when he was temporarily in the high rhetorical mode of "Spring" in *Walden*. If Thoreau could generate an authentically positive attitude toward this beach piled with human flotsam, it was because these people were beyond suffering. "It is hard to part with one's body, but, no doubt, it is easy enough to do without it when once it is gone" (13). Thoreau viewed that act of separation with such complacency that he transformed it into a trope of a sailor met by "a skillful pilot," then moving through "the fairest and balmiest gales" until his ship "makes the land in halcyon days, and he kisses the shore in rapture there, while his old hulk tosses in the surf here" (13). It is a haunting farewell to a world of pain and darkness, one quite at odds with any position posited in the conclusion of *Walden*, and one already effectively repudiated by the nineteenth century. Thoreau was driven to this sentimental expedient because he could derive no validation of a harmonious life from nature, since nature proved at times to be amoral, cruel, repugnant, indifferent. But his whole philosophy depended on opposite assumptions, even as the harsh imperatives of nature forced themselves on him.

The sheer statistics of nature's operation sometimes astonished Thoreau, as in 1856: "I have not done wondering at that voracity of the pickerel,—three fresh perch and part of another in its maw! If there are a thousand pickerel in the pond, and they eat but one meal a day, there go a thousand perch or shiners for you out of this small pond. One year would require 365,000! not distinguishing frogs. Can it be so?" (*J*, VIII, 103). Here was the other side of that "quite dazzling and transcendent beauty" of the Walden pickerel that

Thoreau had celebrated in the pond book (*Walden*, 284). But although he did record numerous instances of nature's voracity, that appetite symbolized something he could not address directly. I can think of but one occasion when Thoreau acknowledged the cruelty of the system in which he found himself enmeshed. He came upon a small painted turtle on its back, stretching out its head. When he stooped down to look more closely, it withdrew its head, but Thoreau also saw that the turtle's shell was partially empty, "its entrails having been extracted through large openings just before the hind legs. . . . The flies had entered it in numbers" (*J*, XIII, 345–346). After speculating on what might have done this, Thoreau concluded that the predator had been a bittern with its "long and powerful bill." Then, before continuing his thoughts about the behavior of the turtle, he delivered himself of a single, devastating statement: "Such is Nature, who gave one creature a taste or yearning for another's entrails as its favorite tidbit!!" (*J*, XIII, 346). It is probably significant that this exclamation came quite late in Thoreau's life. The date is June 11, 1860, and in less than two years he himself would be dead.

Even more disconcerting for a consistent philosophic position were those instances of inexplicable, contingent destruction, not for any purpose of feeding and sustaining life, but seemingly meaningless. "The helpless unwieldiness of the oxen is remarkable," Thoreau noted one day in 1852. "I was told yesterday that when a man had got his ox out of Bateman's Pond, the latter gave a spring, and, coming down, his hind legs slipped and spread apart on the ice, and he was split up so that he had to be killed" (*J*, III, 306–307). The next year, apropos of nothing and a little mysteriously, Thoreau entered this question in his journal: "Are not more birds crushed under the feet of oxen than of horses?" (*J*, V, 509). In 1855: "Examined my two yellowbirds' nests of the 25th. Both are destroyed,—pulled down and torn to pieces probably by some bird—though they [had] but just begun to lay" (*J*, VII, 395).

Thoreau's attention was regularly drawn to violent and morbid occurrences that he faithfully recorded in his journal, but the significance of which he rarely assessed in his written work, or, if he did, did so unconvincingly, as in his reaction to the *St. John*'s wreck: "Infants by the score dashed on the rocks by the enraged Atlantic Ocean! No, no!" Let me interrupt to point out that the image of a babe "dashed" against the rocks characteristically heightens the horror by bringing the most vulnerable representative of humanhood into abrupt contact with the most resistant features of nature. Then, the exclamatory denial, "No, no!" is enhanced by the weakest figurative assertion: "If the *St. John* did not make her port here, she has been telegraphed there" (13).

But the job of neutralizing this scene of carnage was not yet completed. A most curious epilogue is attached to this first chapter (which itself, remember, is not concerned with Cape Cod). The epilogue is set "one summer day, since this" (14). (The trip he will describe appears in his journal, beginning July 25, 1851, but it also incorporates material from May 29 of that year.) It begins with some virtually random observations about the spits and coves of the Boston shore. Part of this has to do with a subject Thoreau would later return to: the remorseless eating-away of the land by the ocean. But mingled with it are references to the thorn-apple, which was then blooming profusely along the beach. For this reason, Thoreau proposed that the locals should have, as a device for their shields, a ripple, to symbolize "a wave passing over them," and a thorn-apple "springing from its edge" (15). The referent of "its edge" is ambiguous. It may reasonably refer to "wave," "device," or the sentence's subject, "this isle."

Now I realize that even though I have reduced the Thoreauvian sentence to its essence, it is neither very compelling nor especially clear. Nonetheless, it seems to me a characteristic moment for Thoreau, for it is written badly; it joins separate journal entries carelessly; the details conveyed seem almost incidental; and yet I suspect that, underneath it all, Thoreau felt some intuited truth.

When Thoreau proposed the thorn-apple (otherwise known as jimsonweed, *Datura stramonium*) as a symbolic device, it was because it "is said to produce mental alienation of long duration without affecting the bodily health" (15). To this Thoreau appended a long footnote from Beverly's *History of Virginia* (bk. II, ch. iv, sect. 18). It described how the inadvertent eating of the plant by some soldiers brought about "a very pleasant comedy" in which the men "turned natural fools . . . for several days." One blew a feather in the air, while another darted straws at it. A third sat in a corner "stark naked . . . grinning and making mows at them," while a fourth "would fondly kiss and paw his companions." Although "they were not very cleanly," still "all their actions were full of innocence and good nature." And when they came to their senses after eleven days, they remembered nothing of what had happened (15).

What *is* this all about? These grotesqueries appear in a book about Cape Cod, in a first chapter that concerns a shipwreck off Cohasset (which is not on the Cape), but this is about a *different* walking trip, on which Thoreau proposed an eccentric shield for Hog Island, which he then "explained" by means of a long footnote from Beverly. What has this to do with anything? One tenable answer is, not much. Following through with that answer, one could argue that Thoreau sometimes had minimal control of his materials and wrote (or tied previously written materials together) almost mechanically. Here, for example, the shipwreck took place at Cohasset, and, since he had other entries in his journal concerning events close to Cohasset, he decided to wedge them in. I think this is, in part, what happened. Such an explanation would account for the fact that in his *first* reference to the thorn-apple, Thoreau included his ruminations on it as a plant widely dispersed around the world, "this cosmopolite, this Captain

Cook among plants," and as "not an innocent plant," since it suggested "not merely commerce but its attendant vices" (14). Those associations are the first established in the reader's mind about the thorn-apple, yet they do not fit the later interpretation of it as the agent "of mental alienation of long duration without affecting the bodily health" (15).

But let us try to understand what Thoreau might have felt about the conjunction of a benign wave passing over and a harmless narcotic. It was he after all who developed the symbolism, for his original journal entry had confined itself to observing that the wave and the thorn-apple were each physically characteristic of the locale. Thoreau also noted here in *Cape Cod* that some islands were being eaten away voraciously while still others were being created. New shores were being "fancifully arranged," so that on Hog Island "everything seemed to be gently lapsing into futurity" (15). Generalized, then, the components of the proposed heraldic device were: a passive yielding to nature's constructive energies, even if done, paradoxically, at the cost of destruction, coupled with a period of narcotic release in which men cavorted in innocent lewdness. One must decide whether to entertain some such interpretation or to concede the incoherence of two pages of Thoreau's published work.

Even though the main theme of the balance of the chapter was the overpowering perfection of the scene, it was pitted with marks of disaster, or of its potential. A thundershower approached, but merely touched Thoreau's cheek, "though, within sight, a vessel was capsized in the bay, and several others dragged their anchors, and were near going ashore" (16). However, at Cohasset Rocks, where earlier the *St. John* had been wrecked, the sea-bathing proved to be "perfect. The water was purer and more transparent than any I had ever seen. There was not a particle of mud or slime about it" (16). These last two sentences, which parallel Thoreau's exaltation of his environment at Walden Pond, were added to the original journal entry to heighten the exorcistic effect (*J*, II, 346–

347). The Cohasset beach was now "the most perfect seashore that I had seen" (17).

Still, Thoreau felt compelled to describe a shallow lake formed by the sea in back of the beach. In it, thousands of alewives were trapped, making the inhabitants fear "pestilence" from their rotting. But Thoreau replaced his original observation, "The water was very foul," with the noncommital, guidebook safety of: "It had five rocky islets in it" (17). The whole paragraph seemed so obviously out of place that the editor George William Curtis excised it when he published the chapter in *Putnam's* (June 1855, p. 636).

Then, to conclude the chapter, Thoreau made the emphatic point that the ocean no longer looked "as if any were ever shipwrecked in it. . . . Not a vestige of a wreck was visible, nor could I believe that the bones of many a shipwrecked man were buried in that pure sand" (18). Those words both acknowledged the existence of fatality and effectively neutralized it. Thoreau was trying to handle the worst and to go beyond it. Menace was not concealed; rather, reality was reformed.

Chapter two of *Cape Cod*, "Stage-Coach Views," gives the reader his first bouncing glimpses of the Cape from Sandwich to Orleans, or from the shoulder to the elbow along the inner arm. It is a jokey chapter, set in a dreary landscape. The rain comes down hard through "driving mists"; the Cape is "composed almost entirely of sand," although it probably has "a concealed core of rock"; the country is almost bare "or with only a little scrubby wood left on the hills"; and these "barren hills," like much of the rest of the landscape, are "all stricken with poverty grass" (19, 20, 20, 22, 25). In the area around Dennis, punctuating this "exceedingly barren and desolate country," are a few houses "standing bleak and cheerless" (25). Here are "almost no trees," and the few Thoreau saw were all, evidently, dead (26). And yet, for all this, Thoreau says he liked Dennis better than any town yet seen on the Cape, "it was so novel, and in that stormy day, so sublimely dreary" (27).

So the Cape landscape was an unusually bleak one, a desert of sorts, and yet on it Thoreau found simple, good-humored natives. These Cape Codders did not live by the "foolish respect . . . claimed for mere wealth and station" (23). In contrast to the coddled bourgeois tradesmen of Concord sunning in their complacent illusions, the Cape provided Thoreau instructive models. More significant, the inhabitants of this forbidding land were cheerful, so that they promised to show how to live in a world as dangerous as the initial ship-wreck had shown it to be.

The subject of surviving adversity became more sharply focused in chapter three, "The Plains of Nauset." Now Thoreau explicitly stated that "every landscape which is dreary enough has a certain beauty to my eyes" (32). The Cape afforded him a true abundance of dreariness. "The barren aspect of the land would hardly be believed if described" (36). The rain and mists continued as he and Channing proceeded by foot through this hellish environment. The soil was "white and yellow, like a mixture of salt and Indian meal" (36). There were blackbirds molesting the crops, and boxes of tar were set out to catch cankerworms (38, 33). The apple trees were either narrow and high with flat tops or dwarfish, and in one yard there was but a single healthy-looking tree, the rest all dead or dying, apparently because they had been "manured" with blackfish (34). Although kept in good repair, the houses were "small and rusty," and the windmills struck Thoreau as resembling "huge wounded birds, trailing a wing or a leg" (32, 34).

In some respects, though, appearances were deceiving. In spite of being stunted, the apple-trees were fruitful, and al-though the soil was apparently barren, in fact substantial crops were taken from it. Still, Thoreau ultimately concluded that "by far the greater number of acres are as barren as they appear to be" (39). He "never saw fields of such puny and unpromising-looking corn" as those of Eastham, but "the vegetables raised in the sand, without manure, are remarkably sweet." When vegetables succeeded at all, they looked "remarkably green and healthy," although Thoreau speculated that this was perhaps "partly by contrast with the sand" (39, 40).

The pattern is consistent. Thoreau repeatedly described an essentially forbidding environment, then found positive elements in it, which he then qualified a bit. The final clause specifying that perhaps the excellent appearance of the vegetables was partly caused by the contrast with the sand is a clear example. Thoreau was affected by this unpromising and even threatening environment, for it accorded more closely with his rarely admitted sense of existence in general. "The most positive life that history notices," he observed, "has been a constant retiring out of life, a wiping one's hands of it, seeing how mean it is, and having nothing to do with it" (*J*, I, 133). Still, he managed to generate some affirmative features from the general dreariness, but, having done so, was uneasy at proposing that the vegetables looked healthy, so covered his vulnerability with further qualification.

The latter part of the chapter involved crossing a plain to the eastern shore. The storm still "raged," which made the plain appear "more vast and desolate than it really is" (41). The travelers could hear the sea roaring—"a very inspiriting sound to walk by"—and Thoreau pronounced himself happy to be away from human communities "where I am wont to feel unspeakably mean and disgraced" (40, 41–42). His loathing was particularized against "the bar-rooms of Massachusetts" where men practice "savage and filthy habits" such as "sucking a cigar" (42; see also 29 for other temperance sentiments).

Thoreau then turned, appropriately, to the past history of Eastham, concentrating on the ministry. Abundant quotation was followed by sardonic commentary, both on the dubious piety of the community and on the ministers themselves. Thoreau turned respectfully to the first minister, the Reverend Samuel Treat, who interested him because he worked with Indians as well as whites, so sympathetically, in fact, that on his death he was borne by his Indian parishioners through an arch of snow to his grave (52). As the Reverend Mr. Treat was a "consistent" Calvinist "of the strictest kind," Thoreau quoted extensively from his uncompromising hellfire sermons, but noted that nonetheless Treat was known as a cheerful, pleasant man, fond of humor (49, 51). He concluded his long account of the minister with the story of how Treat once delivered a sermon to the congregation of another minister known for his "graceful delivery" (51). His performance "excited universal disgust," but then the host minister begged a copy of the sermon and delivered it to the same congregation several weeks later, to the pleasure of the audience (51–52).

Thoreau makes no comment whatsoever on this life to which he devotes so much space, but one can see in Treat the lineaments of a Thoreau, or at least of a man Thoreau could relish: an Indian appreciator, an uncompromising moralist, a severe judge, and yet a fundamentally cheerful man, even though his seriousness of manner often offended people. Similarly, Thoreau was engrossed by the history of the Reverend Samuel Osborn, who "taught his people the use of peat" and "introduced improvements in agriculture" (52–53). "A man of wisdom and virtue," Osborn became ensnared in doctrinal disputes until finally dismissed by a church council. But, said Thoreau, recognizing a practical prophet without honor, "he was fully justified, methinks, by his works in the peat meadow" (52, 54).

After mentioning a couple of other ministers briefly and facetiously, Thoreau then came to "probably the most just and pertinent character of all." This assessment of the Reverend Ephraim Briggs Thoreau quoted as given "in the language of the later Romans," but "which not being interpreted, we know

not what it means" (55). This sardonic dismissal is supplemented by Thoreau's saying that these ministers all deserved the attention they received in the town histories and
that, if only he could "hear the 'glad tidings' of which they tell,
and which, perchance, they heard, I might write in a worthier
strain than this" (55–56). That seems to be a humorously
tinged was of saying that he could believe in the jeremiads as
well as in the necessity of changing one's slovenly ways, but
that he could not accept the reality of "those glad tidings of
great joy" preached by ministers whose "thoughts were so
much in heaven that they seldom descended to the dismal
regions below" (55). To use the contrasting terms provided by
the local history, Thoreau was "a son of thunder" rather than
"a son of consolation" (54).

"The Beach" took Thoreau into direct contact with the
elemental world. Dark, stormy, and overcast, it was presided
over by a weather-beaten wrecker, "too grave to laugh, too
tough to cry; as indifferent as a clam" (59). The kingdom of this
"true monarch" was "a perfect desert of shining sand" (60, 62).
Here was the true Cape Cod, "huge and real . . . the thing
itself . . . where man's works are wrecks" (65). Thoreau was
exhilarated by it, "wholly absorbed by this spectacle and
tumult," which was quite unlike the torpid flow of the Concord River and Concord life (66). The experience transported
him sufficiently outside of predictable existence for him to
regard the kelp washing ashore as symbolizing "those grotesque and fabulous thoughts which have not yet got into the
sheltered coves of literature" (70). Along the shore "a sort of
chaos reigns still," in spite of the benevolent intentions of the
charity-houses established there for the solace of shipwrecked
mariners (71).

Thoreau examined in rueful detail one of those
"Humane-houses," there discovering all the evidence he
needed of man's dubious humanity. Despite the fine descrip-

tions of these havens in the guidebook, the first that he and Channing encountered was unequipped, as Thoreau discovered by peering at length through a knothole into its interior darkness. Once his eye had adjusted itself to the gloom, he perceived "the wreck of all cosmical beauty there within," by which he meant that this shelter demonstrated man's actual indifference toward others (78). Looking through the knothole "into the very bowels of mercy," he discovered the house to be essentially empty (78). It "*was not* supplied with matches, or straw, or hay, that we could see" (77–78). Thoreau pressed the disillusioning point hard: "There we thought how cold is charity! how inhumane inhumanity!" (78). The essential impression this experience made on Thoreau was that of looking onto a "night without a star" (78). Human solace was at best untrustworthy, if not illusory. Thoreau noted that Channing had previously declared him to possess "not a particle of sentiment" and to have affirmed it in such absolute terms as to astonish him. But he concluded firmly, "I did not intend this for a sentimental journey" (78). Nor was it.

The next—and for dubious reasons the most famous—chapter of *Cape Cod*, "The Wellfleet Oysterman," offers specific evidence of the kind of world it actually was and how one might deal with it. It displays a realistic family, a coarse means of coping, enigmatic symbols, greed deliberately creating human suffering, and an indifferent contemplation of the spectacle of death. The chapter's reputation is based on Thoreau's characterization of the oysterman as "the merriest old man that we had ever seen" (91). The actuality of the old man's presence is rather different, though. He is garrulous, cantankerous, and opinionated, comfortably established in an ugly and irritating world. As he remonstrates with his wife, who had suggested that he eat his breakfast: "Don't hurry me; I have lived too long to be hurried" (99). He complains of being "under petticoat government," but, unprepossessing as it may be, it is plain enough that he is master of his household, which is composed of his wife and daughter (both deaf), a middle-aged, "brutish-looking" grandson, and a boy of ten (81). The grandson, mentally deranged and sullen, interrupts one conversation to mutter. "Damn book-pedlers,—all the time talking about books. Better do something. Damn 'em. I'll shoot 'em," whereupon his grandfather orders him to sit down (90).

If the oysterman's stories sometimes have a pungency to them, they are not notably humorous, let alone Rabelaisian, as they have sometimes been described. And although he is uncorrupted by formal education—"I never had any learning, only what I got by natur"—his knowledge is by no means infallible (95). He imparts dubious information about an oyster's capacity to move; he asserts that George the Third had a road built straight down the whole length of the Cape but cannot specify where that road is now; and when he claims that an earthquake "cracked the pans of the ponds, which were of iron, and caused them to settle," even Thoreau comments soberly, "I did not remember to have read of this" (83, 87–88, 89).

Although Thoreau is amused by this household, its features are closer to a Gothic nightmare than to a charming bucolic romance. In the evening, Thoreau vomits up a poisonous clam he had eaten earlier in the day. That night the winds howl around the house. The next morning, he and Channing eat selectively because the old man is spitting tobacco juice onto the hearth where the breakfast dishes are being prepared. These occasions are treated lightly, and yet the ugliness permeates and poisons the atmosphere.

In the previous chapter, Thoreau had mentioned the wreck of the *Franklin*. It had evidently been deliberately perpetrated, since "a letter was found in the captain's valise, which washed ashore, directing him to wreck the vessel before he got the America" (73). The old oysterman provided a model of how to behave in the face of unchangeable tragedy. Hearing a vessel (the *Franklin*) was in distress, he first finished his breakfast, then walked over to the top of the hill "and sat down there, having found a comfortable seat, to see the ship wrecked" (93). The deliberateness, the concern for his own comfort, is quite extraordinary, not unlike Thoreau when he found that he could not stop the fire he had accidentally set. "I walked slowly through the wood to Fair Haven Cliff, climbed to the highest rock, and sat down upon it to watch the progress of the flames" (*J*, II, 23). The old man watched nine passengers get into a boat. A wave washed over them, "and when they came up there were six still clinging to the boat; I counted them" (93). The next wave overturned the boat "and emptied them all out. None of them ever came ashore alive" (93). This laconic factuality was not the result of a feeling man restraining powerful emotions. It was the account of a morning's entertainment.

And why not? The old man, an attentive Bible-reader, had concluded that "man is a poor good-for-nothing crittur, and everything is just as God sees fit and disposes" (82). Such fatalism proved remarkably good for the digestion.

Later, there was an extended exchange about the meaning of a girl's name, which concluded with Thoreau agreeing emphatically with the opinion of a schoolmaster who had told the old man that the name "had no more meaning that a beanpole" (95). What did have meaning, then? Chance. Fate. As Thoreau and Channing left, they saw a fish-hawk pluck a fish from a pond, then drop it, "and we did not see that he recovered it" (101). The incident possessed no significance that Thoreau wished to confront, but the absence of inspirational meaning was striking.

"The Beach Again" is a slovenly chapter with idle, mechanical stretches, but also with moments of great intensity and revelation. At its actual and thematic center are two grotesque but important images, "A Religious Fish" and man seen as "a half-emptied bottle of pale ale" (116–117).

The fish emerges in a paragraph reflecting on what fishes have swallowed—"jugs, and jewels, and Jonah" (116). Then Thoreau quotes a newspaper story concerning a fish found with a certificate of church membership in its belly. The certificate included a pietistic verse: "O what are all my sufferings here, / If, Lord, thou count me meet / With that enraptured host t'appear, / And worship at thy feet" (116). The bizarre context of this official certificate with its religious conventionalities is a prologue to the more audacious reflections that immediately follow. Finding a partially full bottle on the beach, Thoreau reflected: "As I poured it slowly out on to the sand, it seemed to me that man himself was like a half-emptied bottle of pale ale, which Time had drunk so far, yet stoppled tight for a while, and drifting about in the ocean of circumstances; but destined ere-long to mingle with the surrounding waves, or be spilled amid the sands of a distant shore" (117). Fish now belonged to the Methodist Church, but men were "half-emptied" bottles drifting in an "ocean of circumstances" until at last they were by chance broken or poured out, without reason or notable consequence. Thoreau's image accorded quite accurately with his own frame of mind. Again, it is important to note how clearly the conception is expressed, for here Thoreau was creating not against his deeper instincts, as when he felt obliged to argue a springtime renewal and the ever-higher ascendancy of man, but in images that corresponded to his own largely unacknowledged ideas and feelings about existence and its essential fruitlessness.

The new day walking along the beach began in an atmosphere of conventional optimism. In contrast to the previous stormy days when in fact Thoreau was exuberant, now "the air was beautifully clear" and the sea was "no longer dark and stormy . . . but sparkling and full of life" (104). The clarity of the day, however, only heightened Thoreau's pessimism. Seeing, for example, a ship heave to and anchor, his anxious imagination initially supposed that the ship was in distress but that he and Channing had failed to understand its distress signal. His second conjecture was that the ship contained smugglers. Only after these dire interpretations had arisen did he think that perhaps the crew wished "to catch fish, or paint their vessel" (105). A similar sequence in which Thoreau's imagination conjured up dark visions occurred when he saw "a large black object" cast up on the beach behind him. "As we approached, it took successively the form of a huge fish, a drowned man, a sail or a net, and finally of a mass of tow-cloth"—which it was (107). This particular scene's ominousness was heightened by the inexplicable appearance of two wreckers darting out from the bank "where no human beings had appeared before, as if they had come out of the sand" (107).

Remembering when he had found "some bones with a little flesh adhering to them" on the beach at Fire Island, Thoreau found the remains grew "more and more imposing" in his imagination until they excluded "my snivelling sympathies." The "dead body had taken possession of the shore, and reigned over it as no living one could" (108). Thoreau was in the domain of the inhuman, where nature's presence overwhelmed, and of death, whose king was a dead body. Sharks prowled along the shore of the Cape, entering the bathing coves, and the prevalence of scavengers along the shore made Thoreau inquire, "Are we not all wreckers contriving that some treasure may be washed up on our beach, that we may secure it" (115). The alliance between the sea and the wreckers was a grim and repellent one but, for all of that, no less true. The coast was a vomitorium. "The sea, vast and wild as it is, bears thus the waste and wrecks of human art to its remotest shore. There is no telling what it may not vomit up" (115).

When the surface of the sea was populated by ships, the sight stimulated Thoreau. Seamen inspired him, especially the audacity and curiosity of the maritime explorers, for they struck him as heroic dreamers like himself. He celebrated these men because, again like himself, "referred to the world's standard, they are always insane" (121). Nonetheless, reflect-

ing on the terrible oceanic indifference, Thoreau acknowledged that "I felt that I was a land animal" (123). Looking out
to sea, Thoreau was impressed by "the vast spaces" between
ships, by "a sense of the immensity of the ocean" (122). And as
he gazed still further out, he could see "the water growing
darker and darker and deeper and deeper . . . till it was awful
to consider" (123). In *Walden,* Thoreau retold with some
relish the joke about the traveler asking a boy if the swamp
ahead had a hard bottom. Informed that it did, the traveler
proceeded, and his horse began to sink, whereupon he pro-
tested, " 'I thought you said that this bog had a hard bottom.'
'So it has' " the boy replied, " 'but you have not got half way to
it yet' " (330). But now Thoreau felt less jaunty—"of what use
is a bottom if it is out of sight, if it is two or three miles from the
surface, and you are to be drowned so long before you get to
it" (123). The dimensions of the ocean, like those of Katahdin,
dwarfed Thoreau's philosophic pretensions. Mountain and
ocean alike appalled him. The idea of shallows seen from a
bank at sea was "something monstrous" to his imagination,
"more awful than its imagined bottomlessness." Then Thoreau
reverted to that powerful image that had been haunting his
imagination of late. The visible bottom in the shallows was
really "a drowned continent, all livid and frothing at the nostrils, like the body of a drowned man" (124). Even the temporary calm of the restless sea was—at least according to a letter
Thoreau quotes from Daniel Webster—the result of large fish
"chopping up their prey," biting them into acceptable pieces
until "the oil from this butchery, rising to the surface, makes
the 'slick' " (125). But such placidity was temporary, Thoreau
remarked, whereupon he launched into yet more violent images of the sea's power. It will "ruthlessly" break ships into
pieces, it will play with castaways, and then, having drowned
them, will "distend them like dead frogs" and present them to
the fishes to nibble at. Yielding to the sea's deceptiveness was
fatal: "This gentle ocean will toss and tear the rag of a man's
body like the father of mad bulls" (125).

Still, in spite of the sea's viciousness, Thoreau sought for a positive, quasi-scientific interpretation of it, namely that the land and its various creatures have invariably moved out of and up from the sea on their "way to the heavens" (127). But this fancifulness hardly offset the disturbing power of the principal images of the chapter. Perhaps this explains why Thoreau ended on the otherwise inconsequential topic of sore mouths and throats. In any case, the chapter veers back and across, expressing various apprehensions of the sea, then ostensibly neutralizing them. It is chaotically revelatory.

"Across the Cape" offers some of the most desert-like scenery Thoreau would ever encounter. "Barren," "desolate," and "bleak" are the words he used over and over, especially "barren." The landscape was "exceedingly" desolate and "singularly" bleak. The very desolation made Thoreau "frequently think . . . you were on top of a mountain" (129). Still, although the notion of living here made Thoreau and Channing "shudder," the novelty of the bare landscape made it "agreeable" to them (136). Its lesser features continued to be unattractive: wood ticks, dwarfish trees, and valleys like circular holes where the sand had run out and the houses had been swallowed up (133).

The other dominant subject was the slaughter of a kind of whale called a "blackfish." Some schools ran ashore accidentally, but more often hundreds were driven ashore by local residents, then, by Thoreau's description, were decapitated and stripped of their blubber, which was rendered into valuable oil. Thoreau was intrigued by this activity. The corraling of the whales he found "an exciting race" (145). He displayed no concern or regret for the carnage, only typical chagrin at the stench of the decaying carcasses. Virtually the only wild quadruped he observed on the whole trip was a fox, but even then the story swiftly took a morbid turn as Thoreau reported that sometimes the foxes "died off in great numbers by a kind of madness" in which they whirled "round and round as if in pursuit of their tails" (149).

This persistent turn to disaster is a prominent feature of the next chapter, "The Highland Light." After counting bank swallows, Thoreau then not only reported that a boy collected eighty eggs from them ("tell it not to the Humane Society!") but further mentioned that many young birds had fallen from their nests to their deaths (164). Reference to the upland plover led to this gratuitous information: "The keeper had once cut off one's wing while mowing, as she sat on her eggs there" (164). Moreover, "this is also a favorite resort for gunners in the fall to shoot the golden plover" (164). We are also told that many birds were found dead around the lighthouse and—an exquisite crescendo—that the keeper had sometimes "seen where a golden plover had struck the glass in the night, and left the down and the fatty part of its breast on it" (170). All in all, it was indeed a murderous beach. "Think," remarked Thoreau, "of the amount of suffering which a single strand has witnessed!" (163). His specific illustration of this proposition shows, however, the facetiously grotesque side of his mind. He recounted a story he had been told of the bodies of a man and woman found on the shore. "The man had thick boots on, though his head was off." Thoreau's phrasing here is as ponderously playful as is his summarizing reflection: "Perhaps they were man and wife, and whom God had joined the ocean currents had not put asunder" (163). We again see at such moments Thoreau's preoccupation with the truly Gothic aspects of nature at its most powerful, along with his attempt to master them, here through an insensitive humor.

If the thematic word of the previous chapter was "barren," this one's are "wasting" and "wearing away." Thoreau reported in detail the gradual encroachment of the sea on the Cape, playing with the land, "holding a sand-bar in its mouth awhile before it swallows it, as a cat plays with a mouse; but the fatal gripe is sure to come at last" (155). The Cape's dubious advantage, then, was that it remained ever in the presence of the world's reality. Almost every family had lost someone to the sea. In spite of the lighthouses, ships were wrecked in almost every storm. "The inhabitants hear the crash of vessels going to pieces as they sit round their hearths" (159). One story Thoreau retold has all the elements of horror multiplied by horror. A ship was taken by pirates, but then the captured master deliberately led the pirate fleet aground in a storm. The result was that "more than a hundred dead bodies lay along the shore." That was not all, though. There was no succor. "Six who escaped shipwreck were executed" (160).

Watching a sloop dragging for anchors and chains, Thoreau drew back for some metaphorical philosophizing. Could one drag "the roadsteads of the spiritual ocean," he wrote, "what rusty flukes of hope deceived and parted chain-cables of faith might again be windlassed aboard!" (162). There can be no doubt that Thoreau intended this, for he underlined his revulsion by elaborating the basic imagery. "If we had diving-bells adapted to the spiritual deeps," he went on, we should see sights as hopeless as they are repulsive—"anchors with their cables attached, as thick as eels in vinegar, all wriggling vainly toward their holding-ground" (163). At last Thoreau made a hollow gesture toward other possibilities. We should not search for what others have lost—"rather it is for us to seek what no other man has found or can find" (163). Not even the model of Jesus Christ or of Buddha was brought forward this time. The inspirational value of Thoreau's admonition was low, and it was virtually canceled when he immediately began a new paragraph on "the annals of this voracious beach!" (163).

That night, lodged at the Highland lighthouse, Thoreau lay quietly, thinking of "how many sleepless eyes" of sailors at sea "were directed toward my couch" (175). This extremely odd notion had little to do with the lighthouse as a beacon of security. Thoreau had already specified the problems of the lighthouse—a poor quality of oil, lights dimmed by frost or moths, mariners mistaking a cottager's light for that of the lighthouse or miscalculating distances. Those sleepless eyes gazed on Thoreau, then, from a remorseless, killing ocean.

Perhaps because Thoreau did not live to see *Cape Cod* through the press, its last two chapters are particularly unkempt. An equally plausible explanation might be, however, that Thoreau again barely had his materials under control. He responded in bursts of shocked imagery to the alarming reality that challenged him along the shore, but was unprepared to revise his fundamental assumptions about the world to accommodate the evidence flung in his face that "the ocean is a wilderness reaching round the globe, wilder than a Bengal jungle, and fuller of monsters" (188). Furthermore, the very same experiences that obsessed Thoreau also exhilarated him. This seashore might well be "a vast *morgue,* where famished dogs . . . range in packs, and crows come daily to glean the pittance which the tide leaves them" (186–187). But Thoreau had no great conception of mankind anyway—"we, too, are the product of sea-slime" (186). In any case, the positive feature of the awesome shore was that "it is a wild, rank place, and there is no flattery in it" (186). It was quite simply superior to any anthropocentric system. "There is naked Nature,—inhumanly sincere, wasting no thought on man" (187). It could also be cruel and degrading, as when Thoreau approached the carcass of a horse on the beach, whereupon "a dog would unexpectedly emerge from it and slink away with a mouthful of offal" (186). When he lived on Staten Island in 1843, Thoreau had observed similar scenes on the beach, so that by 1858 his revulsion finally overflowed openly in his journal: "How dogs will resort to carrion, a dead cow or horse, half-buried, no matter how stale,—the best-bred and petted village dogs, and there gorge themselves with the most disgusting offal by the hour" (*J,* X, 499).

The balance of the two final chapters, "The Sea and the Desert" and "Provincetown," is a mix of tedious detail and undigested quotations, puns, and historical summaries, all interspersed with yet more evidence of "the universal barrenness" (which was nonetheless "an autumnal landscape . . . beautifully painted") (193). Thoreau was plainly taken by the sight of the large mackerel fleet at work, more than two hundred sails pouring around the Cape to anchor in Provincetown harbor. Yet the life of a fisherman-sailor was not for him. Sailing once for three miles in a mackerel schooner had been quite sufficient: "I had seen the whole of it" (184). When he turned back to land, though, "It was the dreariest scenery imaginable," which then generated unpleasant descriptions and stories of spiders, "venomous-looking" worms, toads, snapping turtles, snakes, and the ever troublesome mosquitoes (201, 202). Even in the community of Provincetown, Thoreau observed workers spitting tobacco juice "repeatedly" on the fish curing in the air (212). This insult to his sensibility he purged with a pun, by remarking of the Cape and its fish, "that is where they are cured, and where, sometimes, travellers are cured of eating them" (213).

Thoreau devoted some thirty pages of "Provincetown" to reviewing various histories of Cape Cod, a section that might have been more stimulating than it is in its present untoward state. Thoreau showed the various confusions and prejudices animating these histories as well as the inevitable ambiguities surrounding exploration and early colonization. In fact, Thoreau's skeptical conclusion to this extensive review is: "I believe that, if I were to live the life of mankind over again myself . . . I should not be able to tell what was what" (250). Even the Pilgrims seemed to Thoreau to have been deluded by subjective enthusiasm into finding the Cape's soil rich and black and its forestation ample, for he assessed their account as "generally false," even though he generously ascribed the inaccuracies to their fervor. "We must make some allowance for the greenness of the Pilgrims in these matters, which caused them to see green." (255)

Not Thoreau. He saw simple, resourceful people living on a narrow desert under constant assault by an irresistible sea. It was a disturbing but also a bracing experience. It gives him a sense of superiority over his sequestered townsmen, to whom the Cape might seem "strange and remote" (269). And it gratified his sensed perceptions of the world as a dangerous and even appalling place that could nonetheless be survived. For a moment in "Walking," Thoreau comprehended the paradox. "My spirits infallibly rise in proportion to the outward dreariness. Give me the ocean, the desert, or the wilderness!" (*W,* V, 228).

The seashore was a reassuringly objective place, one that fulfilled its role without sentimentality and with a ferocious directness, quite beyond the time-serving irritations of daily life in the domesticated interior. The imaginative act of turning his back on a contemptible human society and gazing out at sea is the note on which Thoreau ended *Cape Cod.* He moved to it through an odd apostrophe—"Here is the spring of springs, the waterfall of waterfalls"—then set the austere terms of his admiration of the Cape: "A storm in the fall or winter is the time to visit it; a lighthouse or a fisherman's hut, the true hotel." Finally, the desirable condition: "A man may stand there and put all America behind him" (273).

Primitives: *Reform Papers*
and *The Maine Woods*

> I have almost a slight, dry headache as the result
> of all this observing. How to observe is how to
> behave. O for a little Lethe!
>
> *Journal*, V, 45

AFTER MAKING his first trip to the Maine Woods, Thoreau had
felt rather less enthusiastic about the wilderness. Initiated by
an invitation from his cousin George Thatcher but a month
after he had been jailed overnight for failing to pay his poll tax,
the adventure took place in the late summer of 1846 while he
was still living at Walden Pond. His account of the trip was
composed in first draft while he was at the pond, then completed and delivered as a lecture shortly after he left Walden.
The essay appeared as "Ktaadn and the Maine Woods" in
monthly issues of *The Union Magazine* from July through
November, 1848, and was then reprinted in 1864 as the first
chapter in the posthumous volume *The Maine Woods*.

Thoreau had originally traveled to Maine in 1838,

searching for a teaching position. On that trip he got no further than Oldtown, just north of Bangor, where he sat with an old Indian who whetted his appetite by pointing up the Penobscot and observing, "Two or three mile up the river one beautiful country!" (*J,* I, 49). Now, eight years later, offered companionship, Thoreau eagerly headed north, still possessed of certain implicit assumptions about nature and the wilderness that were shortly to be challenged, if not dispelled. Throughout the trip, Thoreau's inclination toward correspondence and transcendental symbolism clashed with the unpleasant verities of Maine's backwoods wilderness. If "Ktaadn" is "an Indian word signifying highest land," summer in the woods was the season of "myriads of black flies, mosquitoes, and midges" that made "travelling in the woods almost impossible" (3). Those were the poles between which Thoreau oscillated.

From the beginning of "Ktaadn," Thoreau emphasized a sense of destruction and negativity. Using an 1837 source, he specified that there were "two hundred and fifty saw mills on the Penobscot and its tributaries above Bangor," and he cited these figures and the function of a saw mill with a sarcastic indignation, comparing the original white pine with its ultimate destiny as a friction-match (5). Over against this he set the batteau-manufactory, which attracted Thoreau because the batteau reminded him of the earlier voyagers in the fur trade. "There was something refreshing and wildly musical to my ears in the very name of the white man's canoe" (6).

But reality impinged drearily on this romantic woolgathering in the persons of some Abenakis, the first of whom, although a male, struck him as "a short, shabby washerwoman-looking Indian." The Indian homes he found possessed in general "a very shabby, forlorn, and cheerless look" (6). Thoreau also noted with disapproval that "politics are all the rage with them now," then contrasted this condition with a superior vision—"I even thought that a row of wigwams, with a dance of pow-wows, and a prisoner tortured at the stake would be more respectable than this" (7).

In effect, what one observes at the beginning of "Ktaadn" is Thoreau's disapproval of most of what he encounters, from saw mills to shabby Indians, and his attempt to counter this depressing reality with his imagination: the white pine, the "highest land" signified by "Ktaadn," the former life led by Indians. But these attempts at recovery were perfunctory. They are nothing like the dreamy meditations of the *Week,* many of which, to be sure, were taken in whole from earlier journal entries and incorporated into the manuscript—which is why the composition of the *Week* was in large measure retrograde activity for Thoreau. The *Week* represented his mind in 1845–1846 encountering and working with his imagination of earlier years, rather than, as here in Maine, his mind forced to deal freshly with the resistant materials of the present.

Thoreau was observant now, willing to make note of what he saw, even if no longer inclined to draw higher truths from it. In fact, he was ready to describe "an orchard of healthy and well-grown apple-trees" that he noted were "comparatively worthless" because all they bore was "natural fruit." What was needed, Thoreau thought, was grafting. So here he enthusiastically conceded the value of human intervention into the natural process. More surprising, he added that, were a Massachusetts boy to travel there in the spring with his grafts, "it would be a good speculation, as well as a favor conferred on the settlers" (8).

The antithesis to this thought was "the grim, untrodden wilderness" that lay a "tangled labyrinth" but a step off the road Thoreau and Thatcher now followed (11). Thoreau's attitude toward it was thoroughly ambivalent. He imposed subjective evaluations on the countryside, their coloration depending on what his subject was, for elsewhere the "grim" wilderness was "the primitive wood" (20). James McIntosh has pointed out that the phrase "grim, untrodden wilderness" was a second thought, inserted later in different ink, even as Thoreau later also added the phrase "stern yet gentle wildness."[1] Similarly, Thoreau came upon a potato field that a settler had created by felling and burning trees, then planting potatoes "between the stumps and charred logs" with the ashes serving as fertilizer (14). This sight generated an impatient digression concerning the unimaginative "emigrant." "Let those talk of poverty and hard times who will, in the towns and cities." Cannot the emigrant find the money to come north "where land virtually costs nothing . . . and he may begin life as Adam did?" (14). To be sure, the smouldering scene sounds rather more like hell than the garden of Eden.

A few pages later, their trail crossed a tract "of more than a hundred acres of heavy timber, which had just been felled and burnt over, and was still smoking" (17). This scene too was desolate. "The trees lay at full length . . . crossing each other in all directions, all black as charcoal" (17). Here Thoreau's reaction was no longer admiration for the settlers' enterprise in preparing to transform a forest into a cultivated field. Rather, the scene triggered an atypical expression of concern for those same poor of Boston and New York, for here were thousands of cords of firewood, and even though "the whole of that solid and interminable forest" was "doomed," no man would be warmed by it (17). Yet Thoreau very soon gave a partial answer as to why emigrants were not flocking to Maine. "When I asked McCauslin why more settlers did not come in, he answered, that one reason was, they could not buy the land, it belonged to individuals or companies who were afraid that their wild lands would be settled, and so incorporated into towns, and they be taxed for them" (24). That knowledge failed, however, to modify Thoreau's impatience with those poor in the cities who were suffering hard times.

Such inconsistent attitudes are to be expected in a journal, but when the entries are recast for a book, one might expect their author not to conceal or eliminate them by simple excision, but to think through the situations he had encountered. But mass poverty interested Thoreau much less than did the opportunity for explosions of indignation at others' mismanagement of their lives. This, after all, was the man who, when he lived on Staten Island in 1843, observed with equanimity "whole families of emigrants cooking their dinner upon the pavements." Encounters with these "mere herds of men" rapidly hardened him to their misery. "Seeing so many people from day to day one comes to have less respect for flesh and bones" (*Corr.*, 142). But, from the start, Thoreau had been revolted by New York City. "It is a thousand times meaner than I could have imagined. . . . The pigs in the street are the most respectable part of the population" (*Corr.*, 111–112).

After pausing at Mattawamkeag until their two (white) companions arrived, Thoreau and his cousin symbolically leaped a fence and headed up the northern bank of the Penobscot through "a wholly uninhabited wilderness, stretching to Canada." Yet, in the next paragraph, Thoreau would begin by describing the "three classes of inhabitants, who either frequent or inhabit the ["wholly uninhabited"] country which we had now entered" (16). One supposes that Thoreau meant that the settlers were only along the river bank for the most part, so that the interior remained uninhabited. But it was he who used the words "inhabit" and "inhabitants." "Ktaadn" cannot be said to be a carefully written essay, although that is not to say it is unattractive, for compared to the *Week* it has a welcome directness.

Most of the signals Thoreau gave as they set off "buoyantly" were unmistakably positive. He was happy to break free from civilization's constraints. The evergreen woods had a "sweet and bracing fragrance." The only sounds were from the river and the birds. "This was what you might call a bran new country." For the moment, the sinister, dark mystery of the wilderness went unmentioned. And yet Thoreau concluded the paragraph with an otherwise unexplained (but for him not inconsistent) statement: "Here, then, one could no longer accuse institutions and society, but must front the true source of evil" (16).

That implicit promise was in fact never fulfilled, not in "Ktaadn" nor in the full *Maine Woods*. But it is worth under-lining Thoreau's overt consciousness of evil abroad, his assumption that it had a specific source, and, in oft-reiterated imagery, his sense that one must confront that evil somewhere, initially in an attic, more recently in a wilderness, and subsequently as a glittering scimitar or hard rock in place, and that it might well scalp you, cleave you, or otherwise prove viciously fatal. At the beginning of 1853, Thoreau consolidated his misanthropy into a couplet for his journal: "Man Man is the Devil / The source of all evil" (*J*, IV, 445; see also *Poems*, 186, the version I follow here). The couplet emerges from a long reflective passage contrasting man's constraints with nature's freedoms. Man, wrote Thoreau, "makes me wish for another world" (*J*, IV, 445).

The physical attributes of this particular Maine retreat hardly fulfilled Thoreau's wishes, for it proved to be "drear and savage," swamplike in its "wet and spongy" ground, and on this day "so smoky" that the travelers could not see Katahdin (19, 21, 21). Further, they were stalled at McCauslin's by a rainstorm, and even after they delayed a full day, the Indians they had hired still failed to show up. On the other hand, McCauslin was "a man of dry wit and shrewdness, and a general intelligence," so that Thoreau posited that the deeper one penetrates into the woods, the more intelligent and worldly the inhabitants were (22). This notion, comparable to assuming that the higher one lives, the better one is, as he had proposed in the *Week*, provided Thoreau the occasion to give his home neighbors a backhand slap by remarking that "for a narrow, uninformed, and countrified mind," look to those living in "an old-settled country," more specifically, "in the towns about Boston, even on the high road in Concord" (22–23).

Further along at Old Fowler's, having been told of attacks made on sheep, Thoreau observed utterly without comment: "There were steel traps by the door of various sizes, for wolves, otter, and bears, with large claws instead of teeth, to catch in their sinews" (30). As if that relish in detail were not enough, he added, "Wolves are frequently killed with poisoned bait" (30). Thoreau lived a safe, domestic life for the most part. He never had to face bears, black or grizzly, mountain lions, rattlesnakes, or alligators. He was rarely obliged to accommodate the full dimensions of nature to his attitude toward life. But, in a moment like this, when he described the mechanisms for trapping animals potentially dangerous to him, Thoreau accepted with equanimity the suffering involved in their being trapped.

Nonetheless, his romanticism went deep. As they hauled their batteau over some rocky hills, Thoreau gratuitously remarked: "This portage probably followed the trail of an ancient Indian carry" (30). Why he assumed so, he did not explain. His practicality remained in force, however. In regard to shooting some dangerous rapids, Thoreau wrote how fortunate they were to have gained the services of the men they had induced to replace the Indians who had failed to show up. They were at once "indispensable pilots and pleasant companions," whereas, Thoreau tells us, the Indian was reputed to be less skillful with a batteau, and, moreover, "he is, for the most part, less to be relied on, and more disposed to sulks and whims" (32). On the whole, Thoreau preferred the storybook Indian whom he could associate with the artifacts he found, particularly when his own safety was at issue.[2]

After encountering a logger's camp, then occupied only by a cook, the party had apparently reached the genuine wilderness at last. If at Mattawankeag they were at the edge of "a wholly uninhabited wilderness, stretching to Canada," with only an obscure trail available, now the camp "was the last human habitation of any kind in this direction" and "beyond, there was no trail" (16, 35). Thoreau was determined to find himself (and his party of six) truly out of society, even though that was evidently not possible. On the solitary Ambejijis

Lake, he observed a ring-bolt anchored in a rock and, later still, a hand-bill glued to the trunk of a pine (42, 50).

One of the first attractions of the deep wilderness specifically mentioned by Thoreau was that he could feel himself unobserved. The stealthy roamer of the back lots of Concord himself disliked being the object of attention. He particularly celebrated being free from "any lover of nature or musing traveller watching our batteau from the distant hills" (36). Such an observer would have seen a comedy, for having built a fire "some ten feet long by three or four high" and set up a lean-to made of cotton cloth, the party soon found that sparks from their giant fire were burning the cloth, which forced them to prop up the batteau and sleep under it (39). The next morning, they launched their boat, "leaving our fire blazing" (41). As Thoreau had but two years earlier burned the Concord woods through carelessness, here in mitigation he offered a series of defensive propositions: (1) "The lumberers rarely trouble themselves to put out their fires, such is the dampness of the primitive forest." But the implicit assumption that the fire cannot sustain itself in the swampy ground proved erroneous, for (2) "this is one cause, no doubt, of the frequent fires in Maine, of which we hear so much on smoky days in Massachusetts." But this seemed to have meant nothing to the loggers, for (3) "the forests are held cheap after the white pine has been culled out." Still, this was thoughtless of them, if not crudely destructive, for (4) "the explorers and hunters pray for rain only to clear the atmosphere of smoke." (It will be remembered that Thoreau's party could not initially see Katahdin because "it was so smoky" [21]). Nonetheless, (5) "The woods were so wet to-day, however, that there was no danger of our fire spreading" (41).

It does seem curiously and unnecessarily negligent to leave a "blazing" fire on the shore, but in the context, guided by skillful woodsmen, Thoreau probably felt disinclined to challenge their practice. Later in their encampment on the lower slopes of Katahdin, they proved equally casual about fire danger. Thoreau tells us that the wind rushed through the ravine in which they were sleeping, "dispersing the embers" of their fire, until once, they were awakened by a "sudden blazing up to its top of a fir-tree, whose green boughs were dried by the heat" (62).

On the whole, though, Thoreau found himself comfortable, as if in the presence of a "stern yet gentle wildness" (40). He tells us that he felt "strangely affected" by the sight of the ring-bolt fastened to the rock, but does not say which way his feelings went—although what immediately follows is a quite long and enthusiastic celebration of the romance of logging (42–44). There is very much an admiring tone in this account of men victorious over a dangerous environment, a tone that would not readily please a conservationist. Having discovered a brick, "clean, and red, and square," Thoreau even remarks that "some of us afterward regretted that we had not carried this on with us to the top of the mountain, to be left there for our mark. It would certainly have been a simple evidence of civilized man" (45). This observation indicates Thoreau's feeling of being in the presence of a distinctly antagonistic adversary that needs to be bested. It should be remembered that this was written *after* his shocked encounter with the overpowering brutality of Mt. Katahdin. But he had already had intuitions of its danger in bears and wolves, in the plunging, roaring rapids, and in the very tracklessness of the backwoods, where Thoreau was told of "a gang of experienced woodmen . . . who were thus lost in the wilderness of lakes" (37). All in all, despite its natural grandeur, Maine seemed a threatening environment, so that a brick would have been a reassuring symbol of man's capacity for mastering it.

When Thoreau's party examined a log jam above Aboljacarmegus Falls, the sight produced an analogy to his own life as he sat later at Walden Pond recreating this trip. "Methinks that must be where all my property lies, cast up on the rocks on some distant and unexplored stream, and waiting for an unheard-of freshet to fetch it down." As the occasion was not ironic, we must suppose that Thoreau's "property" is to be understood as spiritual rather than material. The freshet needed to free that property was "unheard-of," perhaps because of the magnitude Thoreau felt was necessary to liberate himself. He wished it urgently, though. "O make haste, ye gods, with your winds and rains, and start the jam before it rots!" (52–53).

Having established a camp, preparatory to striking north from the West Branch of the Penobscot, the party fished prodigally, showering the shoreline with trout and roaches. Thoreau having always been responsive to fish, this vision of "these bright fluviatile flowers, seen of Indians only," occasioned an observation of considerable insensitivity. The fishes were "made beautiful, the Lord only knows why, to swim there!" (54). If the Lord kept his silence, Emerson had not. In 1839 he published "The Rhodora," in which the poet says to the flower blooming in the woods, "if the sages ask thee why / This charm is wasted on the earth and sky, / Tell them, dear, that if eyes were made for seeing, / Then Beauty is its own excuse for being."[3] In any case, Thoreau evidently thought the Indians incapable of appreciating piscine beauty, since their acknowledged presence was insufficient explanation for the fish.

The climactic ascent of Katahdin had several peculiar features. The party started out together and ascended gradually and with difficulty. As the summit was not in view, they depended on a compass for direction. "It was the worst kind of travelling" (59). At four in the afternoon, while the others were seeking a place suitable for camp, Thoreau climbed on alone, a practice normally discouraged by outdoorsmen for good reason. On reaching the margin of the clouds obscuring the summit, Thoreau finally turned back. This first reconnoitering effort was marked by the extraordinary picture of Thoreau scrambling and walking for an eighth of a mile on the tops of black spruce trees that had been leveled by the wind and the spaces between them filled in with rocks.[4] His trip resembled, Thoreau thought, Satan's journey through Chaos. More ominous yet, once when his foot slipped through the branches he looked "down ten feet, into a dark and cavernous region" and realized that such "holes were bears' dens, and the bears were even then at home" (61). All this seems somewhat improbable: Thoreau walking precariously on the tops of trees over the dens of actual bears. Such an encounter would have been the most dangerous in Thoreau's life, so that one might have expected some evidence to prove that the bears were there—the crackling of twigs, bulky shifting, musky odors, deep-throated grumblings, black forms dimly perceived—but it seems more likely that Thoreau's imagination momentarily filled those shadowy recesses with active dangers, perhaps with the later consent of his companions. Thoreau was feeling distinctly uneasy and menaced. It was "certainly the most treacherous and porous country I ever travelled" (61). The tracks of moose seen everywhere on the mountainside evoked some second-hand accounts of them, within which comes the information, again perhaps heightened by his experienced companions, that the moose "are sometimes dangerous to encounter, and will not turn out for the hunter, but furiously rush upon him, and trample him to death" (57). This too seems an exaggeration. In *The Moose Book*, Samuel Merrill writes that, "In common with some other creatures of the woods, the moose has gained a reputation as a dangerous animal which his disposition does not justify. Attacks upon men made by moose are very rare, even in the rutting season. . . . Wounded, and at close quarters, with all chance of escape cut off, a moose will of course attack a man as a measure of self defence: a squirrel would do as much."[5]

Some of this apprehension was surely derived from Thoreau's characteristic timorousness. The dangers of his ascent, involving moose, bears, rapids, and the threatening severity of the mountain-top itself, are illuminatingly glossed by Thomas Wentworth Higginson's account of a climb he made to the summit of Katahdin nine years later in the company of five young ladies clad in "free and happy Bloomers."[6]

The next day, Thoreau again started out with the party, but then without explanation he forged ahead to make the climb by himself. We are simply told, "soon my companions were lost to my sight" (63). If we are interested in the motivation of others in the party, Thoreau was not, here or ever. On rare occasions, we are permitted a glimpse that may encourage conjecture, but that is all. Returning from his evening scramble, Thoreau mentioned that "one was on the sick list, rolled in a blanket," but whether that information explains why he previously referred to this as "rather an invalid party," and whether that explains why the others failed to make the climb, we have no way of telling (62). Thoreau's relationship with others in the party certainly seems distant and informal when he tells us that he took his whole pack to the summit because he was not sure whether he might descend "alone and by some other route" (65). As was the case in the *Week*, one often feels in Thoreau's journeys that one is moving through an obscure terrain with occasional glimpses of familiar behavior but with the action generally dominated by the illogic of a dream.

The mountain was anything but receptive. Ascending toward the summit, which was "concealed by mist," Thoreau found himself "deep within the hostile ranks of clouds" (63). He tried to lighten the impression with some witty comparisons: "It was like sitting in a chimney and waiting for the smoke to blow away. It was, in fact, a cloud-factory" (63–64). Nonetheless, the prevailing impression given is of malaise. "Vast" and "Titanic" are the words that repeatedly occur to him to describe this disturbing scene where the beholder "is more lone than you can imagine" (64). Climbing appeared literally to debilitate Thoreau. Some vital part of him "seems to escape through the loose grating of his ribs as he ascends" (64). He was threatened by an adversary who turned out to be his beloved Nature. Listen to how she was characterized: "Vast, Titanic, inhuman Nature has got him at disadvantage, caught him alone, and pilfers him of some of his divine faculty" (64). His reactions were somewhat distanced by being put in the third person; nonetheless, the situation is that, like a luckless tourist, having intruded where he does not belong, he is "caught" and "pilfered." In a moment Thoreau revised that lowly imagery to that of the stern parent who reminds the child that his arrival is premature. "Why came ye here before your time?" But almost at once the issue shifted again. It was not the premature arrival but the intrusion on alien ground that was reprimanded. "I have never made this soil for thy feet, this air for thy breathing, these rocks for thy neighbors" (64). Finally, Thoreau was led to conclude that savages wisely do not climb mountains, since their summits are the "unfinished parts of the globe, whither it is a slight insult to the gods to climb" (65).

Thoreau descended, he said, because he feared his "companions would be anxious to reach the river before night" and because he knew the clouds might not lift for days (65). Rejoining the party, he then traveled down a winding ravine holding a mountain brook until they reached open land that sloped down toward the Penobscot. There, rather like a delayed reaction, Thoreau's full response to Katahdin emerged in a justly famous passage. It should be noted that this did not occur on the summit ridge, where Thoreau said it was as if it had rained rocks and where the atmosphere was cool, damp, and alien. Only as the party emerged on the lower slopes was it that Thoreau "most fully realized that this was primeval, untamed, and forever untameable *Nature*, or whatever else men call it" (69). It was not bare and forbidding here, but more like "some pasture run to waste" with low poplars and patches of blueberries (70). So this lower slope alone could not have inspired the feelings that Thoreau recounted. It had to be joined with the summit area to justify the language he used to describe what he called "pure Nature"—"vast," "drear," "inhuman," "savage," "awful," and "beautiful" (70). One might have expected Thoreau to be responsive to this fruitful natural beauty, but the combination of his memory of the summit and other matters in his mind produced a series of exclamations. This was "Matter, vast, terrific," this was "the home . . . of Necessity and Fate" (70). It was in fact what he would search for metaphorically in *Walden*—"some hard matter in its home!" (71).

The reality of it all quite overwhelmed him. Here was substance apart from man, "a specimen of what God saw fit to make this world." Although there was no immediate, specific incident or perception to account for it, the experience was transferred to Thoreau's own body. *It* awed him, too, because it too was matter, and he was bound to it. The same Titan that ruled Katahdin "has possession of me." This made Thoreau exclaim with more passion than he ever before or again would display at the mystery of the actual, of the materiality that surrounded him in every sense, even the most intimate—"the *solid* earth! the *actual* world! the *common sense! Contact! Contact! Who* are we? *Where* are we?" (71). Then, abruptly, the fit was over.

Central to it were the terms "untamed" and "untameable." Previously, Thoreau remarked that "it is difficult to conceive of a region uninhabited by man" (70). This in fact seemed the basis of his exclamatory responses. Although Thoreau enjoyed nature, it was the controlled and domesticated nature of Concord and its environs. On this trip through the Maine wilderness, Thoreau had admired the mastery that the woodsmen displayed on the river, shooting the dangerous rapids. He had celebrated the intrepid loggers. He had looked on animal traps without criticism. He had seen the ring-bolt fixed to the rock with positive feeling. He had left the fire blazing on the shore of the lake. He had contemplated taking a brick to the summit of the mountain. All of these acts and responses were on the side of the controllers of nature. Thoreau was not inclined to be admiring of his compatriots at Concord who had inherited an already mastered land and then merely kept it subdued, with no appreciation or understanding of its intricate beauty. Of them he was largely contemptuous, and preferred to contrast them with the hardy pioneers, the *coureurs de bois*, the settlers, and most of all, the Indians. To be sure, the dismal reality of the present-day Indian was a severe trial to Thoreau. Even more difficult to absorb was the gigantic indifference he perceived in the clouds and boulders of Katahdin's summit. His account of what nature said to him was understandably contradictory. He heard her reproving him for coming too soon, for coming before the ground was prepared—no, for coming where he was not wanted. This in turn touched on whether nature could be interpreted positively. Thoreau could not see, let alone admit, in the ant wars and the frogs half-swallowed by snakes, in John's lockjaw and his sister Helen's tuberculosis, the full indifference of the system of which he was a part. He therefore chose to have nature remind him that she smiled in the valleys, that elsewhere than on the mountain-top she was kind and receptive to man.

Thoreau sensed that this was far from true, however, and this distressed awareness lay behind his concluding outburst in "Ktaadn." Thoreau could live with his impossibly idealized versions of existence. He could manage the idea of some few regions existing that were alien to and hostile to man (this parochial figure who had never experienced, let alone seriously thought about the significance of, the Arabian desert, the Amazonian jungle, the Arctic ice-pack, let alone cancer, madness, and congenital imbecility), but the full alienness of nature he could not face, save in these exclamations over his body, which had him so firmly in its possession. That alone was a fearsome enough thought.

The return trip from Katahdin only confirmed the danger of the wilderness, the incomparable value of the experienced woodsman, and the sadly degraded condition of the Indian. The party again ran numerous rapids, making Thoreau feel vulnerable once more, "like a bait bobbing for some river monster," and it was the intrepid skill of the "almost amphibious" boatmen that took them through safely (76). As the party approached Tom Fowler's house, they at last encountered Louis Neptune and his companion, about a week late and still not totally recovered from "a drunken frolic." Thoreau remarked grimly, "We thought Indians had some honor before" (78). The sight of the Indians reminded him again of the city poor. The Indian in fact resembled "the sinister and slouching fellows whom you meet picking up strings and paper in the streets of a city" (78). Thoreau failed to ponder why those "fellows" would choose to engage in this pitiful activity.

Against such debasement, Thoreau set Fowler with a flute and perhaps some literature to read. "He lives three thousand years deep into time, an age not yet described by poets" (79). He exemplified a mode of living not unlike the one that Thoreau was pursuing at Walden Pond—a model of civilized manliness and competence that he could respect. Yet Thoreau remained obsessed by the fantasy of some ultimate purity of existence. Further back than Fowler was the incorrupt Indian, "but dim and misty to me," and although this "still more ancient and primitive man" was conjured up, it was without overt evaluation (79). He merely built a wigwam of skins, not a log house; he ate animals, not breads and cakes; and then quickly he disappeared into the recesses of Thoreau's imagination. Thoreau had long invested a great deal in the idea of the Indian and would continue to do so, but the brutality of the wilderness and the degradation of the Indian's descendants had severely qualified his commitment to them. Thoreau's real enthusiasm went to the white woodsman. The Indian flitted by and was lost. "So he goes about his destiny, the red face of man" (79). It was a thoroughly equivocal conclusion to that line of thought.

At the end of "Ktaadn," Thoreau sought to bring his ideas together. One can discern the strain existing between his desire to render the experience positively and attractively, and his actual feelings, when he asks, "Who shall describe the inexpressible tenderness and immortal life of the grim forest" (81). He had not provided a single instance of natural tenderness anywhere in his account. The more accurate summary was his admission that "it is even more grim and wild than you had anticipated . . . universally stern and savage" (80). He was genuinely appreciative of the lakes—"like amethyst jewels"—and of the evergreen trees, but, for the rest, the impression was one of unease and distance. If the forest was lovely, and resounded "at rare intervals" with bird cries "along the solitary streams," in summer it was "swarming with myriads of black flies and mosquitoes, more formidable than wolves to the white man" (80–81).

Thoreau was struck by the newness of the country, by how America's shores were barely settled and by how the interior remained virtually undiscovered. His point was on the edge of the metaphorical—"New-York has her wilderness within her own borders"—which reenforced the significance of his impression. This country did not seem settled to Thoreau, but rather, "for the most part, like a desolate island, and No-man's Land" (82). Need one do more than point out that there were other ways to describe an unsettled country than through these analogies?

To Thoreau, Maine was still, in the old cliché, a "howling wilderness," which made Bangor seem as "a star on the edge of night" (82). Nonetheless, the imaginative counter-reaction was equally strong. Thoreau was ever enamoured with the idea of an unsullied isolation of the sort that was exalted in the conclusion of the chapter "Sounds" in *Walden*, where he sang of "no path to the civilized world!" (128). So at the end of "Ktaadn," in spite of his generally disconcerting experiences, Thoreau let his desire take over by evoking how quickly out of Bangor one reached purity, even though the constituents of that purity, as previously revealed in Thoreau's account—the degraded Indian, the dangerous rapids, the unreceptive mountain, the damp darkness of the forest, the omnipresent signs of loggers—all challenged the very concept. "Twelve miles in the rear, twelve miles of railroad, are Orono and the Indian Island, the home of the Penobscot tribe, and then commence the batteau and the canoe, and the military road; and sixty miles above, the country is virtually unmapped and unexplored, and there still waves the virgin forest of the New World" (83). But had he forgotten that "the most valuable white pine timber . . . had been culled out"? (36). This conclusion was no more than rhetoric at work, trying to neutralize unwelcome discoveries.

During a very concentrated period, then, Thoreau was being severely tried. Between 1845 and 1847, he completed but could not sell the *Week*; he drafted the uneasy proclamations of *Walden*; he was arrested; and he had to face the harsh enlightenment afforded by the stony indifference of that portion of nature represented by Mt. Katahdin. Although this was Thoreau's most ambitiously productive period, it was also his most disquieting. He was prodigiously active but also often frustrated and graveled. Out of these years came his most famous statement on a public issue, a statement that was in many respects a highly personal eruption caused by the pressure of his offended dignity.

It was while Thoreau was assembling the *Week* at Walden Pond that he underwent the experience of being arrested that two years later resulted in "Resistance to Civil Government." Because Thoreau's antagonism toward society was sharply focused here by his sense of moral probity, the essay is a confident and vigorous one. As its political ramifications have been extensively discussed under its more familiar title, "Civil Disobedience," applied to it after Thoreau's death, I mean here to make only a few neglected points.[7]

The essay's apparent subject is resistance to those poll taxes that contributed to the support of a government that was then prosecuting a war with Mexico, possibly in an attempt to extend the dominion of slavery further across the continent. Although indignation at the plight of slaves is often regarded as at the heart of the essay, in fact it is much less about slaves

206 / Dark Thoreau

than it is about an attempt to sully Thoreau. If establishing a shelter at Walden Pond made it possible for Thoreau to withdraw in large part from the galling and censorious presence of his neighbors, here in the matter of his tax he managed to act without acting. In the whole affair, Thoreau was not obliged to make a single active gesture. Rather, the state was forced to demonstrate its coarseness by moving on him with its clumsy force. No matter that its agent was the amiable Sam Staples, nor that someone then and thenceforth paid Thoreau's tax for him.

Throughout the essay, the government is patronized and mocked as something pitiable and half-witted that nonetheless tries to exercise its control over him. But it fails, the essay implies, because superior moral force will always triumph. The anecdotal center of "Civil Disobedience," whatever its relationship to reality, insists not only that Thoreau was unmarked by the experience of being arrested but that he was diverted by it. "The night in prison was novel and interesting enough" (*RP*, 81). He found the atmosphere casual and friendly. When he arrived, "the prisoners in their shirt-sleeves were enjoying a chat and the evening air in the door-way" (81). Nothing could be more domestic. These circumstances quite fit a "prison" that served hot chocolate to its guests in the morning. Thoreau shared a cell with an accused barn-burner who supplied him with stories of the jail quite unknown to the contemptible outside world—"even here there was a history and a gossip which never circulated beyond the walls of the jail" (82). And in the evening he gained a fresh and welcome perspective on the village and "its peculiar institutions" (82). All of this was to assure us that Thoreau never lost his equanimity (even though Staples said he was "mad as the devil") and indeed was amused and instructed by an experience meant to punish (Harding, *Days*, 204). Such cat-like assertions of dignity are altogether understandable, but the grand moral posturing born of them is quite unmerited.

Thoreau's need in "Civil Disobedience" to show that he

was superior to the whole brutish episode resembles his exaggerated rationalization in his journal of why he was not guilty of starting the fire that burned the Concord woods in 1844. So, Thoreau insists, "I did not for a moment feel confined" (*RP*, 80). He further confers on his cell the purity and simplicity of his house at Walden Pond. "The rooms were whitewashed once a month," he informs us, "and this one, at least, was the whitest, most simply furnished, and probably the neatest apartment in the town" (*RP*, 81). Despite the ironic reverberations of that sentence, its major emphasis is on the cell's pristine quality. The description tells us that, even though the state laid its dirty hands on him, Thoreau remained undemeaned and inviolate. Unsullied by this attempt on his integrity, he emerged the self-proclaimed victor.

His focus remained on himself in contrast to the state, the straight-backed independent versus the monstrous collective will. Emancipation of the black slaves in the American South in all of its terrible complexity yielded to self-liberation, the freedom to be left alone. Two days after he had retired to the pond, Thoreau commented in his journal: "I wonder men can be so frivolous almost as to attend to the gross form of negro slavery, there are so many keen and subtle masters who subject us both" (*J*, I, 362).

Similarly, Thoreau played a quite unearned role of operatic nobility. "I was not born to be forced," he cried out. "I will breathe after my own fashion. Let us see who is the strongest. . . . They only can force me who obey a higher law than I" (80–81). But Thoreau did not then, or ever, face the possibility of being imprisoned for a long period under rigorous conditions, let alone being executed. It was a markedly civil government that reacted to Thoreau's disobedience. One cannot suppose that Thoreau, even in his provincial innocence, never thought of such matters. In fact, he ends his autobiographical account with a reference to Silvio Pellico, the playwright and member of the Carbonari who was arrested by the Austrian police in 1820 and spent the next decade in various prisons. With remarkable complacency, Thoreau tells us that, in sum, he was jailed on his way to the shoemaker's and released the next day, whereupon he secured the shoe and joined a huckleberry party and within a half an hour was in the country, "and then the State was nowhere to be seen." He finishes with an ironic flourish of triumph: "This is the whole history of 'My Prisons' " (84).

Although it may seem so at first glance, Thoreau is not altogether contrasting the insignificance of his experience with Pellico's. The summary of his arrest tells us that no honest man can long be annoyed by the government. We realize, however, that even in civilized and domesticated Concord, it required the intervention of a friend or relative to release Thoreau from jail, so that his self-satisfaction was unearned. And, in comparison to Pellico, who was under the threat of the gallows, who at times was in chains and suffering hunger, who saw several friends die and who held one in his arms while his leg was amputated, Thoreau's experience was decidedly trivial.

After brooding on the illegitimacy of governmental power, the essay concludes on a conceit of its potential perfection. "The authority of government," begins the last paragraph, ". . . is still an impure one" (89). Thoreau's notion of the exercise of governmental authority essentially envisaged its agreeing not to bother him. First, he proposed the patriotic ideal, that the State would come "to recognize the individual as a higher and independent power, from which all its own power and authority are derived," and treat him accordingly (89). Then he elaborated until he reached a point that included himself—that the State would even permit a few "to live aloof from it, not meddling with it, nor embraced by it, who fulfilled all the duties of neighbors and fellow-men" (90). And that vision of special exemption expanded at last to the kind of idealized vision that concluded *Walden*, of "a still more perfect and glorious State, the which also I have imagined, but not yet anywhere seen" (90).

C. Roland Wagner has argued that in his political essays, "Thoreau's struggle for inward identity, his rage against the ideas of passive submission and apparently arbitrary authority, almost makes him lose contact with the real world and express his fantasies only."[8] "Civil Disobedience" certainly is a diatribe against any restrictions on Thoreau's freedom, an assertion that, because he possessed the higher right, he was absolved from civil authority. At the same time, Thoreau utilized his imaginative arsenal to assure his audience that even during this temporary incarceration he remained untouched. But that was not true.

In 1854, similar antagonistic feelings animated Thoreau in those forceful instances of public rhetoric, "Slavery in Massachusetts" and "Life Without Principle." A conflation of several strong currents runs through these speeches: namely, a refusal to accept criticism or correction from anyone; an absolutist's revulsion at political compromise; hatred of the idea of anyone being imprisoned or, worse, enslaved; loathing of lives swayed by mercenary motives; and a readiness to castigate and punish those who were the profiteers of slavery. In "Civil Disobedience," the case had been awkward, since Sam Staples, the agent of the repressive government, was a Thoreau familiar. But when it came to the nameless functionaries of the state and federal governments, Thoreau felt free to exercise his wrath, and did.

These speeches proved to be perfect outlets for Thoreau's passionate resentments. First given as a lecture on July 4, 1854, "Slavery in Massachusetts" was printed soon after in *The Liberator* and the New York *Tribune,* journals that Thoreau would later excoriate for backing away from John Brown's violence ("A Plea for Captain John Brown," *RP,* 125). Although Thoreau slowly moved (or was moved by time) to a state of more or less calm acceptance, slavery was the one subject that could always be counted on to release that emotional violence of his, originating in his resentment at ever being judged or restrained.

Thoreau's revulsion was expressed in terms of filth and of destruction. The "natural habitat" of the Fugitive Slave Law was "in the dirt" (*RP,* 97). The main informational conduits for the politicians who conceived it were sewers called newspapers (101). Everywhere Thoreau perceived "slime and muck" and servile people behaving like dogs returning to their vomit (108, 100). The restitution in particular of Anthony Burns to the slaveholders meant for Thoreau that "I dwelt before, perhaps, in the illusion that my life passed somewhere only *between* heaven and hell, but now I cannot persuade myself that I do not dwell *wholly within* hell" (106).

Insofar as Thoreau now felt there was a possibility of change, it was in the form of destruction. Memorably: "My thoughts are murder to the State, and involuntarily go plotting against her" (*RP,* 108). Or he flatly asserted the sure triumph of moral superiority, but by means of the most dubious and costly imagery, that of the blooming of the sweet-smelling white water lily, the "fragrant flower" that would spring from "the foul slime . . . the decay of humanity" (109). "Slavery in Massachusetts" prophecied an idealistic victory too, but only by similarly ending on the ugly notion of using the defeated metaphorical opponents for "manure." How might this primitive ending be translated into practical terms? "Let the living bury them [slavery and servility]; even they are good for manure" (109).

Thoreau's response in "Slavery in Massachusetts" to the conciliatory meekness of most men, who, however aggrieved they might be by the slave system, would never act to correct it, was cataclysmic. "Rather than do thus, I need not say what match I would touch, what system endeavor to blow up,—but as I love my life, I would side with the light, and let the dark earth roll from under me, calling my mother and my brother to follow" (102). Even though this has been called "one of the most violent statements ever written, or spoken before a mass audience," its imaginative aggressiveness was even more direct in the original journal entry.[9] "Rather than consent to establish hell upon earth,—to be a party to this establishment,—I would touch a match to blow up earth and hell together" (*J,* VI, 315). This apocalyptic violence was fused in the public version with a remarkable but not unfamiliar passivity in which, once Thoreau had chosen the side, it was the dark earth that would roll from under him, with no effort on his part. Something ever held Thoreau back from action, made him retire to Walden, made him refuse to pay his poll tax and be jailed, but did not, except verbally, empower his energies and moral fervor to act as other abolitionists did. Does this not explain the qualifications that hedge Thoreau's promise? "Show me a free State, and a court truly of justice, and I will fight for them, if need be" (106). The exquisite prudence of that final phrase is effectively absolute.

The same aggressively critical tone that marks "Slavery in Massachusetts" as well as those portions of *Walden* that were written late, such as "Economy" and the "Conclusion," obtains in "Life Without Principle," which was also composed in 1854. All of these essays return obsessively to certain social topics such as the rush for California gold and the venality of newspapers, and all share Thoreau's punishing determination to "give them a strong dose of myself" ("Life Without Principle," *RP,* 155).

The question of how one sustains oneself in the world had perforce long been a central one for Thoreau, and although the Walden Pond experience might illustrate one's potential freedom of choice, when Thoreau left the pond he still had not settled on an occupation. As his contribution to household maintenance, he had always been willing to participate inventively in the family's pencil business (see Harding, *Days,* esp. 56–57 and 157–158). Previously, he had expended his energies variously as schoolmaster, handyman, tutor, subsistence farmer, and writer, so that in 1847, when answering an inquiry from his Harvard class secretary, Thoreau designated his various occupations as "some of the monster's heads," and concluded: "If you will act the part of Iolas, and apply a hot iron to any of these heads, I shall be greatly obliged to you" (*Corr.,* 186). Having only just left Walden Pond then, he still felt defensively ironic about his multiple occupational identities. Within the year, though, he had a handbill printed up, offering his services as a surveyor, and by the spring of 1850 he was actively engaged in projects as sizable as laying out some sixty house-lots from a single estate (Harding, *Days,* 235, 274). Surveying was a respected and practical occupation that proved ideal for Thoreau, for it afforded him the opportunity to work out of doors and often alone, while at the same time providing him a modest income.

So, by 1854, "since I am a surveyor," Thoreau was prepared to criticize the occupational choices of his fellows from a rather more secure position ("Life Without Principle," *RP,* 155). No longer just his father's employee in the black-lead business, nor just Emerson's handyman, supported at his pleasure, and no longer the idler, the queer, irresponsible fellow who burned the woods, then sequestered himself in them—"no, no! I am not without employment at this stage of the voyage"—Thoreau was professionally consulted now on the most sacred of New England realities, property lines (159). He realized that the man who spends half the day walking in the woods "for love of them" still ran the risk of being regarded a "loafer," but he was now ready to challenge that assessment (157).

Still, Thoreau's general characterizations of social life were shallow in their contempt. Although he himself acknowledged with some pride that "my connection with and obligation to society are still very slight and transient," it was precisely this unsympathetic distance that permitted Thoreau to make parochially chilling judgments of others (160). "Nations! What are nations? Tartars, and Huns, and Chinamen! Like insects, they swarm" (171). Commerce—which included Thoreau's furnishing of plumbago to electrotypist firms in Boston, New York, and Philadelphia, and which in 1858 required him to cut his family's price in half to fend off competition—commerce, although it supplied the family its main income, became in "Life Without Principle" no more than "the activity of flies about a molasses-hogshead" (Harding, *Days,* 261–263, 396–397; and *RP,* 176). This persistent denigration of complex social units and activities permitted Thoreau to slide easily into the apocalyptic language of "Slavery in Massachusetts." "Of what consequence, though our planet explode, if there is no character involved in the explosion? In health we have not the least curiosity about such events, do not live for idle amusement. I would not run round a corner to see the world blow up" (170.)[10]

Thoreau's dismissal of the newspapers was equally absolute. One must "preserve the mind's chastity" from them (171). He never thought seriously about the place of the newspaper in a democracy so large that its citizens could not communicate directly. He was at his most ferocious in "Slavery in Massachusetts," where the newspapers represented to him "the gospel of the gambling-house, the groggery and the brothel" (101–102). Hampered by such censorious prudery, Thoreau could write complacently that "the newspapers, I perceive, devote some of their columns specially to politics and government without charge . . . but, as I love literature, and, to some extent, the truth also, I never read those columns" (177). In April 1861, as the crisis over Fort Sumter mounted, Thoreau wrote Parker Pillsbury, "What business have you, if you are 'an angel of light,' to be pondering over the deeds of darkness, reading the New York Herald, & the like? I do not so much regret the present condition of things in this country (provided I regret it at all) as I do that I ever heard of it." Hence, "Blessed are they who never read a newspaper, for they shall see Nature, and through her, God" (*Corr.,* 611).

Thoreau remained the absolutist, convinced that the right should prevail, that he had access to its identity, and that insofar as anyone resisted his position, it was treason, perversion, or stupidity. Thoreau had not changed very much in this respect since writing his college essay on "T. Pomponius Atticus as an Example," in which he said flatly, "Truth is not exalted, but rather degraded and soiled by contact with humanity" (*EE,* 111). When Thoreau tried to fuse such cold revulsion onto the social cause of abolitionism, his primary imaginative solution necessarily became the blowing-up of the whole disgusting mess.

Despite the personal urgency of Thoreau's public pronouncements, he had very little of interest to tell about human beings in general. He was more attractive and more perceptive when he followed his own bent, which is to say, into the fields and onto the ponds and rivers.

Thoreau's second trip to Maine was made in September 1853, again in the company of his cousin George Thatcher, this time up the Penobscot River to Chesuncook Lake. His account of that trip was first published in *The Atlantic Monthly,* June, July, and August 1858. "Chesuncook" is, in effect, the moose chapter of the full book, even as "Ktaadn" is the mountain chapter, for even though Thoreau tells us that he and Thatcher had employed an Indian guide, "mainly that I might have an opportunity to study his ways," Joe Aitteon proved to be a singularly unimpressive specimen of natural man, so that it was the hunt and slaughter of the moose that furnished the vital center of the chapter (95). On the journey to Katahdin, the Indians had outright failed to meet their obligations. Here, Joe Aitteon led them through the forest adequately, but, when observed closely, he often failed to impress Thoreau because he appeared "to identify himself" with lumbermen. Hence, "he was the only one of the party who possessed an India-rubber jacket" (90). When he arrived, the upper edge of his canoe had been worn "nearly through by friction" from having been carried on the stage coach (90). Being one of the Indian governor's sons, he remarked at the outset, "We ought to have some tea before we start. We shall be hungry before we kill that moose," and he later surprised Thoreau while paddling by whistling "O Susanna" (95, 107). There was not a great deal to learn about wilderness ways from this man. Although Thoreau does not say so explicitly, Joe Aitteon existed in those unsatisfying half-lights between the woods and the town. He could not read, but neither could he subsist "wholly on what the woods yielded" (107). When Thoreau pointed out that his ancestors could, Joe replied that "he had been brought up in such a way that he could not do it. . . . 'By George! I shan't go into the woods without provision,—hard bread, pork, etc.' " (107). Thoreau had in fact noted that the party carried provisions seemingly sufficient "for a regiment" (86). When Thoreau once asked his guide how the ribs of the canoe were fastened to its side rails, the answer was, " 'I don't know, I never noticed' " (107). So Thoreau gradually had to reconcile himself to the fact that Joe Aitteon was limited as a resource for learning.

On the other hand, it became increasingly evident that Thoreau was in the company of killers. His "companion"—as his cousin is discreetly referred to—was one of those casual but thoughtlessly rapacious predators. "My companion said, that, in one journey out of Bangor, he and his son had shot sixty partridges from his buggy" (87). Later, they heard a slight rustling in the trees and saw something black. Joe identified it first as "bear!" then "corrected himself to 'beaver!' " then at last hit on the correct identification: " 'hedgehog!' " (117). The beast was forthwith shot for no obvious reason, although Thoreau did take advantage of the occasion to measure and examine it closely.

If Thoreau made no direct condemnation of such slaughter, it was evidently out of discretion. Writing to J. R. Lowell in 1858, he said that "the more fatal objection to printing my last

Maine-wood experience [that of 1857, which became "The Allegash"] is that my Indian guide [Joe Polis] whose words & deeds I report very faithfully . . . knows how to read, and takes a newspaper" (*Corr.*, 504). But Thoreau's attitude toward the killing became clear when he declared that hunting the moose was "too much like going out by night . . . and shooting your neighbor's horses" (119). Nor was this casual waste confined to Thoreau's party. When they eventually came on an Indian camp, we learn that these Indians "had killed twenty-two moose within two months, but, as they could use but very little of the meat, they left the carcasses on the ground" (135). And as Thoreau moved through the wet forest, he more than once saw "the red carcass" of a moose, grim as those squirrels that he and his brother had skinned in the *Week*, then "abandoned in disgust," but now a hundred times bigger (122, 132; *Week*, 224).

Apparently in consequence of being in the company of these insensitive sportsmen, a remarkable side of Thoreau emerged, a quiet, amiable, tender man who came closer to the sentimental version of Thoreau extant than any other. Mild and uncomplaining, his composure was only occasionally broken by flashes of sarcasm. This was the man who, finding it unendurable to kneel while paddling, ended sitting on the canoe's cross-bars or standing up in it (96). He seemed to be rather short-sighted, since he once saw "what I thought was an Indian encampment, covered with a red flag, on the bank, and exclaimed 'camp!' to my comrades," but this fantastic interpretation proved to be only "a red maple changed by the frost" (96). There seemed to be a complicated association in Thoreau's mind between the red foliage of the maple in the fall and the Indian, for in "Autumnal Tints," speaking of the red maple, he wrote that "these burning bushes . . . take you by surprise . . . as if it were some gay encampment of the red men" (*W*, V, 259). Such a moment, joined with Joe's rapid-fire misidentification of a hedgehog, suggests some of the blundering anxiety of men rather ill at ease in the wilderness.

Thoreau later tells us that he actually suffered a hallucination while drifting along a moonlit stream. He seemed to see "an endless succession of porticoes and columns, cornices and facades, verandas and churches. I did not merely fancy this, but in my drowsy state such was the illusion" (118). While entertaining this fantasy, Thoreau said that he would be brought back "to a sense of my actual position" by the sound of Joe calling a moose—"*ugh, ugh, oo,oo, oo oo oo oo . . .*" But the return was to a fantasy equally unreal: "I was prepared to hear a furious moose come rushing and crashing through the forest, and see him burst out on to the little strip of meadow by our side. . . . I had had enough of moose-hunting" (118).

This dreamy gentleman, troubled by nightmarish expectations, had already seen two live moose, which were certainly far from threatening in reality. "They made me think of great frightened rabbits, with their long ears and half inquisitive, half frightened looks" (110). But reality failed to control a fundamental uneasiness. With Joe calling the moose with his birch horn one night, "we saw many times what to our imaginations looked like a gigantic moose" (103). But it never was. Later, in the Indian camp, Thoreau asked one "if the moose never attacked him. He answered, that you must not fire many times so as to mad him" (138).

Thoreau's feelings of insecurity in the backwoods may help to explain why, whenever he came to a settlement, no matter how small, his language always posited an urban growth to come. Greenville, at the lower end of Moosehead Lake, was "the nucleus of a town" (91). Seeing some twenty to thirty acres of felled trees, Thoreau supposed a "pioneer" had selected a home site that "will, perhaps, prove the germ of a town" (108). Ansell Smith's clearing on Chesuncook Lake offered "the first rude beginnings of a town" (130). Tedious, complacent, materialistic as it might be, the domesticity of a town had protective features attractive to Thoreau. Out at sea or in the deep forest, severe dangers such as he fancied were genuinely possible, no matter how calm the appearances. The source of Thoreau's prevailing disquiet may be located in his household. His mother had a favorite story of "the shipwreck of a schooner upon which she was a passenger, on a voyage to Maine. The dark night, the sound of the waves, the cries of the people, and all the tragic events, were related with a vividness which photographed it at once, a startling picture upon the mind of the hearer."[11] In "Chesuncook," during Thoreau's boat-trip to Bangor, the sea was smooth, there was singing on the deck, and still, "we passed a vessel on her beam ends on a rock" (84). Mabel Loomis Todd confirmed the power of Cynthia Thoreau's narrative. "I can never forget the stories of startling, terrifying or pathetic import which she told us, evening after evening." They were "blood-curdling tales."[12]

Tossed about by his imagination, because he rarely sought to plumb or reconcile his feelings, Thoreau could hardly assuage his self-victimization. A particularly illustrative instance concerns his feelings about lumbermen. Describing the essay "Chesuncook" to J. R. Lowell, Thoreau said its subjects were "the Moose, the Pine Tree & the Indian" (*Corr.*, 504). His indignation when Lowell excised a passage concerning the immortality of the pine is well known. Thoreau was impressively eloquent in his apostrophe to the pine. It was "no more lumber than man is" and "Every creature is better alive than dead, men and moose and pine-trees, and he who understands it aright will rather preserve its life than destroy it." Who is the pine's friend? The lumberman? "No! no! it is the poet; he it is who makes the truest use of the pine—who does not fondle it with an axe" (121). Of course, "near the end of March, 1845, I borrowed an axe and went down to the woods by Walden Pond . . . and began to cut down some tall arrowy white pines, still in their youth, for timber" (*Walden*, 40). But, Thoreau would argue, his motivation was other, for lumbermen were "all hirelings," moved by "base or coarse" motives, unlike those who engage in "employments perfectly sweet and innocent and ennobling," by which Thoreau meant the person who "comes with a pencil to sketch, or sing" (119,

120). He did genuinely feel animus toward those who kill the moose and cut down the pine, but, as was often the case, he managed to exclude himself from consideration. For example, on February 25, 1854, he wrote to his cousin Thatcher, concerning some land he had been hired to survey: "9 acres and 9 rods are woodland, whose value I have got . . . an old Farmer . . . to assist me in determining." Then followed a detailed specification of the number of cords of various kinds of wood growing there, followed by the specification: "Merchantable green oak wood, piled on cars, brings here 4.75 pr cord/ Pitch pine 4.25/ White 2.50" (*Corr.*, 322).

It all depended on his mood at the moment. One aspect of Thoreau would, speaking of the pine, ask in "Chesuncook" whether it was "the tanner who has barked it, or he who has boxed it for turpentine," who best loved the pine (121). But in "Walking," another Thoreau remembered that "A hundred years ago they sold bark in our streets peeled from our own woods," whereas in "these comparatively degenerate days of my native village . . . you cannot collect a load of bark of good thickness, and we no longer produce tar or turpentine" (*W*, V, 229). Similarly, on the "Allegash" trip, when Thoreau and his companion were introduced to creeping snowberry tea, their reaction was a commercial one: "We thought it quite a discovery, and that it might well be dried, and sold in the shops" (*MW*, 206).

Because of the thinness of Thoreau's arguments (as opposed to the depths of feeling that generated them), he could easily turn his reaction to the lumbermen upside down. For example, earlier in the "Chesuncook" trip, Thoreau's party had come across two men employed to seek out commercially valuable timber. A moment before, Thoreau had been in a solitude that "seemed to be growing more complete every moment" (100). Then suddenly he came on a campfire with the two lumbermen before it, "talking aloud of the adventures and profits of the day," in particular of a bargain in which "somebody had cleared twenty-five dollars" (100). Now one might expect vociferous complaint, if not condemnation, from Thoreau of these "explorers" for their desecration of the wilderness solitude, especially on behalf of profit, and especially given his attack on the base motives of hireling lumbermen. But no. Thoreau commented: "I have often wished since that I was with them" (101). He knew full well that their mission was to locate profitable timber for their employers, but that was not what captured his attention. It was their free life in the outdoors that stimulated Thoreau's enthusiasm—"they two alone, a hundred miles or more from any town, roaming about and sleeping on the ground . . . a solitary and adventurous life" (101). These were not poets, sketchers, or musicians in the woods such as Thoreau had contrasted with the lumbermen. These were men "working ever with a gun as well as an axe, letting their beards grow, without neighbors" (101).

One can sympathize with both of the roles Thoreau would like to play: the writer secluded at a pond, appreciating the trees and the wildlife, and the independent woodsman, ranging freely far and wide with a male companion as experienced in his craft as he. At the same time, the surface contradictions are jarring. Thoreau's insensitivity to the need to acknowledge his contesting views of, for example, the lumberman illustrates why he remained severely limited in his presentation of the flawed human condition.

The central experience of "Chesuncook" was the shooting and skinning of a moose. In "Ktaadn," moose had been mentioned, tracks were seen in the moist ground, and the party had even found a skeleton (40, 51, 55). From secondhand information, Thoreau described the moose in detail, but he never in fact encountered one on the Katahdin trip (57–58). In "Chesuncook," the party again saw numerous signs of moose and imagined catching sight of them, but for all of Joe's calling and exploring likely spots, their only sighting was of a mother and its calf—both of which were immediately fired at. The moment was far from heroic. After all of the imagined aggressive monsters, these moose struck Thoreau as "great frightened rabbits" (110). The yearling, temporarily deserted by its dam, "leaped out into the stream . . . and there stood cowering for a moment . . . uttering two or three trumpeting squeaks." "Our Nimrod," cousin Thatcher, fired at it and it too bounded away (110, 111). Thoreau then found Joe's efforts to track the wounded animals unprofessional. The guide first gave up tracing a trail of blood "too soon, I thought, for a good hunter" (112). Then, when the dead cow-moose finally was located—inadvertently, as the party was making a portage—Thoreau observed, "No doubt a better hunter would have tracked it to this spot at once" (113).[13]

Once presented with a moose, Thoreau examined and measured it with care. What followed, though, the "tragical business" of skinning it, upset him. The sight was presented as Gothic in its horror: "to see that still warm and palpitating body pierced with a knife, to see the warm milk stream from the rent udder, and the ghastly naked red carcass appearing from within its seemly robe"—that distressed Thoreau (115). So, although his companions continued on the prowl that night, Thoreau decided that the "tragedy" had "affected the innocence" and "destroyed the pleasure of my adventure" (118–119). Consequently, he kindled a fire and sat examining "the botanical specimens which I had collected that afternoon" (120). Thoughts of "the murder of the moose" made him uneasy, however, made him imagine that "nature looked sternly upon me," so that he again wondered with some apprehension if there were any bear or moose watching him on the margin of the firelight (120–121).

Yet, when later he spent the night at an Indian camp where they were curing moose-hides and smoking meat, Thoreau was thrilled, even though he knew that the Indians had left most of the carcasses of the twenty-two moose they had killed on the ground. Titillated by certain references to cannibalism, Thoreau found this all in all "about as savage a sight as was ever witnessed" (135). The problem with Joe was that he was not savage enough, not sufficiently primitive to win Thoreau's romantic approval.

Searching for a legitimate reality, Thoreau was capable of eliciting fresh poetic images, such as that the first notice hunters often have of the presence of a moose "is the sound of the water dropping from its muzzle" (102). Or he described the sound of a tree falling, deep in the forest: "a dull dry rushing sound, with a solid core to it, yet as if half-smothered under the grasp of the luxuriant and fungus-like forest" (103). Most remarkable of all was a story elicited from old Governor Neptune of how the moose had originally been the whale and, when it first emerged from the water, had no bowels inside, only jellyfish (147–148). These moments occurred, however, only incidentally as it were. Thoreau's pages are a scramble of the pedestrian, the inconsequential, the pedantic, the cloudy, the perceptive, and, occasionally, the brilliant.

The idea of the "sound of a tree falling in a perfectly calm night" again stimulated Thoreau's negative propensities. The sound led him to posit not only supernatural forces but, worse, treacherously malevolent ones. When the tree fell, it was "as if the agencies which overthrow it did not need to be excited, but worked with a subtle, deliberate, and conscious force, like a boa-constrictor" (103). Then, having indulged himself in suspicions of subversion, Thoreau counteracted them with a scientific explanation of some dubiousness. Perhaps trees fall in calm weather because "with the dews of the night on them [they] are heavier than by day" (104).

Near the end of "Chesuncook," Thoreau made a typically enigmatic remark. He said that on his return to Bangor he went expressly to a nearby hill where "I got my first clear view of Katadn [sic]" (151). Earlier (on Saturday) he had noted "we got our first sight of Ktaadn," but that was all (109). There was no indication that the visibility that day was poor, nor that the sighting of Katahdin was of any significance. It was merely recorded, probably verbatim from his notes. But having, as he told us, gone two miles out from Bangor specifically to look at the mountain, Thoreau had no more to say of it than: "After this I was ready to return to Massachusetts" (151). From what followed, though, a concluding set of reflections on the wilderness, one can perhaps understand Katahdin's prevailing importance for Thoreau. Its hard, impersonal grandeur had shocked him back in 1846, and there was never any indication that he had any desire to climb it again. Nonetheless, its presence was significant enough for him to go out of his way to determine that that awful, impersonal power still existed.

Thoreau began his concluding thoughts with a familiar apostrophe to the primitive forest, to its "wild, damp, and shaggy look," now lost to domesticated areas, save partially in swamps (151). He also lamented the loss of trees in Massachusetts and saw destruction extending to the very invention of a machine with which to chop up huckleberry bushes for fuel. Such indignant keening was all vintage Thoreau. But suddenly he reversed his ground, saying: "Nevertheless, it was a relief to get back to our smooth, but still varied landscape" (155). Thoreau then made quite clear, even to himself, why home was best for him. Wilderness—epitomized by Katahdin—was necessary "for a resource and a background" (155). But for daily life, "the partially cultivated country" seemed preferable, "perhaps our own woods and fields . . . with the primitive swamps scattered here and there in their midst"—this was the perfect compromise. "Or, I would rather say, such *were* our groves twenty years ago" (155, 156). Things were manifestly no longer satisfactory today. Otherwise, why should Thoreau suffer periodic feelings of malaise? The *Week* had opened with the citation of the Concord River's Indian name, "The Musquetaquid, or Grass-ground River" (5). But in Maine, Thoreau twice inquired of different Indians the meaning of the river's name, and each time the answer was similar: "Dead Stream." "Deadwater" (142, 169). For all of Thoreau's idealizing of the Massachusetts village with its common as "its true paradise," this was far from the sum of his feelings (155). He was temporarily reacting to his disillusionment with the deep forest. Nature at its most primitive and powerful had proved excessive. The wilderness was vast, threatening, and at best indifferent. Nonetheless, Thoreau still argued the poet's need occasionally to explore "the recesses of the wilderness" in order to resuscitate himself; therefore, he ended with a plea for establishing and protecting "national preserves" (156).

This conclusion was prophetic in its perception of what was happening to the American continent and of how the ravages might be diminished. Even more impressive was Thoreau's clear articulation of what his own preferences really were. He was not a notably adventurous sort, nor had he ever the taste for the outdoors and the solitary life that a John Muir, for example, would exhibit as a shepherd in the Sierra. "I feel that with regard to Nature," Thoreau wrote in "Walking," "I live a sort of border life" (W, V, 242). In "Chesuncook," he identified himself as a poet, which somewhat shifted his identity from the sarcastic individualist and gadfly of *Walden*. If he himself had largely given up writing poetry, the mild, sensitive mien he associated with the poet best suited the feelings he experienced during the Chesuncook trip.

Something else was at work in changing Thoreau's attitude toward the wilderness world. One had seen a crack in Thoreau's romanticization of the Indian in "Ktaadn" when his party accidentally ran into Louis Neptune after he had failed to show up to guide them as he had agreed. Irritably, Thoreau then remarked that there was "a remarkable and unexpected resemblance between the degraded savage and the lowest classes in a great city" (78). In 1853, although Joe Aitteon fulfilled his formal obligations as a guide, he had not impressed

Thoreau much. Thoreau quietly recorded, then corrected, Joe's fund of misinformation. "Joe said that though the moose shed the whole horn annually each new horn has an additional prong; but I have noticed that they sometimes have more prongs on one side than on the other" (114–115). After skinning the cow-moose, Joe declared the skin weighed a hundred pounds, "though probably fifty would have been nearer the truth" (116).

Thoreau's disenchantment with the Indian as a wasteful slayer crystallized in "Chesuncook," causing him to exclaim, "what a coarse and imperfect use Indians and hunters make of nature!" (120). But old habits of mind then reasserted themselves. When he chose to stay with the Indians rather than the whites at their log-camp, Thoreau emitted another burst of enthusiasm, although even this was tempered by close observation. Listening to the Abenakis gossiping, Thoreau felt himself "as near to the primitive man of America . . . as any of its discoverers" (137). And yet he also found that these authentics "knew but little of the history of their race" (136). Later, he undermined the authority of these men who were supposedly in touch with a genuine past. Having asked the meaning of "Quebec," Thoreau was told by one Indian that it was derived from "go-back." Since the river narrowed sufficiently at that point, ships "must go back." Thoreau observed tersely of this folk etymology: "I mention this to show the value of his authority in the other cases" (142). So, for all of his romantic excitement at spending the night with primitives, Thoreau retained his critical judgment. He also exhibited his prim fastidiousness. "For fear of dirt, we spread our blankets over their hides, so as not to touch them anywhere" (135).

One brief episode illustrates Thoreau's drawing away from his idealization of the Indian. He asks one Sabbatis how he made fire. The Indian displayed matches, flint, steel, and punk. But supposing they were wet? Thoreau then received an answer of stoic practicality such as he might be expected to admire: "Then . . . we wait till we get to where there is some

fire" (140). Thoreau was not impressed. Rather, he triumphantly showed the Indian a waterproof vial of matches "and
told him that, though we were upset, we should still have some
dry matches." The Indian's response was stupefaction: ". . . at
which he stared without saying a word" (140).

Such delicate readjustments of Thoreau's loyalty are visible everywhere. In "Walking" he even professed to "think that
the farmer displaces the Indian even [ever?] because he re-
deems the meadow, and so makes himself stronger and in
some respects more natural" (W, V, 230). Thoreau found
himself at a juncture in his life when he had to learn that
Indians were real, often fallible, men, of unusual interest to
him and possibly in possession of skills and information unknown to the white man, but still no less living men. And he
had to learn, as to his credit he did, not to reject them in
chagrin and disillusionment if they were not gods.

Thoreau kept a series of Indian fact books, starting possibly as early as the period of residence at Walden Pond and
continuing almost to the last year of his life.[14] Twelve of these
commonplace books exist, with extensive information on
various tribes. However, although F. B. Sanborn and others
have believed that Thoreau intended to write an original volume on the Indians, Robert Sayre remarks, "But he did not
write it, and a skeptical critic must also recognize that no
evidence has so far turned up of his explicitly saying he intended to."[15] It was probably not ill-health alone that blocked
this possible undertaking. What Thoreau discovered, in effect,
was that if Indians were of particular interest because of certain habits, skills, and knowledge they possessed, so was
George Melvin, the musquash hunter. The Indians were not
prehistoric divinities. They could not in truth serve as instructive contrasts with which Thoreau might belabor his compatriots. The morning after Thoreau had felt himself "carried
back at once three hundred years" in the camp of the Indian
moose-hunters, he noticed that one of the hunters was "now
very sprucely dressed in a clean white shirt and fine black

pants, a true Indian dandy" who was now going "to show himself to any arrivers on the north shore of Moosehead Lake, just as New York dandies take a turn up Broadway and stand on the steps of a hotel" (135, 144). It is true that Thoreau could not quite bring himself to say that, yes, we are all flawed brothers under the skin, but the making of such a comparison of the Indian and the Broadway dandy, the tolerance displayed of such an exercise of frippery, would hardly have been possible for the Thoreau who had earlier made violent attacks on those who pursued the will-o'-the-wisp of Fashion. He was beginning to make peace with some of the contradictions outside of himself.

The third and last essay of *The Maine Woods,* "The Allegash and East Branch," which memorialized a trip made in the summer of 1857, was first published posthumously in the book in 1864. It contains an admired, romantic little anecdote that dramatizes the multiple influences Thoreau had to reconcile in the woods. One night while his companions were sleeping, Thoreau observed a phosphorescent ring of light on a piece of firewood. It enchanted him sufficiently for him to awaken his companion (who on this trip was not his cousin George Thatcher but his friend Edward Hoar, recently returned from eight years in the California gold fields and evidently none the worse for wear, despite Thoreau's indignant opinion in "Life Without Principle" that "the rush to California" reflected "the greatest disgrace on mankind" and that "the gold digger is the enemy of the honest laborer") (*RP,* 162, 163). Discovery of the phosphorescent wood led Thoreau to draw two conclusions: first, in a typical bit of psychological cost-accounting, he "already felt paid for my journey." Second, "I little thought that there was such a light shining in the darkness of the wilderness for me" (180). This phenomenon had just the features certain to stimulate Thoreau's poetic imagination, but it was a rare moment in a book where otherwise Thoreau was often riven with anxiety and fear. As he himself said, "I was in just the frame of mind to see something wonderful" (181).

Up to that point, there had not been much in the way of symbolic or inspirational sights, unless it was the hunters' dog that was determined not to enter the wilderness, even when tied to the top of the stagecoach, so that "several times in the course of the journey he jumped off, and I saw him dangling by his neck" (160). But just then Thoreau had others things on his mind, so he merely commented sourly, "This dog was depended on to stop bears with" (160). The dog failed to measure up, whereas the phosphorescent wood "was a phenomenon adequate to my circumstances and expectation" (181). Temporarily excited by this unexpected gift, Thoreau "let science slide" and proclaimed, "I have much to learn of the Indian" (181). But as his account of the episode came to an end, Thoreau created a most curious juxtaposition. Having argued the insufficiency of both science and the white man's religion, he asked rhetorically: "Where is all your knowledge gone to? It evaporates completely, for it has no depth." But then, without comment, he finished on a note of negativity: "I kept those little chips and wet them again the next night, but they emitted no light" (182).

The discovery of glowing wood represented a symbolist's yearning for a natural truth signifying a higher, spiritual one—"the light that dwells in rotten wood"—that coupled itself mechanically in Thoreau's mind with a scorn for the values adhered to by whites (or at least by those living along the Concord-Cambridge axis) (182). The immediate result was his excitement on making the discovery, but this was then followed by a failure of the glory. Thoreau refused to interpret this failure, but he did accentuate it, by giving the last sentence its own paragraphing, and by following it with the punctuation of several spaces on the page. How conscious the rhetorical act was, one cannot know. We do know that when on October 4, 1858, Thoreau found some more phosphorescent wood in the rotten base of some old fence-posts just dug up, the chips he took from them were still glowing from the stimulation of water on October 9 (*J,* XI, 195–203).

Thoreau wanted to believe there were hidden secrets in the forest that nature had already revealed to the Indian, but several problems muddied that hope: a nature that was too often grim and threatening rather than inspiring; his own imagination, ever alert for disaster; and Indians who were too severely flawed to function successfully as priests of the mysteries of the wilderness. On the whole, Thoreau's accommodation to these circumstances was level-headed and humane, although the phosphorescent-wood episode shows how vulnerable he still was to romantic interpretations. He himself realized a version of the problem in connection with the sound of waterfalls in the wilderness. His imagination, he said, conjured up dams and mills to go with them, while "the steady rushing sound of the wind" he imagined to be railway cars (203). Thoreau periodically lapsed into highly sensitized states on his wilderness trips, when he was subject to fantasies, daydreams, and barely embodied apprehensions. In connection with his false interpretations of sounds, he made an observation of substantially wider application for him: "Our minds anywhere, when left to themselves, are always thus busily drawing conclusions from false premises" (203).

Thoreau proved to be notably clumsy and amateurish on this particular trip. The competence he felt in the Concord woods again evaporated in the Maine wilderness. The man famous for finding Indian arrowheads picked up a small piece of hornstone and hacked at an aspen branch with it, cutting his fingers "badly with the back of it in the meanwhile" (176). Amusing himself by emptying the remains of the breakfast pork fat into the lake and watching it spread over the lake's surface, Thoreau was reproved by his Indian guide (167). Pleased with an echo one morning, Thoreau "was shouting in order to awake it" when "the Indian reminded me that I should scare the moose" (208). On Moosehead Lake in a canoe, while looking at "the spot where a large fish had leaped, we took in a gallon or two of water, which filled my lap" (170). An even more remarkable moment of distraction occurred when his guide was directing their canoe toward a moose he wished to shoot. Despite the tenseness of the situation, Thoreau tells us that "I for a moment forgot the moose in attending to some pretty rose-colored polygonums just rising above the surface" (265).

This somewhat endearingly inept naturalist found himself in the presence of a powerful reality, centered on real Indians, real midges and black flies and moose flies, and real swamps. Here was no "faint hum of a mosquito" making a tour of his apartment and advertising "the everlasting vigor and fertility of the world" (*Walden,* 88, 89). Here were relentless, stinging swarms of mosquitoes, biting so ferociously that the Indian guide lay with his head wrapped in a blanket at night, or immersed in the smoke of the campfire, while Thoreau anointed himself with a repellent wash and wore a veil. Even when protected by the veil, Thoreau found "their combined hum was almost as bad to endure as their stings" (282).

Nor were the swamps here the sort one would enjoy spending one's afternoon chin-deep in, let alone appreciated primitive spots in the domesticated landscape of Concord. These were exhausting. "We sank a foot deep in water and mud at every step, and sometimes up to our knees, and the trail was almost obliterated" (215). On top of that, "the water softened our feet, and to some extent unfitted them for walking" (220).

Despite the arduousness of the journey, Thoreau remained generally good-humored, talking to a squirrel, for example—"I know your cousins in Concord very well" (218). But an anxious and fearful man still surfaced occasionally in the course of the trip. The lake made Thoreau uneasy. He particularly feared being swamped (239, 241). The waves seemed downright insidious to him: one "will gently creep up the side of the canoe and fill your lap, like a monster deliberately covering you with its slime before it swallows you" (171). Even though their canoe was eighteen feet in length, being out on the surface of Moosehead Lake invariably made Thoreau nervous. "Think of our little egg-shell of a canoe tossing across that great lake," Thoreau brooded (171–172). He did not indicate how well he could swim, nor what plans the party had made if they were in fact inundated, but the subject preyed on his mind, even though their guide, "in answer to our questions," asserted "that he had never upset a canoe himself, though he may have been upset by others" (171). At times such as this, the Indian seemed to have been amusing himself quietly by playing on the apprehensions of the two white men. When Hoar was trolling for trout, the Indian warned him "that a big fish might upset us, for there are some very large ones there" (172).

At another point along the journey, the party set up camp under a tree with a dead branch. On Thoreau's instructions, the Indian tried it with his axe, "but he could not shake it perceptibly," so he and Hoar decided to stay where they were. But Thoreau insisted that they move their campsite: "It is a common accident for men camping in the woods to be killed by a falling tree" (200).

While pushing through the swampy region, Thoreau found himself waiting for Hoar, who had gone back to pick up another load. Their guide was somewhere ahead, transporting the canoe. Dusk was falling. Thoreau described his feelings and his behavior: "As I sat waiting for him, it would naturally seem an unaccountable time that he was gone. Therefore, as I could see through the woods that the sun was getting low, and it was uncertain how far the lake might be, even if we were on the right course, and in what part of the world we should find ourselves at nightfall, I proposed [to himself] that I should push through with what speed I could . . . and find the lake and the Indian, if possible, before night, and send the latter back to carry my companion's bag" (220).

Thoreau's near panic under those circumstances was

matched by his concern when he again became separated from Hoar, this time inadvertently. Thoreau, "very much alarmed," searched for Hoar with the reluctant assistance of the Indian ("he went off calling somewhat like an owl"). His apprehensions were dire. "I feared that he had either fallen from the precipice, or fainted and sunk down amid the rocks beneath it" (259). Thoreau recognized the negative force of his imagination: "For half an hour I anticipated and believed only the worst" (259). The Indian counseled a stoic calm until morning, but Thoreau "lay awake a good deal from anxiety," although gradually his hopes brightened (261). Nature almost certainly did not help, however. "The moon . . . setting over the bare rocky hills, garnished with tall, charred, and hollow stumps or shells of trees, served to reveal the desolation" (261).

Hoar was found next morning, in good shape, but his temporary separation served to dramatize the degree of Thoreau's uneasiness in the wilderness. Twice he conjured up "bear-haunted slopes" and commented that "some idea of bears, wolves, or panthers runs in your head naturally" (184, 236, 224). In fact, his list of "quadrupeds" actually seen on the trip was so sparse that it included a bat, a dead porcupine, a beaver eaten on another trip by his cousin, and the skin of a bear (318). As Thoreau remarked, "When you get fairly into the middle of one of these grim forests, you are surprised to find that the larger inhabitants are not at home commonly, but have left only a puny red squirrel to bark at you" (219). To which he added a perceptive truth: "Generally speaking, a howling wilderness does not howl: it is the imagination of the traveller that does the howling" (219). Thoreau's imagination operated powerfully, but what was a creative faculty in the vicinity of Concord often proved a debilitating force on the Atlantic coast of Cape Cod, or on the slope of Katahdin, or in the dank forests of Maine. Thoreau was too sensitive a man to live away from the society that, ironically, irritated him. Maine was too much, and the Great Plains, or the Rockies, or Hudson Bay, or the Sierra, or the Mojave Desert were unthinkable. But the *idea* of an independent existence in the wilderness could always start a passionate sequence of response in Thoreau's mind.

His party encountered, for example, between the Allegash and the East Branch of the Penobscot, "a solitary hunter" who had already "been out a month or more alone" (243, 244). Although his trade was killing, and although he evidently had no more interesting features than being "quite small" and "sunburnt," Thoreau immediately unleashed an attack, first on villagers, then on city-dwellers, as being inferior to this unknown hunter. "How much more wild and adventurous his life than that of the hunter in Concord woods, who gets back to his house and the mill-dam every night!" (244). By this time, Thoreau knew that, whatever romantic associations were attached to "wild" and "adventurous," the reality itself was often coarse and sordid, involving mud, mosquitoes, rain on an indifferent and engulfing terrain, and the occasional slaughter and bloody skinning of animals. But, though Thoreau could give a relatively truthful account of the rigors of life in the backwoods, he could still yield to stimuli such as the idea of the lone hunter. It is quite remarkable to observe him turning next to contrast the hunter favorably to "the rowdy world in the large cities," where the proletariat cluster "like vermin . . . in alleys and drinking-saloons" (244). This hunter "is comparatively an independent and successful man," as are all pioneers and settlers who draw their "subsistence directly from nature," unlike "the helpless multitudes in the towns who depend on gratifying the extremely artificial wants of society and are thrown out of employment by hard times!" (244).

It is altogether typical that this outpouring should immediately be followed by a new paragraph beginning, "Here for the first time we found the raspberries really plenty" (244). Although Thoreau's social points have some primitive legitimacy and give evidence of a man of concern and sympathy, in their impassioned disorder they serve better as a display of Thoreau's obsessions than as effective rhetoric.

Thoreau's active imagination could always invent a figure or a place with stronger or different attributes than it warranted, the solitary hunter being a typical instance of such creative characterization, John Brown the most prominent one. Interestingly enough, on the Allegash trip Thoreau shifted some of his reverential feelings from the Indian to the white. As the trip began, he encountered a figure of singular attractiveness—a white hunter, "probably the chief white hunter of Maine" (161). He was about thirty, handsome, with "an intellectual face," "quiet manners," and "of gentlemanly address and faultless toilet" (161). As unlikely as it initially seemed to Thoreau, given these civilized features, this man was resourceful, courageous, widely experienced, and skilled. He had heroically saved a stage-driver and two passengers from drowning. Even the Indian designated him "the great hunter" (162).[16]

Thoreau's brief portrait of this white man elevated him to the level of an ideal. His much more extended exposure to Joe Polis, his Indian guide, diminished him, on the other hand, to quite ordinary dimensions. Thoreau never said that he became disillusioned with Polis, but the cumulative effect of his detailed portrait brought the Indian to earth as a distant, self-contained mutant, both businessman and natural man, one who was first discovered dressing a deerskin in the yard before his two-story white house with blinds, and last seen consulting a train schedule in a Bangor newspaper delivered regularly to "Joseph Polis" of Oldtown (157, 297).[17]

In the long run, Thoreau's Indians do not seem especially superior, morally speaking, to the whites. They may have had some skills not known to the more domesticated race— although to judge by Thoreau's evidence, even that was far from certain—and they did have somewhat different manners, but all in all their failings were quite as prominent as their gifts. Although Thoreau mentioned various ways in which an Indian like Polis had assimilated the ways of civilization, he was not prepared to attribute his failings to the infection of the whites.

The Indians did have a certain reserve, according to Thoreau, which in some of its manifestations closely resembled his own—getting along "with the least possible communication and ado" (272). Thoreau also remarked several times on "the peculiar vagueness" of the Indian's replies when addressed, "that strange remoteness in which the Indian ever dwells to the white man" (162, 158). However, this appeared to be less a function of some higher wisdom, more derived from a contempt for or suspicion of whites. At least, Thoreau noted that when asked by a "tipsy Canadian" for the loan of his pipe, Polis answered, "looking straight by the man's head, with a face singularly vacant . . . 'Me got no pipe;' yet I had seen him put a new one, with a supply of tobacco, into his pocket that morning" (162–163). Later, deep in the forest, Thoreau reverted to a sardonic wit when he asked the younger of two Indian hunters whom they had encountered "if they had seen any moose, to which he said no; but I, seeing the moose-hides sticking out from a great bundle made with their blankets . . . added, 'Only their hides' " (209). There was, then, apparently, an unbridgeable chasm between the two races, but not one of any metaphysical significance.

Polis seemed to be as good an Indian guide as was available—"one of the aristocracy"—so that he could serve Thoreau as the superior representative of the race (158). This of course supposed that the Indians were a single, unified race, whereas the diversity of their appearance, behavior, and language on the North American continent indicates how dubious a proposition that was. But as Robert F. Sayre remarks, Thoreau "did not study Indians . . . he studied 'the Indian,' the ideal solitary figure that was the white American's symbol of the wilderness and history."[18] It is true that Polis successfully managed to take Thoreau and Hoar to their northernmost terminus on Eagle Lake, then back home again by a different route, but throughout the trip there were innumerable disconcerting moments for Thoreau that essentially constituted failures of authority. Polis had a powerful sweet tooth—"He would first fill his dipper nearly a third full of sugar, and then add the coffee to it"—but although very adept at making canoe thread out of black spruce roots, when he made a sugar-bowl at Thoreau's request from birch-bark, the bark cracked (239, 204, 203). He knew only the most familiar stars and constellations (223). Once on Moosehead Lake, when asked the way, he answered, "I don't know," since he had never ascended the side on which they were traveling (166). On Second Lake Thoreau and the Indian disagreed on the direction in which the outlet was to be found, and Thoreau proved to be correct (265). Seeing a muskrat swimming in a stream, the Indian called him, making "a curious squeaking, wiry sound with his lips, exerting himself considerably." Thoreau was very attentive, thinking, "I had at last got into the wilderness, and that he was a wild man indeed, to be talking to a musquash!" (206). But the muskrat failed to heed the Indian's call. The Indian had an excuse, as he did when the bark sugar-bowl failed. Nonetheless, it was a negatively illuminating moment for Thoreau.

When the party finally came upon a moose, Polis was so excited "that his hand trembled and he once put his ramrod back upside down." "This," Thoreau observed, "was remarkable for so experienced a hunter," then added that the white hunter had told him that Indian's excitability generally hindered them from being good shots (266). Still, Polis had been sufficiently adept as a hunter to have made the money to purchase a good deal of land (183, 174). In this respect, he revealed himself as both speculative and hard-headed. He possessed fifty acres above Oldtown, had recently bought more—a hundred acres, Thoreau thought—and had in mind buying a few hundred more above Chamberlain Lake (174,

242). Polis believed in education for pragmatic reasons: "If you had been to college and learnt to calculate, you could 'keep 'em property,—no other way' " (293). To work his cultivated land, he "preferred white men to Indians, because 'they keep steady, and know how' " (174).

If these details build an intriguing and plausible picture of a rising Indian entrepreneur, they hardly constitute an inspiring example. Thoreau was then oddly "surprised to hear him say that he liked to go to Boston, New York, Philadelphia, &c., &c.; that he would like to live there" (197). Thoreau was not prepared to address such anomalies directly. His critical attitude was implicit only in the variety of anecdotes and surprises he reported. For example, the party came upon an encampment of St. Francis Indian hunters. "They had got a young moose, taken in the river a fortnight before, confined in a sort of cage of logs. . . . It was quite tame, about four feet high, and covered with moose flies" (188). Why did Thoreau include this fact? Why had the Indians kept the young moose? To protect it? As a pet? To raise and then slaughter it? To manifest their power? And what did Thoreau think of its imprisonment? He never tells us, but, lacking other information, the impression made reflects questionably on the Indians here.

Polis, Thoreau's specimen Indian, from whom he hoped to gain access to the mysteries of the forest, proved overall to be a disappointment. William Howarth has pointed out, concerning Thoreau's Indian notebooks, that "The size of his volumes reflects the scope of his interest, expanding from 60 to 600 pages in six years (1850–1856), and then diminishing to less than 50 pages annually after 1857," which is to say after the trip with Polis. Howarth adds, "As his knowledge grew, his ambition to publish seemed to wane."[19] I think the central reason for this is clear: confronted directly, Indians simply could not win Thoreau's admiration, in spite of his predisposition to admire them. By the end of his trip with Polis, Thoreau had grown quite wary, even though Polis had flattered him by "giving me an Indian name which meant 'great paddler' " (295). As they approached civilization, "he inquired 'How you like 'em your pilot?' " Thoreau's response contains volumes: "we postponed an answer till we had got quite back again" (294). When the trip was over, Polis tried to sell the canoe to them—"said it would last 7 or 8 years, or, with care, perhaps 10," but despite this salesmanship, "we were not ready to buy it" (296).[20]

Even during the trip, Thoreau and Hoar displayed a surprising irreverence for Indian lore. Polis, for example, told a legendary story of how Mount Kineo had formerly been a giant cow-moose. "He told this at some length," Thoreau remarks, "though it did not amount to much." When Polis then asked "with apparent good faith" how an Indian hunter might have killed so mighty a moose, the scoffing answer of the white men might have come from Mark Twain—"a man-of-war to fire broadsides into her was suggested, etc." (172). The reaction is all very merry, but it is far from what might have been anticipated from a respectful student of aboriginal life. In fact, Thoreau added a rather impatient generalization to the anecdote: "An Indian tells such a story as if he thought it deserved to have a good deal said about it, only he has not got it to say, and so he makes up for the deficiency by a drawling tone, long-windedness, and a dumb wonder which he hopes will be contagious" (172). Later, Thoreau again remarked that Polis himself "frequently commenced a long-winded narrative of his own accord," but by then Thoreau's ethnological curiosity was on the wane: "we would fall asleep before he got through his periods" (289).

So, on this trip Thoreau largely divested himself of his remaining illusions about Indians. When Hoar was separated from Thoreau and Polis, the Indian complained of the dankness of their campsite "a good deal" that anxious night, and in the morning he wanted breakfast before recommencing the search (260, 261). Later, the Indian fell sick with the colic and "lay groaning under his canoe . . . looking very woe-begone."

Thoreau's sympathy was distinctly limited. "It seemed to me that, like the Irish, he made a greater ado about his sickness than a Yankee does, and was more alarmed about himself" (290). Even earlier, when the Indian had evidently hurt himself by a heavy fall, Thoreau did not attribute his lying silent for a moment, then springing up without a word and continuing, to stoic endurance. Rather, Thoreau said, this was one of the Indian's characteristic "taciturn fits" (262).

The Indian's propensity for complaint, along with other failures and deficiencies, pretty much completed Thoreau's disengagement from illusions about the red man, which would account for his unexpected response to an exchange with Polis as the trip came to an end. Thoreau asked Polis if he were "not glad to get home again; but there was no relenting to his wildness, and he said, 'It makes no difference to me where I am' " (296). Now that would seem to be a perfect text on which to embroider truths of a transcendental independent, suddenly blessed with the wisdom of a wilderness natural. Thoreau's response, however, was curtly skeptical. "Such is the Indian's pretence always" (296). Those were words spoken from the heights of quite another world. No sympathetic bond connected the two men.

This trip on the Allagash (as it is now spelled) and East Branch nonetheless had moments suggesting impressive growth by Thoreau from the decade earlier when he had composed the *Week*. The priggish young idealist, wincing at human contact and given to dreamy meditations in forest clearings, had become a sharp-eyed, practical, and even sardonic voyager, one still occasionally given to alarm and menaced by the inventions of his imagination, but also a man capable of enforcing his will and of accepting the sheer amusing and incoherent variety of pedestrian existence. "Having resumed our seats in the canoe, I felt the Indian wiping my back, which he had accidentally spat upon." Thoreau made no more of that potentially revolting moment than to report the quite mundane and utterly unlikely interpretation given the accident by this child of the forest: "He said it was a sign that I was going to be married" (210).

Near the end of their journey occurred the only instance I can think of when outright hilarity appears in Thoreau's writings. Although at first Thoreau misunderstood Polis's intentions, the Indian challenged him to a race along a carry, Polis taking the canoe, Thoreau the camp utensils—"gun, axe, paddle, kettle, frying-pan, plates, dippers, carpets, &c., &c., and while I was thus engaged he threw me his cow-hide boots. 'What, are these in the bargain?' I asked. 'O yer,' said he; but before I could make a bundle of my load I saw him disappearing over a hill with the canoe on his head" (285). With much clanking hullabaloo, the race proceeded, with Thoreau, a sooty kettle hugged to his side, finally prevailing. The Indian took the loss with exemplary cheerfulness, laughing, "O, me love to play sometimes" (286). Thoreau had noted before that Polis, whatever his reserve, whatever his materialistic preoccupations, whatever his deficiencies as a woodsman, was "thoroughly good-humored," and it was an attractive development in Thoreau that he could appreciate and convey that side of the Indian (253). Moral indignation was absent from Thoreau's account, replaced by amusement. For example, Polis was a Protestant, and avowed he thought it appropriate for them to "lie by on Sunday" (182, 193). Thoreau quietly insisted, however, that the party move on, to which the Indian assented, saying "that if he no takum pay for what he do Sunday, then there's no harm." "Nevertheless," Thoreau noted coolly, keeping accurate accounts, but giving the Indian rather more tolerance than he did his Concord neighbors, "I noticed that he did not forget to reckon in the Sundays at last" (194). As Robert F. Sayre says, Thoreau gradually overcame "many of the prejudices of savagism to a point where he could present Joe Aitteon and Joe Polis as both Indians and complex, interesting individuals. . . . In recognizing his guides' humanity, he also found a part of his own."[21]

Still, Thoreau's changes were not invariably permanent.

We customarily describe character development as a linear phenomenon, whereas the roots or traces of former prejudices were still visible in Thoreau for a long time, and could readily be reanimated. For example, on his return from the Allagash trip Thoreau wrote three substantial letters about it to friends. To Daniel Ricketson he was flatly factual: "I have made a journey of 325 miles with a canoe & an Indian & a single white companion" (*Corr.*, 490). With Marston Watson he expanded a little: "I have been associating for about a month with one Joseph Polis, the chief man of the Penobscot tribe of Indians, and have learned a great deal from him" (*Corr.*, 488). But to H. G. O. Blake, the one man who invariably drew pious sermons from Thoreau, he reverted to generalized commonplaces about the Indian such as he had long promulgated but that he now well knew should be extensively qualified, for to what specific Indian Thoreau had actually met could any of this panegyric apply? "I have made a short excursion into the new world which the Indian dwells in, or is. He begins where we leave off. It is worth the while to detect new faculties in man,—he is so much the more divine; and anything that fairly excites our admiration, expands us. The Indian, who can find his way so wonderfully in the woods, possesses so much intelligence which the white man does not,—and it increases my own capacity, as well as faith, to observe it" (*Corr.*, 491).

Interrogating Polis on how he made his way through the wilderness, Thoreau had received vague answers. "Sometimes I lookum side hill. . . . Sometimes I lookum locks (rocks)" (184). But as Thoreau reflected on it, he did not perceive new faculties in Polis that enabled him to steer through an unmarked terrain. Rather, "it appeared as if the sources of information were so various that he did not give a distinct, conscious attention to any one, and so could not readily refer to any when questioned about it" (185). When the Indian's knowledge could be isolated and focused, then it was obvious enough. The white hunter explained, for example, that hemlock branches provided direction because they "were largest on the south side" (185). As for the Indian, "not having experienced the need of the other sort of knowledge, all labelled and arranged, he has not acquired it" (185). This was but one more instance in which Thoreau's refusal to ponder the significance of the whole assemblage of his perceptions and reactions to a subject left him in a fragmented, although sometimes freshly revelatory, state. Characteristically, he gathered together materials on a given subject—autumn leaves, let us say—or from a given sequence of experiences—the Allagash trip—and strung them together without attempting to synthesize them. What revisions he did make tended to involve changing a word or phrase, or adding or subtracting related materials, but they did not require extensive rethinking of the materials. This was not from an utter faith in the truthfulness of the immediate, since, as we have seen, he could flatly change natural fact for his own purposes. Rather, it seems to have been from a constitutional aversion to reconciling diverse experiences, particularly when they clashed with long and deeply held beliefs.

On one side were ideal notions to which no human being could conform; on the other, to a lesser degree but no less there, were social prejudices. For example, a section of Thoreau's journal contains material on the Allagash trip that was not included in the *Maine Woods* chapter. One portion involves the search for a guide. Thoreau said that he was "warned not to employ an Indian on account of their obstinacy and the difficulty of understanding one another, and on account of their dirty habits in cooking, etc." but that he persisted because "it was partly the Indian, such as he was, that I had come to see." (*J*, IX, 486). Then, still evidently remembering the drunken irresponsibility of Louis Neptune, whom he had hired for the Katahdin trip in 1846, an unhappy experience perhaps reenforced by the conventional white wisdom about Indians, Thoreau added, "The difficulty is to find one who will not get drunk and detain you wherever liquor is to be had" (*J*, IX, 486). Then a second, unexpected prejudice arose. "A young, very dark-complexioned Indian" volunteered to accompany Thoreau's party, but "he was too dark-colored as if with African blood" for Thoreau's tastes, "and too young for me" (*J*, IX, 486).[22]

In 1861, Thoreau took a trip west to Minnesota for his health. The notes he kept have been preserved, and it is evident that, although Thoreau was in the presence of authentic Indian artifacts and actually observed a Sioux encampment, his reactions to the Indians were few and tepid. He noted the sight of some "Dacotah shaped wigwams" and some Indian graves on a ridge; he recorded how the Indian makes fire with flint and steel; and of a Sioux dance he thought these details important: "30 dance, 12 musicians on drums & others strike arrows against bows. The dancers blow some flutes. Keep good time. Move feet & shoulders, one or both. No shirts."[23] It is true that Thoreau was ill on this journey, but a lack of energy did not prevent him from making voluminously detailed notes on the flora and fauna of the various regions he visited. The point is, the actuality of the Indian had never really interested him very much. His *idea* of the Indian always had.

So, in reflecting on the Minnesota journey, Thoreau wrote F. B. Sanborn that the Indian speeches were superior to those of the whites "in point of truth and earnestness" and that the Indians "were quite dissatisfied with the white man's treatment of them & probably have reason to be so" (*Corr.*, 621). But Thoreau supplied no particulars to support his assertions of Indian superiority, and no wonder. They were no more than fixed assumptions in his mind, assumptions that were not permitted to conflict with the crude and uninspiring actualities that he had been forced to observe this late in the day.

Blood and Ova: John Brown and the Later Journals and Essays

> It is remarkable what a curse seems to attach to any place which has long been inhabited by man. . . . As if what was foul, baleful, grovelling, or obscene in the inhabitants had sunk into the earth and infected it.
>
> *Journal*, XII, 340–341

IN A MARCH 12, 1854, journal entry, Thoreau placed the responsibility for his occasional verbal outbursts on a friend—evidently Channing—with whom he was then taking regular rambles in the countryside. "My companion," Thoreau avowed, "tempts me to certain licenses of speech, *i.e.*, to reckless and sweeping expressions which I am wont to regret that I have used. That is, I find that I have used more harsh, extravagant, and cynical expressions concerning mankind and individuals than I intended." The tempter called; Thoreau could not resist. "He asks for a paradox, an eccentric statement, and too often I give it to him" (*J*, VI, 165). Of course, Emerson complained of this two years later, finding it an irritating habit of mind in Thoreau that hardly required Channing's stimulation. "Always some weary captious paradox to fight you with, and the time and temper wasted."[1] No doubt the malicious Channing did sometimes encourage Thoreau's extravagance, as in this typical provocation: "Does that execrable compound of sawdust & stagnation, Alcott still prose about nothing?" (*Corr.*, 162). But if Channing succeeded, it was because the misanthropy was there, just below the surface, prepared to burst forth. Only a month earlier, Thoreau had noted in his journal, without any external provocation, that Congress "compels me to think of my fellow-creatures as apes and baboons" (*J*, VI, 129).

After almost a decade's frustrated smouldering over the various abuses perpetrated in Massachusetts by the Compromise of 1850 with its fugitive slave provision, Thoreau was finally ignited by the fiery John Brown. He had met and heard Brown on two occasions, in February 1857, and in May 1859.[2] In a well-known journal entry made after Harper's Ferry, Thoreau recorded that "I subscribed a trifle when he was there three years ago, I had so much confidence in the man,—that he would do right,—but it would seem that he had not confidence enough in me, or in anybody else that I know, to communicate his plans to us" (*J*, XII, 437). This entry shows how far removed Thoreau was from the front line of radical abolition efforts, since, in the persons of the "Secret Six," even the genteel worlds of Concord and Boston were covertly supporting Brown's efforts, and although they did not know precisely what Brown had in mind, they did understand that he had insurrectionary intentions. But Thoreau was evidently excluded from the conferences of his subsequent editor and biographer, F. B. Sanborn, with T. W. Higginson, Theodore Parker, Gerrit Smith, Samuel Gridley Howe, and G. L. Stearns.

For a time after Harper's Ferry, though, Thoreau became completely preoccupied with Brown. As he noted in an 1860 memorial, "I was so absorbed in him as to be surprised whenever I detected the routine of the natural world surviving still" ("The Last Days of John Brown," *RP*, 145). Elsewhere he said that because of Brown he no longer got his "usual allowance of sleep," and so tumultuous were his feelings that he kept "a piece of paper and pencil under my pillow, and when I could not sleep, I wrote in the dark" ("A Plea for Captain John Brown," *RP*, 118). The long, furious journal entries after October 19, 1859, testify to the accuracy of Thoreau's remembrance. He additionally wondered in the "Plea," perhaps revealingly, "How many a man who was lately contemplating suicide has now something to live for!" (*RP*, 135). Conflicting emotions boiled to the surface in company with Thoreau's delight at seeing a corrupt government physically attacked: disgust at the public denigration of Brown's character and motives; inspiration at Brown's noble words and demeanor after his capture; pessimism as to whether men would ever be free; and determination to rub the trimmers' noses in the event. Ellery Channing remembered that Thoreau's "hands involuntarily clenched together at the mention of Captain Brown," and, even more significantly, that "Thoreau was driven sick" by Harper's Ferry and its aftermath (*Thoreau*, 245, 8).

No man—or perhaps for the sake of greater accuracy one should say, no symbol—ever had a more immediate and powerful effect on Thoreau than John Brown. Brown's open attack on a government that protected slavery proved irresistible to Thoreau. All of his resentments and frustrations centered in this austere, single-minded man of action. Some of Brown's features, such as "that his grandfather, John Brown, was an officer in the Revolution," were obviously put forth to gain the sympathy of the audience (*RP*, 111). (The grandfather died of dysentery a few weeks after joining the Continental Army.)[3] And, of course, any reader familiar with *Walden*'s sardonic attacks on Thoreau's farming neighbors will blink with disbelief when he hears Thoreau now tell his Concord audience that Brown "was by descent and birth a New England farmer, a man of great common sense, deliberate and practical as that class is" (112–113).

Bronson Alcott understood the situation. For Thoreau, Brown was "a hero and Martyr after his own heart and style."[4] And Minot Pratt, after hearing Thoreau deliver his "plea," wrote wonderingly, "I never heard him before speak so much in praise of any man" (Harding, *Days*, 417). It is clear why. Thoreau was, in effect, speaking of himself. The portrait of John Brown in the "Plea" is remarkable for the number of characteristics that apply to Thoreau as well, as when Thoreau designates the abolitionist as "a transcendentalist above all" (115). Like Thoreau, too, "for a part of his life he was a surveyor" (112). (Brown, however, practiced that trade primarily on behalf of land speculation. In April 1836 he wrote his business partner "that he was trying 'to feel out the public pulse' to decide at what price the other lots would sell.")[5]

Brown was, according to Thoreau, "an old-fashioned man in his respect for the Constitution" (112). In "Slavery in Massachusetts," however, Thoreau had taken the opposite tack concerning the Constitution: "The judges and lawyers . . . consider, not whether the Fugitive Slave Law is right, but whether it is what they call *constitutional*." The only question for Thoreau at that time was whether one would obey "that eternal and only just CONSTITUTION, which He, and not any Jefferson or Adams, has written in your being" (*RP*, 103). Thoreau further claimed that Brown had "faith in the permanence of this Union" (112). But Thoreau had previously argued that so long as Massachusetts suffered under the constraints of the Fugitive Slave Law, there was "no respectable law or precedent which sanctions the continuation of such a Union for an instant" ("Slavery in Massachusetts," *RP*, 104).

For the particular occasion of the "Plea," it was unnecessary, but Thoreau seized the opportunity to point out that Brown "did not go to the college called Harvard. . . . He was not fed on the pap that is there furnished" (113). (Higginson,

Parker, Sanborn, and Wendell Phillips, all much more actively involved in the abolitionist efforts, were all Harvard-educated.) Rather, Brown "went to the great university of the West" and "finally commenced the public practice of Humanity in Kansas" (113). Hindsight gives an odd perspective on this sarcastic populism. Though it is apparently true that before Harper's Ferry Thoreau knew nothing of Brown's Pottawatomie massacre, Michael Meyer has shown that after the raid the Democratic newspapers, which Thoreau was demonstrably reading, published numerous accounts of the story in an effort to discredit Brown. But, says Meyer, "despite this information, Thoreau never revised his view of Brown. It seems clear that he chose to ignore, or not to believe, the accounts of Brown at Pottawatomie rather than that he was ignorant of the details."[6] And there are indications that he would have sanctioned that ruthless exercise of "Humanity" in Kansas when the party led by Brown literally butchered five defenseless pro-slavery men with cutlasses, for in the "Plea" Thoreau quotes approvingly Brown's curt reference "to the deeds of certain Border Ruffians,"—"they had a perfect right to be hung" (115). Ellery Channing, whose last published work was *John Brown and the Heroes of Harper's Ferry*, remembered that remark in connection with one of Thoreau's. "His advice to a drunkard as the wisest plan for him to reform, 'You had better cut your throat,'—that was his idea of moral suasion" (*Thoreau*, 312–313).

There was yet more to Brown that permitted Thoreau to associate imaginatively with the Calvinist avenger. Being of Puritan stock, in his camp no profanity or loose morals were permitted (113–114). He was "a man of Spartan habits" who was particularly "scrupulous about his diet" (115). If from one point of view Brown was Cromwell, from another he was an avatar of Christ. His standards were so high that he could find but a score or so recruits whom he could accept, "and only about a dozen . . . in whom he had perfect faith" (114). Further on, that approximate dozen became specifically "twelve disciples" (126). And a little later: "Some eighteen hundred years ago Christ was crucified; this morning, perchance, Captain Brown was hung. These are two ends of a chain which is not without its links" (137).

This Brown, then, was a mighty instrument that Thoreau had created, one largely shaped and modeled in his own image. No wonder that the accusations that Brown was insane so vexed him. Thoreau returned to argue this point over and over (119, 122, 126, 135, 149). After writing in his journal that "It galls me to listen to the remarks of craven-hearted neighbors who speak disparagingly of Brown," he transformed this in the "Plea" to "It turns what sweetness I have to gall, to hear, or hear of, the remarks of some of my neighbors" (*J*, XII, 401; *RP*, 118). For others, though, a version of that explanation was at least entertained. Lincoln, for example, called Brown "an enthusiast" who brooded "over the oppression of a people till he fancies himself commissioned by Heaven to liberate them."[7]

Thoreau understandably preferred the silenced symbol to the embarrassingly erratic man. "I *almost fear* that I may yet hear of his deliverance, doubting if a prolonged life, if *any* life, can do as much good as his death" (137). In this, he was one with another supporter, Henry Ward Beecher, who had admonished the public: "Let no man pray that Brown be spared. Let Virginia make him a martyr." Reading these sentiments in a newspaper, Brown wrote "Good" above the passage and resolutely refused the plans of Higginson, Sanborn, and others to rescue him from prison. "I am worth inconceivably more to *hang* than for any other purpose."[8] Sharing that mood, Thoreau acknowledged that "I have all along found myself thinking and speaking of him as physically dead" (125). There was a particularly unpleasant savor, though, to his remark of Brown and his men that "they were ripe for her gallows" (132). But for the state to hang Brown would be one more demonstration of the same cowardly brutishness that had operated in jailing Thoreau. Moreover, the dead Brown would be a still vital weapon against corrupt humanity, a perfect and manipulable symbol.

Finally, though, however much Thoreau admired the older man's punishing forcefulness, he was a different man from Brown. Ellery Channing expressed the painful distinction when he said of Thoreau, "His was a more sour and saturnine hatred of injustice, his life was more passive, and he lost the glory of action which fell to the lot of Brown" (*Thoreau*, 244–245). That fundamental passivity is detectable in his far from ringing declaration: "I do not wish to kill nor to be killed, but I can foresee circumstances in which both of these things would be by me unavoidable" (*RP*, 133). Similarly, one can hear all of Thoreau's suppressed reservations and hostilities in the conclusion of the "Plea." Like several of his works, it ends on an apparently positive note that barely conceals a negative. "Civil Disobedience" finishes by describing "a still more perfect and glorious State, which also I have imagined, but not yet anywhere seen" (*RP*, 90). The problem was there: the desire for perfection in a crooked world could not be gratified. "Slavery in Massachusetts" ends on "manure" (109). Even so ostensibly innocent a subject as "The Succession of Forest Trees" concludes, after comparing the genuine richness of a garden with the tawdry deceptions of village entertainers who so enchant the populace: "Surely, men love darkness rather than light" (*W*, V, 204). So the "Plea" "foresees" a time when the scene of Brown lying wounded on the Armory floor will be, like the landing of the Pilgrims and the signing of the Declaration of Independence, the subject of a painting ornamenting a national gallery. Thoreau then characterized that imagined time: "at least the present form of Slavery shall be no more. We shall then be at liberty to weep for Captain Brown. Then, and not till then, we will take our revenge" (138). So ends the "Plea." Those concluding sentiments are singularly ambiguous, but seem in fact to presage the vindictiveness of Reconstruction to come. Dark and alarming, they foresee but a surface eradication of slavery, while expressions of grief precede those of vengeance.

The rest of this account draws primarily on Thoreau's journals. If moods do not precisely follow chronology, one can nonetheless make some preliminary generalizations about the period from 1854, when *Walden* was published, to 1862, when Thoreau grew very feeble, found it difficult to speak above a whisper, and was often bed-ridden until on May 6 he died (*Days*, 456–466). The last entry in the journal itself was made in the fall of 1861. If one summarizes the subject matter and mood of the journals, the period of 1855 was one of fairly haphazard observation—accounts of walks, of surveying work, and of chance occurrences or stories told Thoreau, especially those involving trapping and hunting. Snapping turtles, snow lice, dead honeybees, and dead fish mark the pages. Although Thoreau seemed hardly conscious of the cumulative morbidity of detail, it was new and relatively concentrated. As a counterbalance, he dug a good deal into the nests of deer mice, muskrat houses, and turtle nests, he caught turtles and flying squirrels, and he brought home eggs and plants. He also looked carefully at various animal droppings. Then in the spring of 1855 Thoreau suffered the onslaught of a disorder that doctors could not diagnose. "I have been sick and good for nothing but to lie on my back and wait for something to turn up, for two or three months," he wrote H. G. O. Blake on June 28th (*Corr.*, 376).

As Thoreau moved through 1855–1856, there was a spate of discovery of bodies and bones that did not relent until late 1856, but that was essentially gone by early 1857, when, at least in his journal, Thoreau seemed inspired, confident, and lyrical again. This positive mood continued into 1858. Thoreau was calm, observant, tolerant, and rarely defensive. If not often lyrical either, he was informed and independent in his reporting. He could both accept his role and appreciate eccentricity, especially that associated with age. At this point, Thoreau was working steadily at surveying.

April 1858 was his frog spawn and fish ova month. He did a lot of close inspection and collection and into May noted instances of amphibian coupling. The specific marks and features of his world also preoccupied him in the later years of the journal. During 1858 and 1859, he made many crude drawings of animal tracks, of ice, of feathers, of acorns, of water currents, as well as of an Indian eel-pot, davits, houses, and bridges. In the summer of 1859 he studied the Concord River in detail, observing that "I find myself very heavy-headed these days. It occurs to me that probably in different states of what we call health, even in morbid states, we are peculiarly fitted for certain investigations,—we are the better able to deal with certain phenomena" (*J*, XII, 242). In 1860, trees and in particular wood-lots engrossed him, even as the river had the year before. By 1861, though, the entries thin out, are fairly random, and often concern things that were brought to Thoreau for his inspection, or things he had heard or read. The impression made is weak and desultory.

It is often asserted that in these years Thoreau lost his appetite for making transcendental extensions of natural fact and found himself earth-bound by his inability to do more than report statistics and the dimensions of what he observed. But that is really not accurate. For the sake of a convenient contrast, both Thoreau's symbolizing propensities as a youth and his devotion to fact as an adult are exaggerated. It is true that as early as 1851 Thoreau felt apprehensive about the constriction of his powers. "I fear that the character of my knowledge is from year to year becoming more distinct and scientific. . . . I see details, not wholes nor the shadow of the whole. I count some parts, and say, 'I know' " (*J*, II, 406). But the evidence of his journal shows that this was a needless fear. The volume of his moralizing was certainly reduced. As Thoreau mordantly observed in arguing that New England as a whole had become more pedestrian, "Our winged thoughts are turned to poultry" ("Walking," *W*, V, 244). But his observations remained sharp, even though they yielded to troublesome realities, as when he described his family's cat, Min, having captured and played with a mouse, now sitting, paws tucked under, watching the mouse steal away, when suddenly a robust rooster belonging to a neighbor seizes the mouse by the tail, whacks it on the ground, tosses it in the air, and swallows it whole, all to the apparent indifference of the watching cat (*J*, IX, 154–155).

Thoreau was gradually being forced into dubious acceptance of the given. One can hear him struggling to comprehend his disaffection, confused but yielding to such inexorable verities of the world as disease. In 1851, the year he lost all his teeth, Thoreau tried valiantly to make sense of such deterioration. "It is a very remarkable and significant fact," he wrote in his journal on September 3, "that, though no man is quite well or healthy, yet every one believes practically that health is the rule and disease the exception." Having perceived this unsettling truth, Thoreau then sought to turn it to a positive end. If disease "is one of the permanent conditions of life," it is a cheerful one, because it signals a struggle between man's spirit and his materiality. "Seen in this light, our life with all its diseases will look healthy, and in one sense the more healthy as it is the more diseased." Thoreau had grasped some powerful possibilities, but, lacking a world view that could contain them, he was forced to revert to a crude Manicheanism. "Life is a warfare, a struggle, and the diseases of the body answer to the troubles and defeats of the spirit. In proportion as the spirit is the more ambitious and persevering, the more obstacles it will meet with" (*J*, II, 449–450).

We can see the problems in this argument. Thoreau was not clear whether the appearance of disease signaled the onset of a battle between body and spirit ("Man begins by quarreling with the animal in him, and the result is immediate disease"), or whether it meant that the body was prevailing ("the diseases . . . answer to the . . . defeats of the spirit"), or whether disease was a sign of a triumphant spirit ("In proportion as the spirit is the more ambitious . . . the more obstacles"). What was clear was that Thoreau was being forced to concede the normality of sickness in life and to entertain such paradoxes as that the healthy life is the diseased one.

By October of 1851, Thoreau was lamenting the fact that he was struggling less, that he was accepting his animality—what he called his "meanness"—without remorse. "I seem to be more constantly merged in nature; my intellectual life is more obedient to nature than formerly, but perchance less obedient to spirit. I have less memorable seasons. I exact less of myself. I am getting used to my meanness, getting to accept my low estate. O if I could be discontented with myself! If I could feel anguish at each descent!" (*J*, III, 66). The irony of Thoreau's lament is manifest, since even if his complacency was brought on by the passage of time, it was nonetheless the means for him to live the calmer and more tolerant life readily visible on the Allagash trip.

Now, to return to the original point: it is true that Thoreau sometimes complained about being limited to factuality, but his journal provides less evidence of this than of his preoccupation with such of the dismal facts of nature as were resistant to being transformed into positive symbols. "I would fain make two reports in my Journal, first the incidents and observations of to-day; and by to-morrow I review the same and record what was omitted before, which will often be the most significant and poetic part" (*J*, IX, 306). Often enough, though, only the record was made, not the succeeding interpretation. And for good reason. In the same entry Thoreau added: "I do not know at first what it is that charms me. The men and things of to-day are wont to lie fairer and truer in to-morrow's memory" (*J*, IX, 306). But that could not always be the case. Sights could "charm" him in the sense of attracting his attention and remaining sufficiently prominent in his memory for him to record their presence, but then fail to prove susceptible to an interpretation that could stress the presence of the fair and the true. It is spring, 1854: "I read to-day that a boy found twenty-six bluebirds dead in a hollow tree"—"Saw a dead sucker yesterday"—"Saw a flattened toad on the sidewalk"—"Saw floating a good-sized rooster without a head,—the red stump sticking out" (*J*, VI, 206, 192, 171, 181). Thoreau noted many other instances of mutilation, of killing, of carcasses, but he dared not attempt to incorporate them into his system of assumptions, for they would tear that ramshackle system to pieces. Still, he recorded them, for they served as undeveloped symbols of what was troubling him about his fundamental relationship to the world.

As late as 1858, Thoreau expressed at length his pleasure in the water lily, which led to this statement: "It is the emblem of purity. It reminds me of a young country maiden. It is just so simple and unproved. Wholesome as the odor of the cow . . . a simple maiden on her way to school, her face surrounded by a white ruff. But how quickly it becomes the prey of insects!" (*J*, XI, 70–71). There the comparison finishes, incomplete. What of the maiden? What of the brief tenure of her purity? Is everyone certain prey to insects? Whatever conclusions concerning human life Thoreau might have drawn from his reactions to the lily, he resolutely balked at following out the full implications of his symbol.

As a young man, in "Natural History of Massachusetts," Thoreau had confidently advanced the credo that "In society you will not find health, but in nature. . . . Society is always diseased. . . . There is no scent in it so wholesome as that of the pines. . . . To the sick, indeed, nature is sick, but to the well, a fountain of health" (*W*, V, 105). But, as the years passed, he had to confront the conflicting evidence. On the first of September 1851 he asked himself, "Is not disease the rule of existence? There is not a lily pad floating on the river but has been riddled by insects. . . . If misery loves company, misery has company enough. Now, at midsummer, find me a perfect leaf or fruit" (*J*, II, 440). Now this was written three years before the publication of *Walden*, when several drafts of the book remained to be written, but Thoreau was not going to tear apart the affirmative message of the book as formulated in 1845–1846 at the pond. Nonetheless, he had already conceived a more complex conception of existence, one that, as we have seen, left its dark stain even on *Walden*. By 1858, again only the record was made, without a conclusion being drawn: "I see a pout this afternoon in the Assabet, lying on the bottom near the shore, evidently diseased. . . . Nearly half the head, from the snout backward diagonally, is covered with an inky-black kind of leprosy. . . . It moves with difficulty" (*J,* XI, 87).

Disease in nature, *natural* corruption, was not all that Thoreau had to endure. Slow death by infection graduated into wounding, permanent mutilation, and brutal extermination. Animals were killed accidentally, men were killed accidentally, animals killed animals, men killed animals, men killed themselves. These experiences Thoreau really could not make philosophic use of, but they preoccupied him no less. His journals are full of notations of suffering, of suffering neither used to point a moral nor responded to with sympathy, although they were sometimes crossed with an unspoken irony. "I asked Coombs the other night if he had been a-hunting lately. He said he had not been out but once this fall. He went out the other day with a companion, and they came near getting a fox. They broke his leg. He has evidently been looking forward to some such success all summer. Having done this much, he can afford to sit awhile by the stove at the post-office. He is plotting now how to break his head" (*J,* XI, 350–351).

At other times, Thoreau's record was merely factual. "I see the black feathers of a blackbird . . . which some hawk or quadruped devoured" (*J,* VII, 343). "I have noticed three or four upper jaws of muskrats on the meadow lately, which, added to the dead bodies floating, make more than half a dozen perhaps drowned out last winter" (*J,* VII, 333). "I saw in the pond . . . a mink swimming . . . carrying something by its mouth, dragging it overland. . . . It was a muskrat, the head and part of the fore legs torn off and gone, but the rest still fresh and quite heavy, including hind legs and tail" (*J*, VIII, 22). "We saw a fish hawk eating a fish. . . . He had got the fish under his feet on the limb, and would bow his head, snatch a mouthful, and then look hastily over his right shoulder." In the water beneath, Thoreau found "parts of the fins, entrails, gills"; one fin in particular had "small leeches adhering to it" (*J*, VII, 308). Beneath another branch, where yet another hawk had perched, "many fragments of a pout,—bits of red gills, entrails, fins, and some of the long flexible black feelers. . . . This pout appeared to have been quite fresh, and was probably caught alive" (*J*, VII, 309).

The varieties of slaughter were many and persistent. In one instance, Thoreau seemed on the point of drawing a conclusion. Hearing some splashing in shallow, muddy water, he approached stealthily to discover a mud turtle, which he seized and threw ashore—"and there came out with him a large pout just dead and partly devoured, which he held in his jaws. It was the pout in his flurry and the turtle in his struggles to hold him fast which had created the commotion." Thoreau then imagined at length how the turtle had lain, "probably buried in the mud at the bottom up to his eyes, till the pout came sailing over," then seized it by its "tender white belly. . . . Pouts expect their foes not from below. Suddenly a mud volcano swallowed him up, seized his midriff" (*J*, II, 14–15). The account is so vividly powerful that even Thoreau remarks in an aside, "there are sermons in stone, aye, and mud turtles at the bottom of the pools," but he never preached that sermon. Further (this is May 1850), neither Walden Pond nor its environs would have leeches or turtles to trouble natural existence or to complicate Thoreau's affirmative exhortations. Just once, in a letter on December 5, 1856, to H. G. O. Blake, did Thoreau state the unacceptable: "A cat caught a mouse at the depot, & gave it to her kitten to play with. So that world famous tragedy goes on by night as well as by day, & nature is *emphatically* wrong" (*Corr.*, 443).

Indeed, the carnage was everywhere. "Washed up against this shore, I see the first dead sucker. You see nowadays on every side, on the meadow bottom, the miserable carcasses of the musquash stripped of their pelts" (*J*, VIII, 283). Revulsion played a larger part than sympathy in Thoreau's reaction. He came on a large dead eel hanging on a branch: "What a repulsive and gluttonous-looking creature . . . made to plow the mud and wallow in filth. . . . It is more repulsive to me than a snake. . . . Its dead-white eye-spots . . . and the fringed gelatinous kind of alga or what-not that covered like a lichen the parts submerged made it yet more repulsive" (*J*, X, 114).

When Thoreau did not actually see the misery, he projected it. Coming on a painted turtle in a rut of the road, he observed, "When they get into a rut they find it rather difficult to get out, and, hearing a wagon coming, they draw in their heads, lie still, and are crushed" (*J*, X, 481). If nature failed to furnish examples of the persistence of violence, his neighbors provided a plenitude of evidence, which again, in the late fifties, he recorded without further comment. Reuben Rice's story of "a huddle of men" trying to cut off the head of a mud turtle with a cleaver was set down in zestful detail, as was Rice's account of failing even to injure a goat by striking its skull with a hatchet (*J*, VIII, 32, 25). Jacob Farmer passed along to Thoreau "the head of a gray rabbit which his boy had snared," then a month later told Thoreau "that he once tried to kill a cat by taking her by the legs and striking her head against a stone, but she made off, and in a week was about again, apparently as well as ever" (*J*, VIII, 34, 52–53). This particular spate of violent journal entries occurs during November and December of 1858, although whether the concentration is of special significance is not clear.

Thoreau often found examples of horror or disgust on his rambles. The spectacle of cannibalistic crickets caught his attention in 1857. "There are two broad ruts made by ox-carts loaded with muck, and a cricket has been crushed or wounded every four or five feet in each. It is one long slaughter-house." What was worse, "You may see these crickets now everywhere . . . oftenest three or four together, absorbed in feeding on, *i.e.* sucking the juices of, a crushed companion." After a cart went by, "the survivors each time return quickly to their seemingly luscious feast" (*J*, X, 108).

Thoreau's dilemma was embodied in a journal entry for January 13, 1852. After describing the evanescent transformations of clouds watched in the late afternoon from the Cliffs, he asked himself, "Would not snow-drifts be a good study,—their philosophy and poetry? Are they not worthy of a chapter?" (*J*, III, 186–187). They were, to be sure, and in their pristine clarity easy and attractive for Thoreau. But the messier world of feeling and of blood was ever impinging on him. Thoreau's next paragraph turned to having seen the Wood brothers "snaking trees out of the woods on Fair Haven,—rude Northman work" of the sort that strongly appealed to him, even though their job was the reaping of the forest. Here Thoreau concentrated on the lumbermen's horse, which, growing skittish in face of the falling trees, "began to dash through the woods with his rattling harness on, reckless and horse-like." The gory result seems to have been only an imaginative possibility, but Thoreau fastened on it avidly. The horse was "ready to impale himself upon the first stake and expose his bloody bowels to the air . . . a ghastly sight" (*J*, III, 187). Further, the imagined disaster called up the memory of one actually observed. "I knew one once, tied to a post, that, when a cannon [was] fired, reared and came down upon the post's sharp top, which pierced clean through and came out at his back, impaling him; and so he met his fate and his equine spirit departed" (187).

The evidence of killings affected Thoreau powerfully, eventually overbalancing his idealism. Even when such evidence was not directly forthcoming, his imagination created it, either through the extension of possibility or by consulting his memory. Although this material did not yield itself so smoothly to philosophy and poetry as the snow-drifts might, Thoreau felt compelled nonetheless to collect it, and on at least one occasion—in the ruptured sand-bank of the "Spring" chapter of *Walden*—he made a confused attempt to elevate the jumble of organic existence into affirmation.

Given his numerous accounts of slaughter and the notable paucity of expressions of concern, one might take Thoreau to be callous and unsympathetic. His abrupt harshness at times seemed to support this assumption. But, also, he could not find a way to express his empathy without making himself vulnerable. So, on landing at Quebec, he reported that "a man lay on his back on the wharf, apparently dying, in the midst of a crowd and directly in the path of the horses, groaning, 'O ma conscience!' " This sight produced but a single response from Thoreau, one of quite unparalleled objectivity: "I thought that he pronounced his French more distinctly than any I heard, as if the dying had already acquired the accents of a universal language" (*Yankee,* W, V, 72). Another day, Thoreau went to see Lincoln Bridge, where some ten men had been killed by being swept from the railway cars. "I looked to see if their heads had indented the bridge, if there were sturdy blows given as well as received, and if their brains lay about" (*J,* IX, 175). This defensive and gruesome jocularity quickly turned into a sarcastic attack on the railway company for being executioners without liability.

Very occasionally, Thoreau displayed feelings, especially concerning the killing of domestic animals for their meat. In Canada, although unmoved by the dying man, Thoreau saw a cart loaded with sheep with their legs tied together, "as if the driver had forgotten that they were sheep and not yet mutton,—a sight, I trust, peculiar to Canada, though I fear that it is not" (*Yankee, W,* V, 19). He also revealed in his journal how susceptible to suffering he could be, when he remarked that walking on the road, "There I have freedom in my thought, and in my soul am free. Excepting the omnipresent butcher with his calf-cart, followed by a distracted and anxious cow." Then his indignation burst forth at this exploitation of animal suffering for economic reasons: "Be it known that in Concord, where the first forcible resistance of British aggression was made in the year 1775, they chop up young calves and give them to the hens to make them lay, it being considered the cheapest and most profitable food for them, and they sell the milk to Boston" (*J*, II, 325).

When economic greed was the source of killing, Thoreau was in no doubt where he stood. But the motivations for other kinds of killing—for food, for sport, by accident—left him more ambivalent. Thoreau was faced with the fact that he respected men like Reuben Rice, Jacob Farmer, John Goodwin, the muskrat hunter, and the Indian moose-hunters more than he did the villagers, who, he felt, were not only morally censorious of him but also paid others to do their slaughtering for them—and then complained of the consequences. "I hear that some of the villagers were aroused from their sleep before light by the groans or bellowings of a bullock which an unskillful butcher was slaughtering at the slaughter-house. What morning or Memnonian music was that to ring through the quiet village? What did that clarion sing of? What a comment on our village life! Song of the dying bullock! But no doubt those who heard it inquired, as usual, of the butcher next day, 'What have you got to-day?' 'Sirloin, good beefsteak, rattle-ran,' etc." (*J*, XII, 301).[9]

Such suffering offered easy occasions for indignation. A harder problem Thoreau twice addressed: the trapped muskrat that gnaws off its leg trying to escape. The first time this behavior was described to Thoreau by a reliable source, George Melvin, "our Concord trapper," he responded that he "was not glad to have the story confirmed." He tried to appropriate Melvin's enthusiastic memory of one particular muskrat "that had just gnawed his third leg off, this being the third time he had been trapped; and he lay dead by the trap, for he couldn't run on one leg." Thoreau's reaction was that "such tragedies . . . dignify at least the hunter's trade." His strained explanation for this view was that "even the hunter, naturally has sympathy with every brave effort," so that he "regards with awe his game, and it becomes at last his medicine" (*J*, I, 481–482). There is no evidence that Melvin was either awed or improved by the muskrats' persistent self-mutilation on behalf of freedom, but one can understand Thoreau's need to cast a shielding curtain of words over the grisly and grotesque reality caused by a man whom he admired—as a passionate tribute to Melvin in 1856 indicates. Thoreau reported seeing Melvin with his hound and gun going home in the evening, a sight that produced this: "He follows hunting, praise be to him, as regularly in our tame fields as the farmers follow farming. Persistent Genius! How I respect him and thank him for him!" (*J*, IX, 148). Much more of the same follows.

But Thoreau also had to deal with the misery Melvin caused. Thinking years later "of the tragedies which are constantly permitted in the course of all animal life"—a dangerous but unexplored concession—Thoreau avowed himself improved by contemplating "the muskrat which gnaws its third leg off,—not as pitying its sufferings, but through our kindred mortality, appreciating its majestic pains and its heroic virtue" (*J*, VI, 98–99). It was a rare and central instance of Thoreau trying to reconcile his mind to animals tortured by men. "When I hear the church organ peal, or feel the trembling tones of the bass viol, I see in imagination the musquash gnawing off his leg . . . . which immeasurably dignifies our common fate" (*J*, VI, 99).

Some of Thoreau's suffering came from an affectionate nature that virtually could not express itself. For whatever reason, the possibility of marriage seems to have evaporated rapidly, reenforced by Thoreau's sardonic attitude toward the emptiness of conversation with young women. But, as we have seen, his conditions for friendship were almost as impossible. In 1851–1852 in particular, Thoreau fretted and groaned with frustration. "I think of those to whom I am at the moment truly related," he wrote on January 4, 1851, "with a joy never expressed and never to be expressed, before I fall asleep at night, though I am hardly on speaking terms with them these years" (*J*, II, 137). However opaquely expressed, the yearning in this statement is unmistakable.

Some five years later, positive affection was generated in him by neglect. In a journal entry for December 3, 1856, Thoreau exclaimed: "How I love the simple, reserved countrymen, my neighbors, who mind their own business and let me alone." But consider the turn the entry took next: ". . . who never waylaid nor shot at me, to my knowledge, when I crossed their fields, though each one has a gun in his house!" (*J*, IX, 151). Even after one has made allowance for a dryly humorous exaggeration in those lines, it still remains a thought that would not readily occur to most. Its proposition of violence restrained is as unexpected as is Thoreau's admission that he might have been an annoyance by repeatedly crossing others' property. In *Walden*, by contrast, he had been at pains to assert his superiority to mere land owners who staggered under the burden of mortgages and to insist that he owned the land by the rights conferred on him by his poetic insight. But his mood grew somewhat more conciliatory over the years. Addressing the Middlesex Agricultural Society in 1860, Thoreau told them why he came to the annual cattle show: "I wish to see once more those old familiar faces, whose names I do not know, which for me represent the Middlesex country, and come as near being indigenous to the soil as a white man can" ("The Succession of Forest Trees," *W*, V, 184). And again he acknowledged that he had "been in the habit of going across your lots much oftener than is usual, as many of you, perhaps to your sorrow, are aware" (185). Returning to the journal entry, the mellowing Thoreau continued: "For nearly two-score years I have known, at a distance, these long-suffering

men, whom I never spoke to, who never spoke to me, and now
feel a certain tenderness for them, as if this long probation
were but the prelude to an eternal friendship." We can see
quite clearly where Thoreau's ruminations take a false turn.
There is no doubt that this long, if distant, familiarity was at
last producing a nostalgia, that "certain tenderness" Thoreau
detected in himself. However, the notion that such feelings
presaged an "eternal friendship" was flatly false, being no
more than the stale residue of a Christianity long since lost to
him. But social attitudes associated with New England, concerning endurance and intimacy, put their mark on Thoreau's
response: "What a long trial we have withstood, and how much
more admirable we are to each other, perchance, than if we
had been bedfellows!" (*J,* IX, 151).

Although capable of feeling sentimental about men who
were at best long-time acquaintances, Thoreau was seemingly
writing epitaphs for personal friendship in this year of 1856. "I
had two friends." One of these appears pretty certainly to have
been Emerson: "The one offered me friendship in such terms
that I could not accept it, without a sense of degradation. He
would not meet me on equal terms, but only be to some extent
my patron" (*J,* VIII, 199).

Yet, at a time when his friendship with Emerson was
losing what intimacy it still possessed (if this was Emerson: the
date is October, 1851, and the friendship is said to have been
of "fourteen years" duration), Thoreau could express his
feelings, his needs, in a schematic way. "Ah, I yearn toward
thee, my friend, but I have not confidence in thee. . . . Though
I enjoy thee more than other men, yet I am more disappointed
with thee than with others" (*J,* III, 61). By April of the next
year, the alienation was more directly painful. "I have got to
that pass with my friend that our words do not pass with each
other for what they are worth. . . . He finds fault with me that I
walk alone, when I pine for want of a companion." We glimpse
the terms of the indictment and the degree to which it distressed Thoreau. "Awful as it is to contemplate, I pray that, if I

am the cold intellectual skeptic whom he rebukes, his curse may take effect, and wither and dry up those sources of my life, and my journal no longer yield me pleasure nor life" (*J,* III, 389–390).

If those were the particulars of the rebuke—that Thoreau was a cold, intellectual skeptic—then they were largely, perhaps wholly, wrong. Evidence exists in abundance that Thoreau was a passionate man. His feelings were usually under strict control, however, and, when expressed in public, were likely to be heatedly aggressive rather than warmly appreciative, as in his journal. A few days later, Thoreau tried to make sense out of his emotional behavior, observing: "If I am too cold for human friendship, I trust I shall not be too cold for natural influences. It appears to be a law that you cannot have a deep sympathy with both man and nature. Those qualities which bring you near to the one estrange you from the other" (*J,* III, 400). He offered no evidence for this beyond himself, probably because there was none.

Throughout this period of the early fifties, Thoreau repeatedly returned to the problem to sift the evidence. Accusations rankled, worried, obsessed him. "My nature, it may [be], is secret. Others can confess and explain; I cannot." He imagined saying, "My friends, I am aware of how I have outraged you, how I have seemingly preferred hate to love, seemingly treated others kindly and you unkindly, sedulously concealed my love, and sooner or later expressed all and more than all my hate." But he felt that "I am under an awful necessity to be what I am" (*J,* III, 146).

The concessive part of such admissions displays the extent of Thoreau's inhibitions. He was undemonstrative, not given to expressing confidences, and, when his feelings *were* expressed, it was likely to be in an emotional outburst such as Thoreau described as "all and more than all my hate." We see it directly in Thoreau's attacks on Concord farmers in *Walden,* in his disgust with material greed in "Life Without Principle," and in the heat of his "Plea for Captain John Brown." A particularly powerful instance was the explosive attack on Flint's farm in *Walden*. More often, Thoreau's critical anger was expressed in offhand ironies that, by repeated expression, tended to vent the explosive force.

But Thoreau could not confess his weaknesses for long before he felt the need to reenforce his self-esteem. Was he cold? "It is not that I am too cold, but that our warmth and coldness are not of the same nature; hence when I am absolutely warmest, I may be coldest to you" (*J*, III, 147). This familiar resort to paradox was no solution, though. The metaphorical possibility was perhaps closer to the truth. "I am of the nature of stone. It takes the summer's sun to warm it" (*J*, III, 147). Thoreau could only argue that he differed in kind, not that he lacked feeling. "That I am cold means that I am of another nature" (*J*, III, 147). The problem preoccupied him. In those closing days of 1851, he felt a need to understand the gravamen of his friends' accusations. The next day he returned to the subject with yet another defense. "If I am thus seemingly cold compared with my companion's warm, who knows but mine is a less transient glow, a steadier and more equable heat" (*J*, III, 148).

In the long run, the stone image probably came closer to Thoreau's character than the others. In the *Week*, he had referred to "the stucco which overlies the heart," and in February 1852, as he described the day's condition, marked by a "frozen snow-crust" everywhere, he observed that "I can with difficulty tell when I am over the river," then added, quite gratuitously, "There is a similar crust over my heart" (*Week*, 269; *J*, III, 313).

The long years of protective reserve made it hard to penetrate to Thoreau's feelings, but the estrangement from his friends, and especially their complaints, could sting him, even as he could feel a longing for human contact beneath his crusted surface. One obtains a perspective on Thoreau's behavior from Horace Hosmer, who was as respectful of

Thoreau as he was contemptuous of the Concord villagers. Hosmer remembered that his brother Benjamin, who had been a schoolmate of John and Henry Thoreau, made a special trip to Walden in 1846 "and was coolly received. Henry said that 'he had not time for friendship,' and closed the volume. I remembered it, and only met him in the woods and fields with a pride equal to his own. I never hesitated to pass him without speaking unless I had something to ask about, or to show." Hosmer added later: "Do not misunderstand my saying that Henry did not speak to me. There was no reason why he should, simply a fact."[10] So the aloof manner was a familiar one, easy enough for Thoreau to fall into and readily taken for coldness. In 1852, Thoreau perceived with the utmost clarity what had happened to him in his social world. "If I have not succeeded in my friendships," he wrote in his journal, "it was because I demanded more of them and did not put up with what I could get; and I got no more partly because I gave so little" (*J*, III, 262). Thoreau could not often articulate his failings so directly, so simply, and so undefensively.

Thoreau's lock on his emotions not only permitted him to survive in a world he often regarded as dangerous and disgusting, it seems also to have largely inured him from being affected by pain, even when he was the cause. For example, he says of pickerel: "I have seen a large one with a deep white wound from a spear, cutting him half in two, unhealed and unhealable, fast asleep, and forked him into my boat. I have struck a pickerel sound asleep and knew that I cut him almost in two, and the next moment heard him go ashore several rods off; for being thus awakened in their dreams they shoot off . . . without considering exactly to what places they shall go" (*J*, II, 15–16). Perhaps Thoreau believed that fish felt no pain. Still, he invariably spoke of them in human terms—they sleep, they dream, and when startled they do not consider their course exactly. Thoreau displayed no feeling whatsoever about the method he used—forking—nor about the shock of the surprise attack he made on the sleeping pickerel.

We know that Thoreau also trapped woodchucks and once accidentally caught a skunk when trying to protect his bean field.[11] Further, he set outdoor traps for mice, evidently in order to obtain specimens. The process was difficult—"I have caught a mouse at last"—and yet "all the flesh is eaten out and part of the skin; one fore foot eaten off, but the entrails left" (*J*, VII, 187). For this reason his measurements were uncertain that day. However, four days later: "I have caught another of those mice of February 16th and secured it entire,—a male" (*J*, VII, 197). And February 21, "Another *Arvicola Emmonsii*, a male" (*J*, VII, 202).

One can never tell how Thoreau will respond. In the autumn of 1857, he came across "a large box trap closed" in which he found a dead rabbit. The trap had evidently floated away in a flood, so that the trapper had not found it when he returned to check. The rabbit then starved to death. Thoreau's reaction was: "What a tragedy to have occurred within a box in one of our quiet swamps!" He then dramatized the scene. "After days and nights of moaning and struggle, heard for a few rods through the swamp, increasing weakness and emaciation and delirium, the rabbit breathes its last. They tell you of opening the tomb and finding by the contortions of the body that it was buried alive. This was such a case." But this emotional re-creation was local, specific, temporal. It produced no reflection in Thoreau on, let us say, the feelings of the mice he trapped—especially the one possibly dismembered while still alive—for scientific observation. He did, however, propose one influence the event might have. "Let the trapping boy dream of the dead rabbit in its ark, as it sailed, like a small meeting-house with its rude spire, slowly, with a grand and solemn motion, far amid the alders" (*J*, X, 77–78). This is a quite original and dignified scene Thoreau has conjured up, mysterious and moving, but of imponderable significance to the posited instigator, "the trapping boy." What seems to have happened is that Thoreau moved through the scene of live burial, couched in conventionally melodramatic terms, to an imagined scene of stately acceptance of death, which was very important for him but quite inconsequential for either the rabbit or the rabbit's effect on the boy. Thoreau quite lacked a consistent position on imposed death. The mixed thoughts of "Higher Laws" in *Walden* were as close as he came to systematically reaching a position that could reconcile both his feelings and his observations.

So, in *Cape Cod*, Thoreau could pass on horrendous information on how to catch snapping turtles: "His own method of catching them was to put a toad on a mackerel-hook and cast it into a pond, tying the line to a stump or stake on shore. Invariably the turtle when hooked crawled up the line to the stump, and was found waiting there by his captor, however long afterward" (202). If there is not a word about the suffering endured, it is presumably because Thoreau could identify more readily with a rabbit than a snapping-turtle. Still, this argues a certain failure of imagination, or perhaps the superior force of pleasure taken in man's ingenious traps.

In *Walden*, Thoreau spoke with a cheerful ferocity when he said that "once I went so far as to slaughter a woodchuck which ravaged my beanfield,—effect his transmigration, as a Tartar would say,—and devour him" (59). A more subtle example of this kind of emphasis on violence comes again in *Walden* as Thoreau described the sumach's growth as being such in August that the weight of "the large masses of berries" "bent down and broke the tender limbs" (114). "Tender limbs" is a phrase that enhances the shock of the bush's self-mutilation. Thoreau appeared to try to control the world's vulnerability by displaying and even emphasizing it. At other times, his anger flared forth in descriptions of incoherently surrealistic force. Speaking of the government in his "Plea for

Captain John Brown," Thoreau described it as "A semi-human tiger or ox, stalking over the earth, with its heart taken out and the top of its brain shot away" (*RP*, 129).

Elsewhere, the imagery of hurt stayed with Thoreau. Of crows he wrote, "they often burst up above the woods where they were perching, like the black fragments of a powder-mill just exploded" (*J*, XIV, 101). Something in him translated natural scenes into wounds, vulnerability, the violent exposure of vitals. On the way to Canada by rail, he noticed the woodbine, "its leaves now changed, for the most part on dead trees, draping them like a red scarf." The sight, he said, "was a little exciting, suggesting bloodshed, or at least a military life, like an epaulet or sash, as if it were dyed with the blood of the trees whose wounds it was inadequate to stanch" (*Yankee, W*, V, 3). The association with blood was perhaps readily available, but its gory elaboration, apropos of nothing in particular, suggests Thoreau's special preoccupation with blood-spilling.

In "Autumnal Tints," Thoreau remarked that the leaves of the scarlet oak gave the impression of having "been dipped into a scarlet dye" and that "the whole tree is much like a heart in form, as well as in color" (*W*, V, 281). Further, seeing some scarlet oaks alternating with white pines in a grove, he said they "look like soldiers in red amid hunters in green" (*W*, V, 283). This comparison offered vivid imagery without turning to blood or its production. However, in his journal on September 29, 1854, when the scarlet oak leaves were just turning in places, Thoreau saw gore: "In many cases these leaves have only begun to be sprinkled with bloody spots and stains,— sometimes as if one had cast up a quart of blood from beneath and stained them" (*J*, VII, 59–60).

I would not exaggerate the pressure of such imagery in Thoreau's mind. His class in the nineteenth century was more regularly and directly exposed to blood (and he himself, as well as his sister Helen, was fatally tubercular). Horace Hosmer tells us of five tons of soldier's white shirts being shipped from the Crimean War to a paper mill on the Assabet

River, "just as they were taken off the dead bodies, matted with blood, and were made into writing paper." Hosmer continues that "there must have been the blood of 10000 men coloring the waters of our beautiful river. I sometimes thought the cardinal flowers, and the Maple leaves in Autumn were tinged with it." To which he adds, mordantly, "Poets will please take notice" (*Remembrances*, 63–64).

Thoreau's preoccupation with blood, then, was hardly unique. But it does join a pattern that includes mutilation, bowels, liquidity, and sex. In "Autumnal Tints," Thoreau brings together several journal entries on the pokeweed, in which "blood" has a mixture of meanings. The pokeweed's color is essentially purple, which Thoreau also regards as a form of red—"I love to see any redness in the vegetation"— and blood-colored—"Nature here is full of blood and heat and luxuriance" (*J*, II, 489, 490). Its very swollen, even bursting, fullness stimulated him: "It speaks to my blood" (*J*, II, 489). He was sensuously ravished by it. "I love to press these berries between my fingers and see their rich purple wine staining my hand" (*J*, II, 489). His revision of the passage for "Autumnal Tints" makes his interpretation more specific: "It is the emblem of a successful life concluded by a death not premature, which is an ornament to Nature" (*W*, V, 254–255). Thoreau felt no need to conceal the extent of his feelings: "I confess that it excites me to behold them" (*W*, V, 255).

It was Horace Hosmer's opinion that Thoreau "did not have the 'love-idea' in him; i.e. he did not appear to feel the *sex*-attraction" (*Remembrances*, 131). It is certainly the case that, after his handful of youthful infatuations, Thoreau transferred his sexual feelings to nature. In 1856, waxing enthusiastic over a cranberry bog, he noted: "We are so different we admire each other, we healthily attract one another. I love it as a maiden" (*J*, IX, 45). And the next year he exclaimed: "All nature is my bride." His feelings seemed to him "like a youth's affection for a maiden, but more enduring!" (*J*, IX, 337). On the other hand, he did enclose the essays "Love" and "Chastity & Sensuality" in his September 1852 letter to H. G. O. Blake, showing that he had pondered these related topics. The latter reveals both Thoreau's sense of the centrality of sex and his feeling that discretion about it was the watchword. "The subject of Sex is a remarkable one, since, though its phenomena concern us so much both directly and indirectly, and, sooner or later it occupies the thoughts of all, yet, all mankind, as it were, agree to be silent about it, at least the sexes commonly one to another" (*EE*, 274).

Thoreau believed "that it is unusual even for the most intimate friends to communicate the pleasures and anxieties connected with this fact" (*EE*, 274). That, of course, was partly because he had so few close friends and partly because he had a very attenuated notion of love. "All lusts or base pleasures must give place to loftier delights," and "the only excuse for reproduction is improvement" (*EE*, 275, 278). With this elevated standard, Thoreau was not likely to hear very much conversation on sex. Someone, probably Ellery Channing, offended—no, *hurt*—Thoreau by his habitual "coarse jesting of facts which should always be treated with delicacy and reverence." He could not bear to hear the relations of men and women reduced "to a level with that of cats and dogs" (*J*, III, 406, 407). Talk of sex was virtually off-limits in any practical sense. "Each man's mode of speaking of the sexual relation proves how sacred his own relations of that kind are. We do not respect the mind that can jest on this subject" (*J*, III, 335). Thoreau even believed in whipping twelve-year-old boys and sending them to bed for the sin of "impurity" (*J*, II, 341). And, at the age of thirty-seven, he had developed a distinctly ascetic view of the affliction. "Love tends to purify and sublime itself. It mortifies and triumphs over the flesh, and the bond of its union is holiness" (*J*, VI, 75).

The problem was that the topic could not be kept suppressed. Thoreau himself ultimately conceded: "Nature allows of no universal secrets. The more carefully a secret is kept on one side of the globe, the larger the type it is printed in on the other." He noted with distress or amazement that "in spite [of] whitewash and brick walls and admonitions," the salacious rhymes boys scribbled on privy walls survived. As he continued to brood on this phenomenon, Thoreau temporarily reached a profound truth. Those rhymes, he realized, were "no doubt older than Orpheus, and have come down from an antiquity as remote as mythology or fable. . . . Filth and impurity are as old as cleanliness and purity. To correspond to man completely, Nature is even perhaps unchaste herself" (*J*, III, 255). In this entry, Thoreau had in fact already expanded on Nature's license. "Nothing is too pointed, too personal, too immodest, for her to blazon. The relations of sex, transferred to flowers, become the study of ladies in the drawing-room. While men wear fig leaves, she grows the *Phallus impudicus* and *P. caninus* and other phallus-like fungi" (*J*, III, 255).

Had he absorbed it, this series of observations might have constituted a permanent revelation for Thoreau. But in fact it was later in the same year that he sent Blake his essays "Love" and "Chastity & Sensuality." There was a lack of continuity in Thoreau's thinking; much of it was sporadic and incidental, with new and potentially liberating truths being advanced but then subsequently forgotten or displaced by attitudes powerfully established early in his life. For example, he had apparently never seen the mushroom *Phallus impudicus* in 1852, and when he did at last come across one in October 1856, he characterized it as "in all respects a most disgusting object, yet very suggestive" (*J*, IX, 116). After describing its shape in fascinated detail, and after expressing his revulsion at its swift decomposition and fetid smell, he exclaimed, "Pray, what was Nature thinking of when she made this? She almost puts herself on a level with those who draw in privies" (*J*, IX, 117). But only four years earlier Thoreau had thought through that problem and at least for the moment had come to a philosophic reconciliation with Nature's immodesty. Now in

1856 he encountered *Phallus impudicus* with all the astonished chagrin of a fledgling. Perpetual renewal of springtime innocence incurred severe costs.

Rather than face or hear of the operative vulgarity of sexual behavior, Thoreau was liable to invest his occasional powerful feelings in confused dithyrambs. He set down two passionate addresses to a "sister" in 1849 and 1850. The first, still unpublished as a whole, has been attributed to Thoreau's grief at the loss of his sister Helen when she finally succumbed to her tuberculosis on June 14, 1849. But one sentence in the passage says, "Others are of my kindred by blood or of my acquaintance, but you are mine" (HM13182, II, 15 verso). This does not exclude Helen, but we do know that Thoreau and others of the Concord persuasion were inclined to designate as "sister" someone to whom they were very close. In Thoreau's case, for example, he wrote to Lidian Emerson in 1843: "I think of you as some elder sister of mine. . . . You must know that you represent to me woman" (*Corr.*, 103).

The three-page fragment entitled by him "A Sister" runs on in spasmodic gasps of feeling, characterizing what a sister is but with an intensity that constitutes a kind of imaginative possession. "You are of me & I of you, I cannot tell where I leave off and you begin" (HM13182, II, 15 verso). Thoreau distinguished this fusion from carnal possession. "I can more heartily meet her when our bodies are away. I see her without the veil of the body" (II, 16 recto). And yet the imagery is of a consolidation of a kind. "When I love you I feel as if I were annexing another world to mine. We splice the heavens" (II, 16 recto). Or more explicitly: "Whom in thought my spirit continually embraces. Into whom I flow" (II, 16 verso). Further, the identities, ages, sexes all become mixed, merged, transferred. She is "the feminine of me." Then, "In the hushed dawn—my young mother—I thy eldest son . . . ." "Whether art thou my mother or my sister—whether am I thy son or thy brother" (II, 16 verso).[12]

The dizzied passion of these pages has but a single counterpart in all of Thoreau's writing. It is a journal entry very similar to this fragment. Again there is a crossover of identities. "I am as much thy sister as thy brother. Thou art as much my brother as my sister." There is the romantic location of the relationship in morning freshness. "Thy dewy words feed me like the manna of the morning." And there is the impassioned need for a passive mingling: "My dear, my dewy sister, let thy rain descend on me" (*J*, II, 78).

Suggestively heightened imagery and spiritualized sexual longing are familiar phenomena in the lyrics of an inhibited age. So far as we know, Thoreau had never experienced sexual relations with anyone. But he did not renounce sexuality to adopt formally the ascetic life like the Catholic convert Isaac Hecker. He did not marry like Emerson. He did not turn to males for solace nor invent female liaisons for the public like Whitman. Nor was he a dry, intellectualized, passionless creature. Consequently, as seen in his appreciation of the rich purple of the pokeweed blossom, this long chastity had its effect.

There is also Thoreau's well-known appreciation of a shrub oak. The passage is interesting, even challenging, because one cannot determine with certainty whether it is touched with humor or not. Nonetheless, should one decide that it is, the conditions described in the passage are absolutely consistent with Thoreau's feelings.

I love and could embrace the shrub oak with its scanty garment of leaves rising above the snow, lowly whispering to me, akin to winter thoughts, and sunsets, and to all virtue. Covert which the hare and the partridge seek, and I too seek. What cousin of mine is the shrub oak? How can any man suffer long? For a sense of want is a prayer, and all prayers are answered. Rigid as iron, clean as the atmosphere, hardy as virtue, innocent and sweet as a maiden is the shrub oak. In proportion as I know and love it, I am natural and sound as a partridge. I felt a positive yearning toward one bush this afternoon. There was a match found for me at last. I fell in love with a shrub oak.

(*J*, IX, 146)

Reviewing Thoreau's indirect sexual expressions, one sees that he began, as in "Sic Vita" and "The Gentle Boy," by expressing his sense of loss and of loneliness, trying to attract pity or taking comfort in self-pity. Then, with Lidian Emerson and the other "sisters," he etherealized the possible relationship between them. In the early fifties he consciously translated (as we shall see in a moment) his sexual feeling into artistic creation or into his bee-like flights through the fields. In another five years the iron hardiness of the shrub oak was attracting him. Finally, there was a period in 1857–1858 when he no longer overtly expressed yearnings but, rather, carefully observed sexual behavior in the natural world.

During 1851 and 1852, Thoreau utilized procreative imagery to express his relationship to his materials. "How many ova have I swallowed? Who knows what will be hatched within me" (*J*, II, 393). He argued that the artist must approach his subject with passion. "It is in vain to write on chosen themes. We must wait till they have kindled a flame in our minds. There must be a copulating and generating force of love behind every effort destined to be successful" (*J*, III, 253). His forays into the fields seemed to him to produce a reciprocating impregnation: "While I am abroad, the ovipositors plant their seeds in me; I am fly-blown with thought, and go home to hatch and brood over them" (*J*, II, 339). Although insect and poultry behavior are mixed here, the meaning is clear enough. Two months later in this deep summer of 1851, Thoreau reversed the roles: "I ramble over all fields . . . and am never so happy as when I feel myself heavy with honey and wax." Could Thoreau have thought that bees brought honey and wax home to the hive from flowers? Evidently, for later in this same quotation he says: "Where is the flower, there is the honey,—which is perchance the nectareous portion of the fruit." Therefore, the honey "is a foretaste of the future fruit" (*J*, II, 470–471). The journal entry also remarks: "I am like a bee searching the livelong day for the sweets of nature. Do I not impregnate and intermix the flowers, produce rare and finer varieties by transferring my eyes from one to another?" (*J*, II, 470).

In the later eighteen-fifties, Thoreau temporarily recorded, as he never had to this degree, such sexual congress as he observed. This entry is typical: "I saw wood tortoises coupled, up the Assabet, the back of the upper above the water. It held the lower with its claws about the head, and they were not to be parted" (*J*, X, 115). Of frogs: "I see one or two pairs coupled, now sinking, now rising to the surface" (*J*, X, 351). Another spring day, Thoreau stood barefoot in a meadow pond: "There are a hundred toads close around me, copulating or preparing to" (*J*, IX, 354). Elsewhere, reptilian union was observed, and speculation was reported concerning the propagation of eels and of leeches. (*J*, IX, 371, and X, 343; X, 429, and X, 350).

These metaphors, observations, and discussions were signs of a sexuality generally suppressed and now either permanently discouraged or waning because of illness and the advance of years. In some ways, Thoreau was less defensive in his last years, less given to spiritualizing his feelings and more proccupied with the physical world around him. On the other hand, he also felt with less intensity, except at sporadic moments, as in the one last, prolonged, angry spasm of his defense of John Brown.

An undercurrent of despair still darkened Thoreau's accommodation to such pedestrian enjoyments as the autumnal tints of leaves and the flavor of wild apples. Thoreau was virtually silent as a poet after 1854, writing only a handful of poems, some of which were marked by a severe, if not openly stated, pessimism. One, on a wild apple tree, reads:

> In two years' time 't had thus
>   Reached the level of the rocks,
> Admired the stretching world
>   Nor feared the wandering flocks.
>
> But at this tender age
>   Its sufferings began;
> There came a browsing ox
>   And cut it down a span.
> (*Poems*, 20)

Seen in this austere version, the poem compels a feeling of being undeservedly cut off, of suffering commenced and, by implication, indefinitely continued. The journal version adds two more lines that hardly modify the tone: "Its heart did bleed all day, / And when the birds were hushed,—" (*J*, X, 139). When incorporating this poem into the essay "Wild Apples," however, Thoreau added positive details in the prose. The tree "thus cut down annually . . . does not despair" (*W*, V, 303). Rather, it grows two twigs for every one removed, and, in time, thorns. This was an acceptable enough extension of the original, but it was not the direction in which Thoreau was originally impelled to go. Like "Sic Vita," the early poem whose central image is of the poet as "a parcel of vain strivings," but to which is added a coda making him a useful sacrifice, here Thoreau attempted to neutralize the destructive browsing of the ox on the tender tree.

The essay-lecture "Wild Apples" itself, however appreciative, also ends in a dying fall. The pleasure of the fruit's taste for Thoreau was its tang, "the wild and sharp," "rich and spicy" flavor, which he compared favorably to that of the domesticated fruit, which too often "turn out very tame and forgettable" (*W*, V, 312, 311, 310). These were outdoors apples that "*pierce* and *sting* and *permeate* us with their spirit" (311). Quite understandably, the wild apple gave Thoreau a chance to celebrate what he knew and appreciated, "the sours and bitters of Nature" (313). No assumed ideal world was posited, no ugliness had to be suppressed. Thoreau found a comic joy in praising one wild apple tree whose fruit "smells exactly like a squash-bug," but he nonetheless relished its "peculiarly pleasant bitter tang" (312). To learn to savor what you have is a classic mark of wisdom.

And yet Thoreau could never forget that even the pleasures of the "gnarly," the "crabbed," and the "rusty" must end (314). His imagination ever returned to its true north, the dismal. "The era of the Wild Apple will soon be past" (321). Hence Thoreau chose to conclude this sunnily realistic essay with a series of diatribes from the prophet Joel, ending: "the apple-tree, even all the trees of the field, are withered; because joy is withered away from the sons of men" (322). Judging by the reasons offered for it, Joel's harsh negativity was excessive for the case. For example, Thoreau attributed the decline of the wild apple in part to "the general introduction of grafted fruit" (321). However, the grafting of apple trees was precisely what Thoreau had counseled in "Ktaadn" for the apple trees of Enfield, for they bore only "natural fruit" and were therefore, Thoreau thought, "comparatively worthless for want of a grafter" (*Maine Woods*, 8). In "Wild Apples," he also doubted that "so extensive orchards are set out to-day in my town as there were a century ago," but this seems dubious, and, even if true, the conclusions of doom set down from the Old Testament remain much in excess of the consequences predicted (321). "Awake, ye drunkards, and weep; and howl, all ye drinkers of wine, because of the new wine; for it is cut off from your mouth" (322). The apocalyptic violence of these quotations in context is astonishing. Their presence is explicable only by referring to Thoreau's constitutional pessimism. He may have learned acceptance and celebration of the given, but he still could not prevent his sense of impending misery from entering his work.

Similar shadows fall over "Walking." Drawn from journal material composed largely from 1850 to 1852, the essay was revised several times, used as a lecture, and finally submitted to the *Atlantic* just before Thoreau's death. Again, this is a long essay, singing a subject close to Thoreau's heart. Nonetheless, there are spots of revelatory power in it, suggesting Thoreau's somberness. He refers, for example, to being "in doleful dumps" during the "awful stillness" of an oppressive Christian Sunday, a condition happily broken by a rooster crowing (*W*, V, 246). He also commiserated with mechanics and shopkeepers for having to remain seated indoors all day—"I think that they deserve some credit for not having all committed suicide long ago" (*W*, V, 208). Suicide turns up in "Autumnal Tints" as well, when he invokes two villages, one "embowered in trees," the other "a merely trivial and treeless waste, or with only a single tree or two for suicides" (*W*, V, 277). Thinking about the treeless condition of this village, Thoreau imagined that in it "Every wash-tub and milk-can and gravestone will be exposed" and that the consequence of this exposure, of both the tediously pedestrian and the morbid realities of life, would be a population of "the most starved and bigoted religionists and the most desperate drinkers" (277).

So reality unmediated by trees was linked in Thoreau's mind with that maddening religious bigotry that dared to judge him adversely. His indignation, which could erupt against the censorious, and which sometimes expressed itself in an icy mastery over natural things as well as in an imaginative preoccupation with mutilation and death, more often turned inward into depression, into the "doleful dumps" (*W*, V, 246). Again, as a matter of making the best of what he had, and in contrast to the "dull equanimity" of his Concord neighbors, Thoreau avowed his preference for struggling "through long, dark, muggy nights or seasons of gloom" (*W*, V, 241). He rarely complained openly, even in his journal, yet phrases such as that suggest the burden he often carried, especially when unable to divert himself by walks. The daily life he observed seemed, simply, "this trivial comedy or farce" (*W*, V, 241).

Recovery from depression, if not possible through escape into the fields, might come from the sound of a rooster crowing in the distance, or a barking dog. There are times, Thoreau wrote, when "we do not wonder that so many commit suicide, life is so barren and worthless; we only live on by an effort of the will. Suddenly our condition is ameliorated, and even the barking of a dog is a pleasure to us. So closely is our happiness bound up with our physical condition, and one reacts on the other" (*J*, X, 227).

When the dog's bark or cock's crow was absent, Thoreau was in the habit of summoning up the memory of them to survive. "I have lain awake at night many a time to think of the barking of a dog which I had heard long before, bathing my being again in those waves of sound" (*J*, X, 227). And, in the same entry, Thoreau invoked the image, the model, of the animal to inspirit himself. "Do not despair of life. . . . Think of the fox prowling through wood and field in a winter night for something to satisfy his hunger" (*J*, X, 228). The setting and the famished condition of the fox are singularly appropriate for Thoreau's psychological condition—hungry, on a winter's night. In this general context of recurring despair, there is a special poignancy to Thoreau's remark in "A Plea for Captain John Brown" that since the raid on Harper's Ferry, "How many a man who was lately contemplating suicide has now something to live for!" (*RP*, 135).

The artificial stimulation of that event temporarily flooded Thoreau with energy. But it was hardly a permanent condition. Brown's aggression against a dull society touched some of Thoreau's deepest feelings, but since he was not finally a social activist himself, he had to find some other solution or accommodation.

None was forthcoming, though, except endurance, and

the enjoyment of sporadic pleasures derived from no coherent moral system, simply random but genuine moments, and the final resolution of signing off. One can see evidence of Thoreau's confusion in the letter he wrote Blake on January 1, 1859. Among other topics, he referred to a trip made to the White Mountains the previous July, when his party, which included Blake, had camped in Tuckerman's Ravine (*Corr.*, 521, 536–539). This reference then drew forth a long, rambling series of metaphors centered on the idea of the body as a ravine in which the soul is encamped. Critics have found this image a mediating solution, with the ravine marking "the symbolic and actual point at which life as we know it on the plain exists on a mountain."[13] But the metaphor was mechanically employed: "the real *homes* of the citizens are in the Tuckerman's Ravines which ray out from that centre into the mountains round about, one for each man, woman, and child." Thoreau then formally accounted for this situation: "The masters of life have so ordered it. That is their *beau-ideal* of a country seat. There is no danger of being *tuckered* out before you get to it" (*Corr.*, 538).

The facetiousness here signals, I think, Thoreau's awareness of the analogy's weakness. Nonetheless, sensing some available relevance, he continued: "So we live in Worcester and in Concord, each man taking his exercise regularly in his ravine, like a lion in his cage, and sometimes spraining his ankle there. We have very few clear days, and a great many plagues which keep us busy" (538). After another fifteen lines of free association, Thoreau reached a concluding sentence of considerable interest:

> Let us pray that, if we are not flowing through some Mississippi valley which we fertilize—and it is not likely we are,—we may know ourselves shut in between grim and mighty mountain walls amid the clouds, falling a thousand feet in a mile, through dwarfed fir and spruce, over the rocky insteps of slides, being exercised in our minds, and so developed. (539)

This conception of existence was remarkably close to feelings that Thoreau frequently expressed. He might long for and sometimes proclaim that he enjoyed the richness of a Mississippi Valley life, but here he conceded its unlikeliness. As for what he perceived life to be at this point, it might display a certain grandeur, but it was far from attractive, let alone benign—"shut in" as it was by "grim . . . walls amid the clouds" and "dwarfed" trees, with the fundamental action that of "falling." The most Thoreau could recover from this bleak imagery was that the experience of precipitous descent would exercise and thus develop the mind. That had hardly been the case with him, though. His perceptions did clarify and become more various as his idealism slowly evaporated, and he did become more humanly accepting as a man, but, as we have seen, he frequently reverted to positions that he had already implicitly repudiated, so that it may be said that he vacillated rather than developed. He sensed the conditions of his life well enough. What he rarely could do was entertain, let alone accept, the possibility that their harshness served no higher purpose.

Conclusion

What am I at present? A diseased bundle of nerves
standing between time and eternity like a withered leaf
that still hangs shivering on its stem. A more miserable
object one could not well imagine . . . .

Houghton Library MS Am 278.5
[4e] January 16, 1843

FOR ALL HIS INDEPENDENCE and abrasive outspokenness,
Thoreau was an emotionally vulnerable man. His tears when
his mother suggested he seek his fortune in the world, his
falling ill with sympathetic lockjaw after the death of his
brother John, his long brooding on the character of friendship,
his confessional poetry, all attest to the profundity of his
feelings. But, reserved and proud, he tried to protect himself
from the disapproving world. Emerging from college, he
enacted that familiar American ritual, signifying the taking
charge of one's life and making a fresh start: he changed his
name. But he could not change his nature, nor his townsmen's
perception of him. The remarks of one of Concord's farmers
were remembered: "Henry D. Thoreau—Henry D. Thoreau,'

jerking out the words with withering contempt. 'His name ain't no more Henry D. Thoreau than my name is Henry D. Thoreau. And everybody knows it, and he knows it. His name's Da-a-vid Henry and it ain't never been nothing but Da-avid Henry. And he knows that!'"[1]

Those were the conditions under which Thoreau lived, in a village from which it was psychologically unthinkable for him to move permanently. Contemptuous of his materialistic neighbors and undergoing severe psychic strains, he sought to escape the obligations of the social world without wholly losing its protective company. The rest of his life was spent struggling with, adjusting to, and defending the awkward strangeness he felt. His human reactions were likely to be harsh and imaginatively frozen. Annoyed on a boat trip by some twelve-year-old Irish boys, he responded indignantly: "What right have parents to beget, to bring up, and attempt to *educate* children in a city? I thought of infanticide among the Orientals with complacency" (*J*, II, 342). He was often withdrawn, but his silences sometimes yielded to outbursts of angry aggression on the page and occasionally to public scoldings of cold and insulting fury. Morbidity and pessimism were consistent features of his mind. Both in his critical harshness and in his underlying pessimism, Thoreau exhibited classic features of his region's Calvinism, but, unlike his neighbors, he possessed no substantial conviction of an eternal recompense to come. His negativity was frequently in contest with the professed optimism of his era, which he had partially internalized. He tried to substantiate the transcendental hope in nature, but although he did experience moments of authentic affirmation in the domestic wilderness around Concord, he could not reconcile the persistent cruelty and destructiveness of the world (in which he participated, although he hardly seemed aware of it) with this new philosophy. Yet he felt obliged to maintain an affirmative stance, mocking the philistines publicly, and privately assuring himself that, seen with sufficient perception, this was an ideal world or, at the very least, a world ever improving.

The problem was that he did not believe it. At times he set his goal as the uncovering of reality, whatever it might be, with the promise that, should it prove mean or of the devil, or should we all really turn out to be dying, then he would publish that truth to the world. But as he never did, those hypothetical conclusions have been regarded as no more than proof of his objective earnestness, whereas the truth is, they embody his tentative suspicions. Implicitly, Thoreau has been thought to have been saying, life is not that way. He suspected otherwise, however, for he had experienced the crushing indifference of Mt. Katahdin; he had seen the destructive force of the Atlantic; he had observed snapping turtles erupting out of the mud to seize fish from below, men taking axes to turtles, trains crushing men; he had seen the confusions of love, the deceptions of commerce, the corruptions of slavery; he knew the vulnerability of the flesh to disease and had suffered the world's mire and leeches and mosquitoes; so that, even as he gave positive testimony, blood splashed across it. He knew that nature was sometimes foul and slimy, and sometimes cold, granitic, and murderous; and that sometimes it was himself. But he rarely faced these truths directly. Embarking on his career, he had bravely announced, "Let us not underrate the value of a fact; it will one day flower in a truth" ("Natural History of Massachusetts," *W*, V, 130). But faced with a disgusting or terrifying fact, Thoreau might record it (and did increasingly as the years drew on) but that was all. He rarely attempted to follow out its implications. The result was not often the flower of truth, but rather evasion and blur. When he slept it was no better: "Yesterday I was influenced with the rottenness of human relations. They appeared full of death and decay, and offended the nostrils. In the night I dreamed of delving amid the graves of the dead, and soiled my fingers with their rank mould. It was *sanitarily*, *morally*, and *physically* true" (*J*, IV, 472).

Although he set down thousands of pages of journal entries, Thoreau was not a reflective man. Much that would be essential for even a provisional philosophic understanding he left unexplored, unacknowledged, unremembered. The materials that have been at the center of this study are the consequence—fragmentary programs, ambiguous affirmations, metaphorical attacks and punishments, dark hints, and grisly notations. Psychological brakes impeded his progress; psychological blinders limited his perception. He early formulated a justification for them, asserting that "we may well neglect many things, provided we overlook them" (*J*, I, 161).

Eventually, though, the denied elements forced acknowledgment of their presence. As time went on, Thoreau recorded more and more of the mess of existence in all of its unacceptability, but he did so without undertaking any philosophic revisions or extensions. If he were positive, it was likely to be in the vein of: "The water adder killed on the 15th and left hanging on a twig has decayed wonderfully. I perceive no odor and it is already falling to pieces" (*J*, VIII, 424).[2] Over the years, Thoreau did become somewhat calmer and more tolerant, for learning the flaws of the harsh and alarming wilderness and of the Indian had brought him to an appreciation of Concord's ordered domesticity. But his central problems, whether philosophic or personal, which he had carefully skirted for so long, were not dispelled, but only ignored or suppressed, so that their presences kept gnawing at him and giving him pain, which he in turn, sometimes imaginatively, sometimes overtly, imposed on others.

Notes

Preface

1. James McIntosh acknowledges that this passage is "surprising and even disturbing," but feels that it is true to the logic of Thoreau's understanding of the innocence of nature. *Thoreau as Romantic Naturalist* (Ithaca: Cornell University Press, 1974), p. 246.

2. *The Complete Works of Ralph Waldo Emerson*, ed. Edward Waldo Emerson (Boston: Houghton Mifflin, 1903–04), I, 76.

3. *Anton Chekhov's Life and Thought: Selected Letters and Commentary*, selection, commentary, and introduction by Simon Karlinsky (Berkeley: University of California Press, 1975), p. 66.

4. "The Style of Walden," *Dissertation Abstracts* 28 (June 1968): 5069A. See also Raymond Gozzi, "An Incoherent Sentence in *Walden*," *Thoreau Society Bulletin*, no. 95 (Spring 1966): 4–5.

Chapter 1

1. *Lyra Graeca*, ed. and trans. J. M. Edmonds, Loeb Classical Library, (London, 1924), II, 181. The translations that follow are from: *The Works of*

289

Anacreon, Translated into English Verse, trans. John Addison (London, 1735), p. 205; Thomas Moore, *The Works of Thomas Moore, Esq.* (Leipsic, 1833), p. 363; and Thoreau's *Week*, p. 243. The standard edition of Anacreon is *Poetae Melici Graeci*, ed. D. L. Page (Oxford: Oxford University Press, 1962); this poem is no. 72. For recent discussions of it, see G. M. Kirkwood, *Early Greek Monody* (Ithaca: Cornell University Press, 1974), p. 162, and C. M. Bowra, *Greek Lyric Poetry* (Oxford: Oxford University Press, 1961), pp. 271–272.

2. *Thoreau: The Quest and the Classics*, Yale Studies in English, vol. 116 (New Haven, 1951), pp. 20–21.

3. Louise Osgood Koopman, "The Thoreau Romance," *Massachusetts Review* (Autumn 1962): 63. Edmund was assuredly no timid, ethereal angel. "I & one of the boys . . . climbed up to a fissure in the rock. I rolled down a stone which made the boys below jump out of the way." Clayton Hoagland, "The Diary of Thoreau's 'Gentle Boy,' " *New England Quarterly* 28 (December 1955): 476.

4. See Walter Harding, *The Days of Henry Thoreau* (New York, 1970), p. 99. Hereafter, this indispensable resource will be referred to parenthetically in the text as *Days*.

5. For example, "the 'gentle boy' whose beauty is therein commemorated being in fact a gentle girl," writes Henry Salt, after describing the Thoreau brothers' mutual attachment to Ellen Sewall. *Life of Henry David Thoreau* (London, 1890), p. 39. F. B. Sanborn attributes the identification to "the testimony of both Emerson and Theodore Parker, and of other persons who know the facts." *The Life of Henry David Thoreau* (Boston, 1917), p. 351. The whole episode concerning John and Henry Thoreau's relationships with Edmund and Ellen Sewall has properly received much attention. See Walter Harding, *Days*, pp. 94–104; Perry Miller, *CinC*, pp. 82–86, 95–96; Mary Elkins Moller, "Thoreau, Womankind, and Sexuality," *Emerson Society Quarterly* 22, no. 3 (1976): 129–130; and Richard Lebeaux, "Rivals for the Hand of a Maiden," *Young Man Thoreau* (Amherst: University of Massachusetts Press, 1977), pp. 114–140.

6. *Thoreau* (Boston: Houghton Mifflin, 1939; rpt. Boston: Beacon Press, 1958), p. 110.

7. (New York: Crowell, 1976), pp. 481–494. The issue of Edmund and Ellen Sewall is discussed on pp. 483–489.

8. See Lebeaux, "The Death of a Brother," *Young Man Thoreau*, pp. 167–204, for a detailed and plausible discussion of this psychological issue.

9. William Ellery Channing, *Thoreau: The Poet-Naturalist* (Boston, 1873), p. 24.

10. Edward Waldo Emerson, *Henry Thoreau, As Remembered by a Young Friend* (Boston: Houghton Mifflin, 1917), pp. 22, 127.

11. Ibid., p. 21.

12. Ibid., p. viii.

13. Joel Porte has explored this complex problem at length, centering his sympathetic interpretation on the notion of hate as "a rational and dispassionate critical faculty" that in its "overt antipathy to vice represents a covert sympathy with virtue." "Thoreau on Love: A Lexicon of Hate," *The University Review* 31, no. 2 (December 1964): 114. See also his "Love and Thoreau: A Lexicon of Hate," *The University Review* 31, no. 3 (March 1965): 191–194.

Chapter 2

1. Richard Lebeaux proposes that Thoreau "could not bear fully to confront the memories and feelings associated with his brother." *Young Man Thoreau*, pp. 198–199.

2. "T's ascription of the lines to *Britannia's Pastorals*, also by Browne, is incorrect." William Brennan, "An Index to Quotations in Thoreau's *A Week on the Concord and Merrimack Rivers*," *Studies in the American Renaissance, 1980*, ed. Joel Myerson (Boston: Twayne, 1980), p. 267.

3. To be sure, in *Walden* Thoreau said that in his concern for the preservation of the forest, "if any part was burned, though I burned it myself by accident, I grieved with a grief that lasted longer and was more inconsolable than that of the proprietors" (250). But in the journal entry, he not only reduced the amount of forest burned from three hundred to one hundred acres but also asserted, "It has never troubled me from that day to this" (*J*, II, 23). In an article in the *Concord Freeman* of May 3, 1844 (reprinted in the *Thoreau Society Bulletin* 32 [July 1950]), the loss was estimated "at about $2000," including some sixty cords of wood already cut and stacked. The newspaper noted that "the fire, we understand, was communicated to the woods through the thoughtlessness of two of our citizens, who kindled it in a *pine stump*, near the Pond, for the purpose of making a chowder." The newspaper further "hoped that this unfortunate result of sheer carelessness, will be borne in mind by those who may visit the woods in future for recreation."

4. See Edith Seybold on Anacreon's poems: "their whole basis is sensual in any meaning of the word, and only a very innocent mind could deny it." *Thoreau: The Quest and the Classics*, p. 20.

5. Most of the poetry regarded as authentically composed by Anacreon is fragmentary. Only one of the poems Thoreau translated, that addressing "the Thracian filly," is actually by Anacreon. The rest are later imitations, the so-called "Anacreontea," composed from the Hellenistic to the Byzantine periods. Some sixty of these are collected at the end of the Palatine anthology. Thoreau's selections appears in *Anthologia Lyrica*, ed. Theodore Bergk (Leipzig, 1883): "On His Lyre," 23; "To a Swallow," 25; "On a Silver Cup," 3; "On Himself," 26A; "To a Dove," 14; "On Love," 29; "On Women," 24;

292 / Notes (pp. 54–65)

"On Lovers," 26B; "To a Swallow," 9; "Cupid Wounded," 33. They are translated by J. M. Edmonds in *Elegy and Iambus*, Loeb Classical Library (Cambridge, Mass., 1961), numbered: 23, 25, 4, 26, 15, 31, 24, 27, 10, and 35. I have relied on the kind assistance of Professor Thomas G. Rosenmeyer for orientation in the somewhat bewildering world of Anacreon and his imitators.

6. *The Works of Anacreon*, tr. John Addison, p. 53.

7. Ibid., pp. 30–31.

8. The full Cotton ode, "The World," is a good deal more pessimistic—"Oh! who would live that could but die,"—and misanthropic than the excerpt suggests, praying as it does for "solitude in a dark cave," away from man, for "brutes more civil are, and kind." *The Works of the English Poets from Chaucer to Cowper* (London, 1810), VI, 738–739.

9. Henry David Thoreau (New York: William Sloane Associates, 1948; rprt. New York: Delta edition, 1965), p. 33.

10. *Henry Thoreau*, p. 102.

11. See Perry Miller, *CinC*, pp. 86–100, for a fragmentary and sardonic but sharply penetrating discussion of Concord's notions of friendship. It was, Miller writes, "a hunger which dreads satisfaction more than it suffers from deprivation" (93).

12. Richard Lebeaux discusses the relationship of this dream to Thoreau's rivalry with his brother John in *Young Man Thoreau*, pp. 145–146.

13. Thoreau changed the pleasurable scents of "the sweet-fern" in the original journal entry to "the wild honeysuckle"; and he reduced the height of the sun's climb from "three hands' breadth" to two (*J*, I, 141). The changes are inconsequential, but they demonstrate how carefully attentive Thoreau could be in his revisions, as well as how cavalier toward the details of experience.

14. The historical episode and its interpretation have attracted considerable attention, beginning with Cotton Mather's telling of it as a heroic act by a woman beset by "furious tawnies" in the *Magnalia Christi Americana* (Book VII, Article xxv). When Hawthorne retold the story in "The Duston Family," he expressed horror at Hannah Dustan's savagery. (*The American Magazine*, May 1836; reprinted in *Hawthorne as Editor*, ed. Arlin Turner [Baton Rouge: Louisiana State University Press, 1941], pp. 131–137.) This was in 1836, six years before Hawthorne met Thoreau, whose opinion was otherwise. Leslie Fiedler, in *The Return of the Vanishing American* (New York: Stein and Day, 1968), sees Hannah Dustan as a killer woman who ruins the "blithe world for males only." (108). For more recent interpretations, see Richard Slotkin, *Regeneration through Violence* (Middletown: Wesleyan University Press, 1973), p. 523; Robert F. Sayre, *Thoreau and the American Indian* (Princeton: Princeton University Press, 1977), pp. 47–54; and Eric Sundquist, *Home As Found: Authority and Genealogy in Nineteenth-*

Century American Literature (Baltimore: Johns Hopkins University Press, 1979), pp. 61–62. Sundquist's chapter " 'Plowing homeward': Cultivation and Grafting in Thoreau and the *Week*" is a remarkably perceptive reading of the book.

15. The identical language for the wilderness is used repeatedly in "Ktaadn," which was also composed at Walden Pond. See, for example, *MW*, 11, 16, 19, 38, 70.

16. In *Regeneration through Violence*, Richard Slotkin writes: "The eating of the fruit of the tree thus seems a kind of Indian-cannibal-Eucharist," but then elaborates "the sacramental quality" of this point further than I am prepared to go.

17. Lawrence Buell, in *Literary Transcendentalism* (Ithaca: Cornell University Press, 1973), detects a similar sense of unmonitored, pessimistic drift: "In the later stages of the book, perhaps unintentionally, this impression of flux will conspire with the mood of autumn and the awareness of the circularity of the voyage to convey the same sense of fatality that one gets at the end of 'Concord River,' or at least the sense of drifting toward an unknown and vaguely ominous future" (211).

Chapter 3

1. In acknowledging the book's contradictions, Walter Benn Michaels argues that "the urge to resolve them" is one that Thoreau believed "must be refused," since it represents a fallacious search after permanent authority (*"Walden*'s False Bottoms," *Glyph* I, Baltimore: Johns Hopkins Textual Studies, 1977, 142, 134). As must be clear, Michaels attributes a greater subtlety of order to Thoreau than I am able to.

2. In several respects, including its original subtitle, Thoreau's report of his Walden experience seems a response to the reservations his English friend Charles Lane had expressed in *The Dial* a year earlier. Lane comprehended the motives for such an experiment, but doubted its practicality: "No wonder need be then excited in our minds, when we occasionally hear of the young spirit, to whom the costliest education has been afforded . . . turning after a little experience, his course from the city towards the woods. The experiment of a true wilderness life by a white person must, however, be very rare. He is not born for it; he is not natured for it." What of an amalgamation of town and country modes such as Thoreau would practice? "This is not a very promising course," Lane thought, for after all the labor, "the whole time will be exhausted, and no interval remain for comfortably clothing the body, for expansion in art, or for recreation by the book or pen" ("Life in the Woods," *The Dial* 4 (April 1844): 422).

3. J. L. Shanley, *The Making of Walden* (Chicago: University of Chicago Press, 1957), p. 128.

4. In *Bucky: A Guided Tour of Buckminster Fuller* (New York: Morrow, 1973), Hugh Kenner, after noting that machine-made nails had fallen from 8¢ a pound in 1828 to 3¢in 1842, observes: "It is not clear why three years later the nails to make Thoreau's cabin cost $3.90. Did he really use 130 pounds of nails?" (210). Walter Harding offers a possible explanation: "When the site of the Walden cabin was excavated a hundred years later, the cellar hole was found filled with hundreds of bent nails" (*Days*, 182).

5. Ralph Rusk, *The Life of Ralph Waldo Emerson* (New York: Columbia University Press, 1949), p. 249.

6. *Early Letters of George William Curtis to John S. Dwight*, ed. George Willis Cooke (New York, 1898), p. 81.

7. The first page number in parentheses refers to the first draft of *Walden* as established and reproduced in J. L. Shanley's *The Making of Walden*. The page number following the slash refers to the Princeton edition of the final version of *Walden*, also edited by Shanley. I shall follow this process of documentation henceforth, unless the references happen to be reversed in the text.

8. In *The Annotated Walden* (New York: Clarkson N. Potter, 1970) its editor, Philip Van Doren Stern, prints marginally passages from the somewhat unreliable F. B. Sanborn's "Bibliophile Edition" of *Walden* (1909), which restored some twelve thousand words to the text. Stern also prints other passages drawn from the manuscripts now held in the Huntington Library. The latter are the imperative sources and I have consulted them, but because of the accessibility of Stern's excellent edition, I shall cite it from time to time, referring to it as "Stern." Here, the quotation comes from p. 219, fn. 23.

9. *Thoreau as World Traveler* (New York: Columbia University Press, 1965), pp. 44, 46.

10. In "Scatology and Eschatology: The Heroic Dimensions of Thoreau's Wordplay," Michael West interprets the squatting as a joke about defecation, so that "squatter's rites of any sort served to manure and so improve Emerson's woodlot." *PMLA* 89, no. 5 (October 1974): 1046. However, given Thoreau's strong aversion to the use of manure (also discussed by West on 1047), if one accepts this interpretation of "squatting" then even in West's terms it would not be an act of improvement but one of aggressive debasement of Emerson—a not implausible reading.

11. "Sometimes identified as God, but more probably Pan" is David Rohman's opinion in "An Annotated Edition of Henry David Thoreau's *Walden*" (Ph. D. diss., Syracuse University, 1960), p. 229. In *The Magic Circle of Walden* (New York, 1968), Charles Anderson argues that the settler "corresponds to Pan only in the sense of the Great All . . . but this is only another way of saying the universal god" (77). The old settler is also mentioned as carrying on conversations on winter nights with Thoreau and

Alcott—"Ah! such discourse we had, hermit and philosopher, and the old settler I have spoken of" (*Walden*, 270).

12. Michael West locates Thoreau's indignation in his vision of how "the living poison themselves by consuming produce raised upon their own offal mingled with that of beasts" ("Scatology and Eschatology," p. 1047). In the course of ruminating on Thoreau's emotional reactions to death and decay, Joel Porte finds this "twisted description" derived from Thoreau's need "to escape both houses and fungi—at once emblems and embodiments of mortality." *Emerson and Thoreau: Transcendentalists in Conflict* (Middletown: Wesleyan University Press, 1965), p. 188.

13. See Charles Anderson's *The Magic Circle of Walden*, pp. 135–143, for a more appreciative reading of both this paragraph and of the whole chapter.

14. In the original journal entry, Thoreau called the infant "crone-like." To the journal observation that the chickens in the house "pecked at my shoe" he later added the splendid adverb "significantly." (*J*, I, 383, 384.)

15. *Henry D. Thoreau*, University of Minnesota Pamphlets on American Writers, no. 90 (Minneapolis, 1970), p. 27.

16. See Harding, *Days*, 312–314; Rohman, "An Annotated Edition of . . .*Walden*," 280–281; George E. Ryan, "Shanties and Shiftlessness: The Immigrant Irish of Henry Thoreau," *Eire-Ireland* 13, no. 3 (Fall 1978): 54–78; and especially Frank Buckley, "Thoreau and the Irish," *New England Quarterly* 13 (September 1940): 389–400.

17. Although today "venison" is reserved uniquely for the meat of the deer, in the past it referred to the flesh of any game animal. Judging from the paucity of reference to deer in Thoreau's journals, they must have been pretty well eliminated from the environs of Concord. In fact, Thoreau once went out of his way to record the killing of a wild deer in Northboro, February 10, 1855 (*J*, VII, 178).

18. "Fate," *Complete Works*, VI, 6.

19. *Thoreau's Minnesota Journey: Two Documents*, ed. Walter Harding, Thoreau Society Booklet No. 16 (Geneseo, New York, 1962), pp. 51, 51, 54.

20. Thoreau evidently meant a muskrat here. Cf.*J*, VII, 132: "I saw one poor rat lying on the edge of the ice reddened with its blood."

21. The various manuscript versions of *Walden* held at the Huntington Library are classified under the general heading of HM924, followed by the number of the draft and the page number of that draft. Here, then: HM924, V, 102. Henceforth cited parenthetically in the text.

22. See Mary Elkins Moller, "Thoreau, Womankind, and Sexuality," *Emerson Society Quarterly* 22, no. 3: 123–148, for a full and sensible discussion of this subject.

23. In the fourth and fifth drafts of *Walden*, he was "John Spaulding," a

name that never appears in Thoreau's journals. See HM924, IV, 118, and V, 113.

24. "Thoreau," *Complete Works*, X, 454, 456.

25. (New York, 1941), p. 166.

26. In "Thoreau's 'Smoke,' " Delmar Rodabaugh argues that the flame is clear because an independent Thoreau pays no obeisance, offers no burnt offering, to the gods. But, if so, why then does he ask pardon for the clear flame—assuming that he is not being sarcastic? *Explicator* 17 (1959), no. 47. See also Charles Anderson, *The Magic Circle of Walden*, pp. 275–276.

27. See Shanley, pp. 67, 68, and 72–73.

28. George Hendrick, ed. *Remembrances of Concord and the Thoreaus: Letters of Horace Hosmer to Dr. S. A. Jones* (Urbana: University of Illinois Press, 1977), pp. 40, 41.

29. An earlier sentence says of Zilpha, "She led a hard life, and somewhat inhumane." This observation does not occur in the journal, although in an earlier draft, "inhumane" read "witch-like" (Stern, 383, fn. 6; HM924, V, 166). The change to "inhumane" was misleading, since it is not synonymous with "inhuman"—which seems to be what Thoreau meant.

30. *Remembrances*, p. 20.

31. Concerning the ministers, Mary Elkins Moller remarks: "And here, again, the figurative 'bowels' becomes literal, and the word is dwelt upon to a degree that can only be called obsessive." *Thoreau in the Human Community* (Amherst: University of Massachussetts Press, 1980), p. 11.

32. However, see "Henry Thoreau and the Wisdom of Words," in which Philip Gura argues that Thoreau was here following the linguistic theories of the Hungarian Charles Kraitsir in order to show "how words, derived from the basic 'germs' of sound . . . are reflections of nothing less than the grand purpose of nature." *New England Quarterly* 52, no. 1 (March 1979): 49.

33. *Putnam's Monthly Magazine* (May 1856), p. 475. For a comparison of the two versions, see Frank Davidson, "Melville, Thoreau, and the Apple-Tree Table," *American Literature* 25 (1954): 479–488.

34. *The Shores of America: Thoreau's Inward Exploration* (Urbana, 1972), pp. 352–353; *The Magic Circle of Walden*, p. 278.

35. Bibliophile *Walden*, II, 259; Stern, p. 447, fn. 56.

Chapter 4

1. See William L. Howarth, *The Literary Manuscripts of Henry David Thoreau*, (Columbus: Ohio State University Press, 1974), E13a through E15b.

2. Some confusion still exists in various accounts as to who accompanied Thoreau on this trip, because both William Henry Channing and

William Ellery Channing were on Fire Island with Thoreau, William Henry having accompanied him from Concord, Ellery having come out from New York to join them. See Thoreau's note to Horace Greeley in which he says: "If Wm E Channing calls—will you say that I am gone to Fire-Island by cars at 9 this morn. via Thompson. with Wm. H. Channing" (*Corr.*, 261). Also on July 25 he writes Emerson: "*Wm* H Channing came down with me" (*Corr.*, 262). In addition, there is Emerson's letter to his brother William, July 27, 1850, in which he says: "Ellery Channing also writes me from N. Y. that he goes to Fire Island—W. H. C. is already there." *The Letters of R. W. Emerson*, ed. Ralph L. Rusk (New York: Columbia University Press, 1939), IV, 220.

3. William White, "Three Unpublished Thoreau Letters," *New England Quarterly* 33, no. 3 (September 1966): 373.

4. Marie Urbanski concludes that although their relationship was mutually rewarding, "it was largely an intellectual rather than an emotional friendship." "Henry David Thoreau and Margaret Fuller," *Thoreau Journal Quarterly* 8, no. 4 (October 1976): 29.

5. Walter Harding, *A Thoreau Handbook* (New York: New York University Press 1959; rpt. New York, 1961), p. 76. The book *Cape Cod* did not appear until 1865, but its first chapters were printed in *Putnam's Monthly Magazine*, June, July, and August 1855. A disagreement between Thoreau and the editor then terminated the series prematurely. See Francis H. Allen, *A Bibliography of Henry David Thoreau* (Boston: Houghton Mifflin 1908), p. 71.

6. *Thoreau*, pp. 368, 371; *Henry David Thoreau*, 251, 277.

7. Thoreau's first publication was an obituary, entitled "Died." *EE*, 121, 304.

8. James McIntosh detects a "moral indignation" in Thoreau's description, and generally takes a more positive view of this chapter than I do, although he does acknowledge that Thoreau's conception of nature as "an indifferent and voracious power, is not incorporated in any distinctive way in his later work." *Thoreau as Romantic Naturalist*, pp. 227, 235.

Chapter 5

1. *Thoreau as Romantic Naturalist*, pp. 190, fn. 4; 192, fn. 8.

2. Thoreau was well known, even fabled, for his ability to find Indian relics, and his collection of arrowheads, axes, pestles, mortars, and chisels numbered over nine hundred items (*Thoreau Society Bulletin* No. 105 [Fall 1968]: 8). However, to put this in perspective, see Laurence Richardson's *Concord River* (Barre, Mass.: Barre Publishers 1964), where he notes of the Nipmucks, the local sub-tribe of Indians: "Over 25,000 specimens of their stone weapons or implements have been found in Concord alone" (9).

3. *Complete Works*, IX, 38.

4. The possibility of this unlikely mode of travel has been attested to in H. Walter Leavitt, *Katahdin Skylines*, Maine Technology Experiment Paper No. 40 (Orono, Maine: University of Maine Press, May 1942), p. 64 and fn. 97, quoting from R. S. Tarr's "Glaciation of Mount Ktaadin, Maine," *Bulletin, Geological Society of America* (1900), II, 443.

5. 2d. edition (New York, 1920), p. 76.

6. "Going to Mount Katahdin," *Putnam's Monthly* (September 1856): 246.

7. For a recent and full review of the literature on the essay, see Michael Meyer, *Several More Lives to Live: Thoreau's Political Reputation in America* (Westport, Conn: Greenwood Press, 1977).

8. "Lucky Fox at Walden" in *Thoreau in Our Season*, ed. John H. Hicks, (Amherst: University of Massachusetts Press, 1966), p. 130.

9. Truman Nelson, "Thoreau and John Brown," *Thoreau in Our Season*, p. 143.

10. C. Roland Wagner writes: "Thoreau's uncompromising moral idealism, despite its occasional embodiment in sentences of supreme literary power, created an essentially child's view of political and social reality. Because his moral principles were little more than expressions of his quest for purity and of hostility to any civilized interference with the absolute attainment of his wishes, he was unable to discriminate between better and worse in the real world." "Lucky Fox at Walden," *Thoreau in Our Season*, pp. 130–131.

11. William S. Robinson, *"Warrington" Pen-Portraits*, ed. Mrs. W. S. Robinson (Boston, 1877), pp. 68–69.

12. *The Thoreau Family Two Generations Ago*, Thoreau Society Booklet No. 13 (Berkeley Heights, N. J., 1958), p. 9.

13. Faulty prose causes a confusing ambiguity at this point. Thoreau wrote: "Joe exclaimed from the stream that he had killed a moose" (112). This and an earlier comment by Thoreau that he "was not sorry to learn how the Indian managed to kill one" (99) made Philip Gura, for example, refer to "Aitteon's slaughter of the moose" ("Thoreau's Maine Woods Indians: More Representative Men," *American Literature* [November 1977]: 375). However, in the description of the shooting, the person who fires one barrel of his shotgun at each moose is described as "our hunter," a man who had "never seen a moose before"—manifestly not Aitteon, but Thatcher (111). Further, Joe gives the cry that "he had killed a moose" when "he had found the cow-moose lying dead" (112–113). So, although the syntactical indication of the original sentence is that the referent of "he" is Joe, the pronoun must refer to Thatcher.

14. Robert F. Sayre, *Thoreau and the American Indians* (Princeton: Princeton University Press, 1977), p. 110.

15. P. 103. Sayre's chapter, "A Book About Indians?" provides an

excellent description, dating, summary, and analysis of these fact books. See also William J. Howarth, *The Literary Manuscripts of Henry David Thoreau*, 294–295.

16. This was Hiram L. Leonard, a market hunter, "who was destined to become even more famous as the inventor of the split bamboo fly rod." Lew Dietz, *The Allagash* (New York: Holt, Rinehart, Winston, 1968) p. 157.

17. I cannot agree with Philip F. Gura when he argues that "Joe Polis stands as a central figure in any pantheon of representative men Thoreau established." "Thoreau's Maine Woods Indians," *American Literature* (November 1977): 377. Thoreau himself evidently felt his portrait of Polis was not particularly complimentary, for he refused to submit the "Allegash" essay for publication in the *Atlantic*, on the grounds that since Polis could read, "I could not face him again" (*Corr.*, 504).

18. *Thoreau and the American Indian*, p. x.

19. *The Literary Manuscripts of Henry David Thoreau*, p. 294.

20. In *Old John Neptune and Other Maine Indian Shamans* (Portland: Southworth-Anthoensen Press, 1945). Fannie Eckstorm records another lengthy instance of Polis's "high-pressure salesmanship." She also claims that Polis was known as "a powerful magician, a shaman," but that Thoreau had failed to detect it (186).

21. *Thoreau and the American Indians*, p. xiii.

22. Cf. Thoreau's reference in one of his drafts of *Walden* to "this fair-complexioned Caucasian race—so many ages in advance of its sunburnt brothers" (HM924, VIII, 14).

23. Walter Harding, ed., *Thoreau's Minnesota Journey*, pp. 4, 10, 21, 22.

Chapter 6

1. *Journals*, ed. Edward Waldo Emerson and Waldo Emerson Forbes (Boston, 1913), IX, 16.

2. See Leo Stoller, *After Walden: Thoreau's Changing Views on Economic Man* (Stanford: Stanford University Press, 1957), p. 144, fn. 27, for an extensive review of the dating problems of these encounters.

3. Stephen B. Oates, *To Purge This Land With Blood* (New York: Harper & Row, 1970), p. 4.

4. A. Bronson Alcott, *The Letters of A. Bronson Alcott*, ed. Richard L. Herrnstadt (Ames, Iowa: Iowa State University Press, 1969), p. 306. Cf. Carl Bode: "There can be little doubt that the strongest aggressions in him found an outlet through Brown. He identified himself with Brown and fought by empathy at his side." "The Hidden Thoreau," *The Half-World of American Culture* (Carbondale: Southern Illinois University Press, 1965), p. 12.

5. Oates, *To Purge This Land*, p. 35.

6. "Thoreau's Rescue of John Brown from History," *Studies in the American Renaissance, 1980* (Boston, 1980), p. 303.

7. "Address at Cooper Institute, New York City" (February 27, 1860), *The Collected Works of Abraham Lincoln*, ed. Roy P. Basler (New Brunswick, N. J.: Rutgers University Press, 1953), III, 541.

8. Oates, *To Purge This Land*, pp. 319, 335. See also T. W. Higginson to his mother: "Of course I *think* enough about Brown, though I don't feel sure that his acquittal or rescue would do half as much good as his being executed." *Letters and Journals of Thomas Wentworth Higginson*, ed. Mary Thatcher Higginson (Boston: Houghton Mifflin, 1921), p. 85.

9. "Rattleran" is not in the *Oxford English Dictionary*, the *Dictionary of American English*, or *The Dictionary of Americanisms*. "Ratel" is shown in the *OED* as both a honey badger and the spleen, the latter perhaps bearing on the quotation.

10. *Remembrances*, pp. 14, 70.

11. *Walden or Life in the Woods*, ed. with intr. F. B. Sanborn (Boston: Bibliophile Society, 1909), I, 27 n.

12. The fragment is printed in part in Canby's *Thoreau*, pp. 160–162, where he argues its subject is Lidian Emerson. Perry Miller in *CinC* follows F. B. Sanborn in attributing the source of the feelings to Helen Thoreau (101–102).

13. John G. Blair and Augustus Trowbridge, "Thoreau on Katahdin," *American Quarterly* 12 (Winter 1960): 516.

Conclusion

1. Mrs. Daniel Chester French, *Memories of a Sculptor's Wife*, quoted in Raymond Adams, "Thoreau and His Neighbors," *Thoreau Society Bulletin* No. 44 (Summer 1953): 13.

2. See also *J*, VIII, 412, which suggests that it was Thoreau himself who killed the snake, since "Amid the high grass or rushes by that meadow-side started a water adder." This is followed by a detailed description of it, possible only through close examination.

Acknowledgments

I THANK Alex Zwerdling, Henry Nash Smith, and Elena Bridgman for their generous, wise, and candid counsel: they helped both to temper my ideas and to improve their presentation. And, while firmly separating himself from the main thesis of this book, Walter Harding has nonetheless kindly reduced its errors.

This work was done with the material assistance of fellowships from the American Council of Learned Societies and the University of California, as well as with funds disbursed by the Berkeley Academic Senate Committee on Research. I very much appreciate all of this support.

Index

303